DATE DUE

The agrarian policy of the Russian Socialist-Revolutionary Party from its origins through the revolution of 1905–1907

The National Association for Soviet and East European Studies exists for the purpose of promoting study and research on the social sciences as they relate to the Soviet Union and the countries of Eastern Europe. The Monograph Series is intended to promote the publication of works presenting substantial and original research in the economics, politics, sociology and modern history of the USSR and Eastern Europe.

SOVIET AND EAST EUROPEAN STUDIES

BOOKS IN THE SERIES

A. Boltho *Foreign Trade Criteria in Socialist Economics*
Sheila Fitzpatrick *The Commissariat of Enlightenment*
Donald Male *Russian Peasant Organisation before Collectivisation*
P. Wiles, ed. *The Prediction of Communist Economic Performance*
Vladimir V. Kusin *The Intellectual Origins of the Prague Spring*
Galia Golan *The Czechoslovak Reform Movement*
Naum Jasny *Soviet Economists of the Twenties*
Asha L. Datar *India's Economic Relations with the USSR and Eastern Europe, 1953–1969*
T. M. Podolski *Socialist Banking and Monetary Control*
Rudolf Bićanić *Economic Policy in Socialist Yugoslavia*
S. Galai *The Liberation Movement in Russia 1900–1905*
Richard B. Day *Leon Trotsky and the Politics of Economic Isolation*
G. Hosking *The Russian Constitutional Experiment: Government and Duma 1907–14*
A. Teichova *An Economic Background to Munich*
J. Ciechanowski *The Warsaw Rising of 1944*
Edward A. Hewett *Foreign Trade Prices in the Council for Mutual Economic Assistance*
Daniel F. Calhoun *The United Front: the TUC and the Russians 1923–28*
Galia Golan *Yom Kippur and After: the Soviet Union and the Middle East Crisis*
Gabriel Gorodetsky *The Precarious Truce: Anglo-Soviet Relations 1924–27*
Paul Vyšný *Neo-Slavism and the Czechs, 1894–1914*
James Riordan *Sport in Soviet Society: Development of Sport and Physical Education in Russia and the USSR*

The agrarian policy of the Russian Socialist-Revolutionary Party

from its origins through the revolution of 1905–1907

MAUREEN PERRIE
Lecturer in Modern History
Centre for Russian and East European Studies
University of Birmingham

CAMBRIDGE UNIVERSITY PRESS
CAMBRIDGE
LONDON · NEW YORK · MELBOURNE

Published by the Syndics of the Cambridge University Press
The Pitt Building, Trumpington Street, Cambridge CB2 1RP
Bentley House, 200 Euston Road, London NW1 2DB
32 East 57th Street, New York, NY 10022, USA
296 Beaconsfield Parade, Middle Park, Melbourne 3206, Australia

First published 1976

Photoset and printed in Malta by Interprint (Malta) Ltd

Library of Congress Cataloguing in Publication Data
Perrie, Maureen, 1946–
The agrarian policy of the Russian Socialist-Revolutionary Party from its origins through the revolution of 1905–1907.
(Soviet and East European studies)
Rev. and expanded version of the 2d pt. of the author's M. A. thesis, University of Birmingham, 1971, which was entitled, The social composition and structure of the Socialist-Revolutionary Party, and its activity amongst the Russian peasantry, 1901–1907.
Bibliography: p.
Includes index.
1. Agriculture and state–Russia–History.
2. Partiia sotsialistov–revoliutsionerov. I. Title: The agrarian policy of the Russian Socialist-Revolutionary Party ... II. Series.
HD1993 1901.P47 1976 338.1'847 76–644
ISBN 0 521 21213 8

To Bill and Martin

Contents

Preface

This book represents a much revised and expanded version of the second part of my MA thesis, 'The social composition and structure of the Socialist-Revolutionary party, and its activity amongst the Russian peasantry, 1901–1907' (University of Birmingham, 1971). I am most grateful to my colleagues, both past and present, in the Centre for Russian and East European Studies at Birmingham, who have taken a constant interest in the progress of my work and provided me with so much valuable advice. Professor R. E. F. Smith, Professor R. W. Davies, and Dr Moshe Lewin have read and commented on various drafts. Professor Teodor Shanin, now of the University of Manchester, and Dr David Lane, now of the University of Cambridge, encouraged me in the early stages of the research. My work on the original thesis was supported by an SSRC studentship.

Research visits have been paid to the British Museum in London, the International Institute for Social History in Amsterdam and the Lenin Library in Moscow, and I should like to thank the staffs of these libraries for their assistance. The bulk of the research, however, has had to be done in Birmingham, and I am deeply indebted to Miss Barbara Ronchetti and her staff in the Inter-Library Loans section of the University Library and to Mrs Jennifer Brine of the Alexander Baykov Library, for their efforts on my behalf.

August 1975 M.P.P.

Acknowledgements

The author gratefully acknowledges permission from The Past and Present Society to reproduce material from her article 'The Russian peasant movement of 1905–1907; its social composition and revolutionary significance', published in *Past and Present. A journal of historical studies*, no. 57 (November 1972). World copyright: The Past and Present Society, Corpus Christi College, Oxford, England.

Note on dates and transliteration

The dates used throughout are in the Old Style (Julian) calendar, which was twelve days behind the Western (Gregorian) calendar in the nineteenth century and thirteen days behind in the twentieth century.

The transliteration system used is a slightly modified version of the simplified form of the British Standard (BS 2979 – 1958), the main difference being that for diphthongs the forms *ay*, *ey*, *iy* (except in endings), *oy* and *uy* are preferred to *ai*, *ei*, *ii*, *oi* and *ui*.

Some of the more common terms which appear in the text in transliterated form have been anglicised in the formation of their plurals, e.g., kulaks, guberniyas. Other Russian terms have been retained in their original form and italicised; explanations for these terms have been provided in the text and in the Glossary.

Regions and guberniyas of European Russia.

Introduction

The most striking feature of the revolutions of the twentieth century which describe themselves as socialist is that they have taken place, not in the advanced industrial societies of Western Europe and North America as the predictions advanced by Marx in the mid-nineteenth century had assumed, but in predominantly peasant countries, such as Russia and China, whose industrialisation was only in its infancy. Any modern sociology of revolution must account for the fact that it is the land-hungry peasantry – numerically if not organisationally stronger than its ally, the industrial proletariat – which has guaranteed success for socialist parties in many areas of the world.

Although ultimate victory in 1917 went to the Bolshevik party, Lenin was not the first Russian socialist to appreciate the revolutionary potential of the peasantry. Many of the Populists of the 1870s had considered that the transition to socialism could be made on the basis of the institution of the peasant commune, avoiding the stage of capitalist development. The failure of their 'movement to the people', however, and the apparent indifference of the peasantry to revolutionary ideas, discredited Populism in the subsequent decades, and industrialisation lent greater credibility to the Marxism of the rival Social-Democratic groups. A reassessment of the rôle of the small agricultural producer came only at the turn of the century with the formation of the Agrarian-Socialist League, and the later formation of the Socialist-Revolutionary (SR) party. It was in the course of polemics with his SR rivals concerning the nature of the peasant movement which developed at the beginning of the twentieth century that Lenin's attitude towards the peasantry was formed.

This study is concerned with the agrarian policy of the SR party in the early years of the twentieth century: its political sociology of the peasantry, its programme for the 'socialisation' of the land, and its attempts to organise the peasantry as a revolutionary force. According to SR theory – which Chernov, the party leader, claimed to have a more valid Marxist basis than that of the Social-Democrats (SDs) – the small, peasant producers formed part of the working class with a similar interest in socialism to that of the proletariat. In addition to this purely objective criterion of class position, there were also subjective factors which made the peasants receptive to socialist ideas: the egalitarian views fostered by the institution of the repartitional commune, and the traditional peasant belief that only personal labour gave rights to the use of land. The SR proposals for the socialisation of the land were designed to correspond to the peasants' own concepts of social justice and to prepare the way for socialist agriculture.

In the period from the formation of the party in 1901 to the outbreak of war in 1914, the SRs had no real opportunity of putting these ideas into practice. Their campaign for the peasantry was launched only in 1902, and the revolution of 1905 had overtaken them before they could establish their influence in the countryside. At the same time, the SRs were probably closer to the peasantry than any other revolutionary group in Russia, and more aware of the problems presented by the socialist transformation of the countryside. They had few illusions about the individualist streak in the peasantry but were optimistic that this could be overcome by patient propaganda and education.

The events of 1917 mean that the SR agrarian programme has been consigned to the political limbo of unsuccessful revolutionaries. After 1917, it was the agrarian policy of the Bolsheviks, and the Leninist analysis of the class structure of the countryside, which guided Russian peasant agriculture towards socialism. Recent studies of Soviet agrarian policy in the 1920s, however, have suggested that the failures of this policy, culminating in the forced collectivisation drive of 1929–30, were derived from the inadequacy of the Bolsheviks' theoretical understanding of the dynamics of peasant society.[1] In this context, a re-examination of the views of the Bolsheviks' chief ideological opponents may not be without interest.

[1] M. Lewin, *Russian peasants and Soviet power; a study of collectivisation*, (London, 1968); D. J. Male, *Russian peasant organisation before collectivisation; a study of commune and gathering, 1925–1930* (Cambridge, 1971); T. Shanin, *The awkward class; political sociology of peasantry in a developing society: Russia 1910–1925* (Oxford, 1972).

Part I

FROM POPULISM TO THE SR PARTY
(1881–1901)

1
The Populist legacy

Historically, the origins of Socialist-Revolutionary activity among the peasantry can be traced to the 'movements to the people' of the 1870s. After the failure of these attempts by the Populist intelligentsia to convert the peasantry to the cause of revolutionary socialism, their secret organisation, *Zemlya i volya* ('Land and liberty'), split into two groups, *Chernyi peredel* ('Black repartition') and *Narodnaya volya* ('People's will'). These two parties represented the two major trends which had developed within the Populist movement after the failure of the 'movements to the people'. *Chernyi peredel*, while retaining the essential programme of *Zemlya i volya*, with its faith in a peasant revolution, in practice concentrated its efforts on the urban workers. Its leaders, Plekhanov and Aksel'rod, soon left Russia for Switzerland, where they later created the first émigré Marxist group. In view of the prevailing disillusionment among the revolutionaries concerning the possibilities of a mass socialist movement, the organisation in Russia soon petered out. *Narodnaya volya*, on the other hand, rejected the policy of propaganda among the masses in favour of a campaign of systematic terrorism aimed at the political overthrow of the autocracy, which overthrow they considered to be a necessary prerequisite of socialist revolution in Russia. The organisation had a brief but spectacular career which culminated in the assassination of Alexander II in 1881. This act, however, brought down upon the terrorists the forces of reaction and repression, and the organisation of *Narodnaya volya* was virtually destroyed.[1]

The decade which followed saw the complete stagnation of the Populist movement in Russia. The events of the preceding few years had shown that neither of the courses of action which the Populists had proposed was practicable under existing conditions. The peasants' lack of receptivity towards socialist propaganda suggested that the prospects of a mass revolutionary movement were poor;

[1] The standard account of Populism to 1881 is F. Venturi, *Roots of revolution* (London, 1960).

and the ease with which the government had suppressed *Narodnaya volya* meant that the alternative course of political terrorism was equally doomed to failure. In the eighties the widespread disillusionment of the intelligentsia with the revolutionary potential of the peasantry and with political terrorism created a favourable intellectual climate for the popularity of the rival Marxist view of Russia's path to socialism; and it was in the eighties that the first Social-Democratic groups were formed in several Russian cities. The rapid industrialisation of Russia in the latter part of the nineteenth century also served as a justification of the Marxist thesis that the bearers of socialism in Russia would be not the peasantry but the urban proletariat. Although scattered groups of *narodovol'tsy* who had survived the destruction of the central party organisation still existed in various places, the eighties and much of the nineties saw Populism gradually replaced by Marxism as the fashionable ideology of the revolutionary intelligentsia.[2] It was not until the formation of the Socialist-Revolutionary party at the beginning of the twentieth century that the twin pillars of Populism – peasant socialism and élite terrorism – were restored to the forefront of the revolutionary movement, albeit with a Marxist facelift applied by Chernov.

However, if the eighties were the decade of the decay of the old Populism, they were also marked by developments of considerable significance for the emergence of the new. The educational reforms of Alexander II had brought increasing opportunities for upward social mobility through the professions for members of the lower strata of society.[3] This new generation of *raznochintsy* inherited the intellectual atmosphere of the aftermath of the Populist débâcle

[2] The term 'Populism' is used here in the accepted broad, if anachronistic sense, to describe that school of revolutionary thought which believed that Russia could avoid the capitalist stage of development and make a direct transition to socialism on the basis of her existing institutions, such as the peasant commune. See R. Pipes, '*Narodnichestvo*; a semantic inquiry', *American Slavic and East European Review*, vol 23 (1964), pp 441–58. Although many Populists were influenced by Marx, the orthodox Marxists considered themselves, and may be considered by historians, to represent a distinct new school of thought, which stressed the inevitability of Russian capitalism. Populism and Marxism co-existed as rival ideologies in the 1880s and 90s, and were eventually to crystallise in the Socialist-Revolutionary and Social-Democratic parties respectively. Valuable studies in English of aspects of Populist and Marxist thought in the 1880s and 90s are: J. H. Billington, *Mikhailovsky and Russian Populism* (Oxford, 1958); A. P. Mendel, *Dilemmas of progress in Tsarist Russia; Legal Marxism and Legal Populism* (Cambridge, Mass., 1961); and A. Walicki, *The controversy over capitalism; studies in the social philosophy of the Russian Populists* (London, 1969).

[3] See V. R. Leykina-Svirskaya, *Intelligentsiya v Rossii vo vtoroy polovine 19 veka* (Moscow, 1971).

with its indifference towards political activism. Theories of 'small deeds' gradualism, the belief that the perfection of the individual must precede that of the social order, and new religious teaching (such as that of Tolstoy) dominated the intellectual horizon of the eighties.

Among a considerable section of the intelligentsia, however, these ideas found their expression in 'service to the people', and the decade saw a great influx of *raznochintsy* into the *zemstva* – the local government institutions established in 1864 with broad responsibilities for education and welfare – where they comprised a group which later came to be known as the 'third element'.[4] The intelligentsia of the seventies had made a 'movement to the people'; their successors in the following decade accomplished a 'settlement among the people'.[5] The new rural intelligentsia were dedicated to serving the people, not as revolutionary leaders but in their professional capacity as doctors, teachers, nurses, veterinary surgeons, lawyers and agronomists. Insofar as they saw their rôle in any light other than that of the ideal of public service, it was as the bearers of cultural, rather than political, enlightenment to the peasantry among whom they lived and worked. What political aspirations they had were channelled not to socialist propaganda among the peasantry, but to demands for greater autonomy and wider powers for the *zemstvo* itself, which was under attack in the eighties from the government of Alexander III through a series of acts of restrictive legislation. In this conflict between *zemstvo* and government, the third element found allies in the more progressive gentry landowners, and the rapprochement of these two groups created the social base for the '*zemstvo* liberalism' of the next decade.[6]

Historians of the Socialist-Revolutionary movement see the famine year of 1891 as a crucial date for the revival of revolutionary Populism.[7] In that year, famine throughout the Central Black Earth

[4] The 'third element' comprised the hired professional employees of the *zemstva*, as opposed to the appointed officials (the 'first element') and the elected councillors (the 'second element'). See N. Potresov, 'Evolyutsiya obshchestvenno-politicheskoy mysli v predrevolyutsionnuyu epokhu', in *Obshchestvennoe dvizhenie v Rossii v nachale 20 veka* (4 vols, St Petersburg, 1909–14), vol 1, pp 538–9; N. Cherevanin, 'Dvizhenie intelligentsii', in *ibid*, vol 1, p 268.

[5] I owe this phrase to an early publication of the Agrarian-Socialist League: *Ocherednoy vopros revolyutsionnago dela* (London, 1900), p 3.

[6] Potresov, *Obshchestvennoe dvizhenie . . .*, vol 1, pp 539–40.

[7] S. N. Sletov, *K istorii vozniknoveniya Partii Sotsialistov-Revolyutsionerov* (Petrograd, 1917), p 23; A. Spiridovitch, *Histoire du terrorisme russe, 1886–1917* (Paris, 1930), p 35. Sletov's book is a posthumous reissue of his 'Ocherki po istorii Partii Sotsialis-

agricultural region was accompanied by a widespread outbreak of cholera and by sporadic peasant disturbances. For the first time since the seventies the attention of the urban intelligentsia was focused on the plight of the peasantry, and a large corps of volunteers, mainly students, went to the countryside to join in the famine-relief work which was being organised there by the *zemstvo* third element.[8]

The survivors of the Populist movement of the seventies sought to take advantage of the famine situation to reach revolutionary ends. A group of émigrés in Geneva issued proclamations appealing to revolutionary circles in Russia to exploit popular discontent in the famine-stricken areas in order to reactivate the revolutionary movement. In Paris at the end of 1891, Lavrov founded a 'Society to combat the famine', which issued appeals laying the blame for the famine on government policy towards the peasantry and calling for the concentration of all revolutionary forces against the government.[9] Within Russia in 1892, a 'Group of *narodovol'tsy*', based in St Petersburg, published a 'Letter to the starving peasants' by the Populist writer Astyrev, in which he explained the connection between the famine and government policy as a whole and why the authorities were persecuting members of the intelligentsia who had tried to help the peasants.[10]

These appeals, however, were largely unheeded by the majority of the *intelligenty* and students who 'went to the people' in 1891. Their motives were humanitarian rather than political,[11] and to this extent the government's grave misgivings failed to take into account the change in mood of the intelligentsia since the seventies. Insofar, however, as any increased contact between the peasantry and the intelligentsia could not fail to have undesirable consequences for the conservative policies of Alexander III's government, official concern was indeed well-founded. The intelligentsia's work in the field of famine relief and medical aid to the cholera victims was

tov-Revolyutsionerov', published under his party nickname of 'S. Nechetnyi' in *Sotsialist-Revolyutsioner*, no. 4 (1912), pp 1–101. Spiridovich's history is a translation and revised edition of his *Partiya Sotsialistov-Revolyutsionerov i ee predshestvenniki, 1886–1916*, the first two editions of which appeared in Petrograd in 1916 and 1918. Sletov, who was killed on active service in France in 1915, was a prominent member of the SR Central Committee, and the brother-in-law of Viktor Chernov; Spiridovich was head of Nicholas II's personal security police.

[8] Cherevanin, *Obshchestvennoe dvizhenie* . . ., vol 1, pp 268–9.

[9] Spiridovitch, p 36 (footnote).

[10] A. Egorov, 'Zarozhdenie politicheskikh partii i ikh deyatel'nost'', in *Obshchestvennoe dvizhenie* . . ., vol 1, p 373; Sletov, p 34.

[11] Cherevanin, *Obshchestvennoe dvizhenie* . . ., vol 1, p 269.

soon extended to cultural and educational activity, such as the organisation of public lectures, the opening of libraries and reading rooms, and the free distribution of books and pamphlets on scientific, moral and literary themes. Other activities, which received a great impetus at this period and evoked considerable concern on the part of Durnovo, the Minister of the Interior, included the establishment of various 'Sunday schools' for adult education and 'Committees for the elimination of illiteracy' in many provincial towns.[12]

This cultural and educational activity, which was intensively conducted in many guberniyas, undoubtedly played a considerable rôle in achieving the rapprochement between the peasantry and the intelligentsia which was a prerequisite for successful revolutionary work in the countryside. By the end of the nineties, the humbler strata of the rural intelligentsia, especially teachers, were being recruited in increasing numbers from the peasantry[13] and could, therefore, share in and sympathise with their problems on the basis of personal experience. The heterogeneity of the rural intelligentsia in terms of social composition was reflected in the range of political allegiances which they were to manifest in 1905. The doctor or lawyer with a higher education and professional training, who hobnobbed with the local gentry on the *zemstvo* board, was more likely to favour plans for liberal reform; whereas the village teacher or medical assistant, whose education had frequently reached little more than primary level and whose way of life was often little different from that of the peasants among whom he lived, represented the backbone of the Socialist-Revolutionary organisation in the countryside.[14]

The political fruits of the 'settlement among the people', however, were not to be gathered until the end of the decade. Various groups and circles of students and intellectuals with more or less Populist sympathies existed in the nineties, calling themselves either *narodovol'cheskie* or 'Socialist-Revolutionary', but they remained largely divorced from the cultural movement. Indirectly, however, the general upsurge of 'Populist' feeling among the intelligentsia, which had been evoked by the famine of 1891, contributed to a revival of the urban revolutionary movement. The young people, returning

[12] Sletov, p. 24; Spiridovitch, pp 35–6. For an account of this 'enlightenment' activity by the intelligentsia, see Leykina-Svirskaya, pp 255–76.

[13] *ibid*, pp 163–4; L. K. Erman, *Intelligentsiya v pervoy russkoy revolyutsii* (Moscow, 1966), p 29.

[14] On the social composition of the intelligentsia, see Erman, pp 18–33.

to their studies in the towns and cities after participating in the relief work in the villages, sought some alternative outlet for their idealistic aspirations to serve the people, and this mood was utilised by both Social-Democratic and Socialist-Revolutionary groups, who set up circles of 'self-instruction' among the students. These were primarily discussion groups, but the members also undertook to distribute revolutionary literature to the workers and the intelligentsia.[15]

The main difference between the groups calling themselves Social-Democratic and Socialist-Revolutionary, at this time, was that the latter revealed a greater ideological eclecticism and laid more emphasis on purely political forms of action, including political terrorism, than did the Social-Democrats, whose prevailing trend was 'economist'.[16] In addition, the Socialist-Revolutionary groups were united, in spite of various differences on points of ideology, by a feeling that they were continuing the native Russian revolutionary tradition of *Zemlya i volya* and *Narodnaya volya*.[17] This awareness of a common heritage was strengthened in the middle and later nineties when the exiled and imprisoned Populists of the seventies began to return to the provincial towns of European Russia, thus constituting a living revolutionary link with the past. These 'elders' of the movement exerted a strong influence on the younger generation and formed the centre of many new Socialist-Revolutionary groups.[18]

In general, the groups of the nineties showed little interest in the peasantry.[19] Both ideological and practical considerations contributed to this situation. The influence of Russian Marxism on Socialist-Revolutionary thought at this period was considerable, and the Social-Democratic view – that the commune, which the Populists had seen as the potential basis of agrarian socialism in Russia, was disintegrating under the influence of capitalist development and that the peasantry was being differentiated into a bourgeois element of prosperous kulak farmers, on the one hand, and a landless or near-landless agricultural proletariat, on the other – was widely

[15] Spiridovitch, pp 42–3; Sletov, pp 40, 45ff.
[16] Sletov, pp 41, 46.
[17] *ibid*, p 41.
[18] *ibid*, pp 42–5.
[19] For details of these groups, their programmes and activity, see Sletov, p 32ff; Spiridovitch, p 12ff; Egorov, *Obshchestvennoe dvizhenie* . . . , vol 1, pp 372–5; V. Meshcheryakov, *Partiya Sotsialistov-Revolyutsionerov* (2 pts, Moscow, 1922), pt 1, pp 7–52.

shared by the Socialist-Revolutionaries.[20] The hopes of the Russian revolutionaries were placed now on the emergence of the rural proletariat, which, it was assumed, would soon display the same revolutionary socialist zeal as the Marxists attributed to its industrial counterpart. It followed, however, that since the process of social differentiation among the peasantry was only in its initial stages, propaganda and organisational work in the country by a socialist party were still premature.

Even those groups and individuals who rejected this analysis[21] and retained their Populist faith in the socialist potential of the mass of the communal peasantry were reluctant to institute a new 'movement to the people', for purely practical reasons. It was felt that, in view of the numerical weakness of the movement and the shortage of revolutionaries even for urban work, it would be a foolish over-extension of their forces to attempt to include the countryside in their sphere of activity.[22] Most groups, however, recognised the value of the work conducted among the peasantry by individuals who lived and worked in the countryside – such as members of the rural intelligentsia, industrial workers who moved to factories in rural localities, and urban workers on regular visits to their relatives in the villages – since such activity could have no detrimental effect on the movement's efforts in the towns.[23] On the contrary, the utilisation of such forces would increase the potential number of cadres at the movement's disposal, by defining a rôle for the young people of provincial areas that had no industry, no proletariat, and, consequently – in terms of Social-Democratic theory, at least – no opportunities for revolutionary action. Allegiance to the Social-Democrats would logically have condemned them to political impotence; the Socialist-Revolutionaries, on the other hand, could make use of their energy in the countryside. But the influence of Marxism was strong, and throughout the nineties the younger generation of revolutionaries continued to think of work among the peasantry as the eccentric delusion of an older generation out of touch with contemporary Russian reality.[24]

[20] As noted with approval by Meshcheryakov, pp 15–25. The author is critical of the SRs from a Bolshevik standpoint.

[21] The most eminent of the anti-Marxists were the old Populists Lavrov and Breshkovskaya; Sletov, pp 52–3.

[22] *ibid*, pp 51–2, 77, 91.

[23] *ibid*, pp 60–61.

[24] As Breshkovskaya discovered when she returned from Siberian exile in 1896; see E. Breshkovskaya, 'Vospominaniya i dumy', *Sotsialist-Revolyutsioner*, no. 4 (1912), pp 122–3.

Such work as was conducted in the countryside in the nineties was largely the result of the efforts of isolated individual members of the rural intelligentsia. In addition to the work which he and Chernov conducted in Tambov guberniya, Sletov cites work in Saratov guberniya by a village teacher, Viktorin Aref′ev, and by a doctor, Chenykaev; in Pereyaslav uezd in Poltava guberniya by a village schoolmistress, Maksimovich, and a medical assistant, Glukhnov, and in Mirgorod uezd by a local doctor. In Samara guberniya, a circle of peasants was formed in 1893 by the secretary of the Literacy Committee, aided by a student named Khmelnitskii. In 1895 a circle of former pupils of the theological seminary in Vladimir conducted propaganda among the peasantry and, according to a police report of 1901, 'in the session 1898–99 there existed in the Novgorod teachers' seminary a circle whose aim was to inculcate into future village teachers anti-government and atheistic ideas which were later to be conveyed to the peasantry'. In Penza in 1895, a circle of young people under the direction of P. P. Kraft spread propaganda in a number of villages in the province. Sletov claims that, in addition to these cases of peasant propaganda for which he can cite details of names and places, there is evidence of similar activity in the guberniyas of Voronezh, Vyatka, Kazan′, Pskov, Smolensk, Tver′ and Ufa. However, he believes the most intensive activity to have taken place in the guberniyas of Tambov, Saratov and Penza.[25]

Sletov characterised the work conducted in the villages at this period as follows:

The work is carried on by isolated individuals and small, scattered groups with neither contacts nor finance. After the long interval since the period of the 'movement to the people', things have to be started again from the very beginning. Until very recently, work among the peasantry has been the work of the solitary pioneer, brought by the will of fate into the countryside. The work has assumed two main directions: some have tried to revolutionise the peasants' outlook on the basis of 'propagation of enlightenment' activity; others have attempted to organise the discontented elements of the village by agitating on behalf of their immediate interests.

The success of such propaganda and agitation has depended largely on the personality of the individual *intelligent*. There have been cases where persons inspired by the very best intentions have spent years in the countryside and have come away having accomplished nothing, with a bitter conviction of the

[25] Sletov, pp 55–60. Spiridovitch (p 108) gives an identical list of guberniyas in which there were cases of work among the peasantry during the nineties, but claims that the most intensive work was in Tambov, Saratov and Voronezh (not Penza).

peasants' irremediable apathy. On the other hand, some had only to appear in a given locality and strike up an acquaintance with the peasants for the revolutionary elements of the village at once to gather round them.[26]

The handful of successful propagandists of the nineties claimed to have made an important discovery: that the peasants were now increasingly responsive to radical ideas. The significance of this discovery for the revolutionary movement was of course immense: to those who believed, it meant a vindication of the Populist idea. What was needed now to convert peasant revolution from potentiality to actuality was, firstly, a theoretical justification of agrarian socialism which would take into account the Marxist critique of the Populism of the seventies; and, secondly, the formulation of a programme of agitational and organisational activity in the countryside on a coordinated, nationwide basis. Both of these requirements were to be fulfilled by Viktor Chernov, as a result of his experience in Tambov.

[26] S. Nechetnyi, 'U zemli', *Vestnik Russkoy Revolyutsii*, no. 2 (Feb. 1902), section 2, p 72.

2
The first peasant Brotherhood

It was in Tambov guberniya, where he spent a period of 'administrative exile' under police supervision from 1895 to 1899, that Viktor Chernov, the future leader of the Socialist-Revolutionary party, became involved in the organisation of the first 'peasant brotherhood' in Russia. On his arrival in Tambov, at the age of twenty-two, Chernov was already a veteran of the revolutionary movement. The grandson of a serf – his father had risen to gentry rank as the result of a successful career in the Tsarist civil service – Chernov's first association with revolutionary circles had been as a schoolboy in Saratov in the 1880s. In 1891, to escape police persecution, he left Saratov to complete his secondary education in Derpt. The following year he entered the Law Faculty of Moscow University, where he was soon elected to the students' 'Union council' and became a leading member of a group of 'young *narodovol'tsy*'. In 1894 he was arrested and imprisoned for nine months as a result of his connection with the short-lived 'Party of the people's rights' (*Partiya narodnogo prava*) founded by the old Populist, Mark Natanson. Following this period of imprisonment, he had to undergo the term of 'administrative exile' under police supervision in the provinces. This exile he spent in his native town of Kamyshin on the Volga, in Saratov for a brief time, and finally in Tambov.[1]

Chernov belonged to a new generation of Socialist-Revolutionaries for whom the Populism of the seventies had already acquired an aura of romance. The idealism of the Populists, especially their faith in the revolutionary potential of 'the people', made a strong impression on the young Chernov, who as a schoolboy was deeply influenced by the poetry of Nekrasov. His ideological mentors were Mikhaylovskii and Lavrov, but he shared the impatience of many of his contemporaries with the gradualist policies which were currently being advocated by the older generation. The famine and

[1] Chernov's career to 1899 is described in his autobiographical *Zapiski Sotsialista-Revolyutsionera* (Berlin, 1922). Extracts from this work can be found in his *Pered burey* (New York, 1953).

cholera years of 1891–2 had failed to produce the popular movement that Chernov had hoped to see, but his belief in the possibility of a peasant revolution remained strong. His exile to a provincial centre such as Tambov gave him a unique opportunity to discover for himself the real mood of the contemporary peasantry.

In Tambov, Chernov found himself in congenial company among the local intellectual community. The Tambov *zemstvo* was relatively enlightened, and the more radical members of the third element gathered around the small nucleus of political exiles, among whom were several of Chernov's contemporaries, as well as some representatives of the older generation of revolutionaries. Chernov naturally gravitated towards the 'Sunday school', or institute for adult education, supervised by A. N. Sletova, who was later to become Chernov's wife. The Sunday school soon became the hub of agitational activity, by the Populist intelligentsia, among the young workers and artisans who attended it. Discussion groups and circles were formed, and Chernov succeeded in organising some of the artisans – cobblers and hatters – in a cooperative, and even in leading a strike.[2]

However, after a series of conflicts with the authorities Sletova was forced to resign her position as head of the Sunday school. The centre of revolutionary activity shifted to another 'cultural' institution – the 'Society for the organisation of popular readings'. This body, whose major function was the selection of books suitable for inclusion in the village libraries, had previously been totally in the hands of the more bigoted and reactionary section of the local clergy and schoolteachers, who ensured that only works of an edifyingly moral and patriotic nature were passed. Chernov, however; appreciating the opportunities which control of such an institution would afford for influence on the peasantry, organised a vigorous campaign to persuade the liberal intelligentsia to play a more active rôle in the Society. Behind the scenes, the colony of exiles was drawn into the task of book selection, and they in turn recruited the students of the local secondary schools, the seminary, the teacher-training institute and the college for medical workers, in order to compile a catalogue of literature which would genuinely educate the peasants and promote their intellectual development in a critical spirit. As soon as the authorities realised what was happening, however, the Society was dissolved.[3]

[2] Chernov, *Zapiski Sotsialista-Revolyutsionera*, pp 249–65.
[3] *ibid*, pp 265–7.

After the failure of these two attempts to conduct political propaganda on the basis of legal 'cultural' activity, the work was continued illegally. Their involvement in the Sunday school and the Society for popular readings had provided the revolutionaries with extensive contacts among the local student body. A whole network of revolutionary circles was formed in the various educational establishments in Tambov, with a central library of illegal literature on various aspects of socialist theory. Many of the students, on completing their courses, took up posts as rural teachers or medical workers in various parts of the province, and Chernov decided to take advantage of this to implement his cherished project of extending revolutionary propaganda to the countryside. The former students would act as local agents of a 'Socialist Populist party', whose programme Chernov had drafted as a basis for uniting the non-Marxist revolutionaries in Tambov, and would conduct socialist propaganda among the peasantry in the villages in which they worked.[4]

As the first group of Chernov's protégés took up their new appointments in the countryside, the problem of providing the young missionaries with literature suitable for the peasants to read immediately arose. The group unearthed a few old pamphlets which had been used in the 'movement to the people', but the contents of these proved to be somewhat dated. For instance, 'A cunning ploy', the most popular of these pamphlets in the seventies, dealt with the way the government exploited the peasantry through the tax system, but it contained numerous references to imposts such as the salt tax, which had since been abolished. The students then turned their attention to a survey of legal literature and succeeded in building up a collection of works dealing with the topic of peasantry and revolution: Erckmann-Chatrian's novels of the French Revolution; the works of Zola and Bellamy; stories by Russian authors with Populist sympathies, such as Leskov; and various novels, stories and articles dealing with the Razin and Pugachev risings, the agrarian movement in Ireland, the peasant war in Germany, the French *jacqueries*, and any other situations and events which they considered relevant to the position of the contemporary Russian peasantry.[5]

The literature compiled and collected by the students was divided into a number of 'mobile libraries' and dispatched to different areas in the charge of a teacher, medical assistant or peasant with

[4] *ibid*, p 273.

[5] *ibid*, pp 266–300.

whom the Tambov circle was in contact. Periodically the libraries were exchanged among the various districts, to ensure that each work had the maximum possible circulation. Occasionally this extended beyond the boundaries of Tambov to the neighbouring guberniyas of Saratov and Voronezh. The peasant response was gratifyingly favourable. Chernov recalls that:

> The little books would return dog-eared from being thumbed through by the peasants' horny hands, but they were always returned with remarkable conscientiousness and consideration. I cannot recall a single case of a book going missing. Sometimes we would lose track of a book as it travelled from district to district, but after a time it would suddenly turn up in quite an unexpected quarter. 'These are blessed books', we would be told. The audience was invariably extremely grateful and receptive.[6]

The establishment of contacts with the peasantry through the rural intelligentsia was Chernov's major achievement during his years in Tambov, and it was the activity of one of these young teachers, Petrukha Dobronravov, that was to convince him of the feasibility of creating a revolutionary organisation from the peasantry. Before this, however, he had explored another possible channel of revolutionary influence on the peasantry – through the rationalist religious sects who had already been brought, through their religious views, into conflict with the state and the Orthodox church.

Chernov's contacts with the sectarians developed out of a chance encounter with a pedlar who turned out to be a self-appointed propagandist among the peasantry. As a young apprentice in Saratov, this man had been influenced by a group of schoolboys, including Chernov's older brother, Vladimir, who introduced him to revolutionary Populist ideas. After this circle was broken up by arrests, his contact with the revolutionary intelligentsia had been broken. He had continued his own campaign, however, among the sectarians, inspired by an article he had read about Herzen's attempts to utilise the schismatic Old Believers for revolutionary ends. He joined the sect of the *Molokane* and began to travel the whole of Russia as a wandering pedlar, making use of his widespread network of contacts in sectarian villages and preaching a curious amalgam of religious and political millenarianism, which identified the achievement of socialism with the realisation of the kingdom of God upon earth.[7]

[6] *ibid*, p 300.

[7] *ibid*, p 281.

The pedlar introduced Chernov to other *Molokane* in the town, and through the latter Chernov became acquainted with the leaders of the sects in the villages, including a learned peasant *Molokanin*, Timofey Fedorovich Gavrilov, who had corresponded with Tolstoy. Discussions with Timofey Fedorovich reinforced Chernov's belief that the sects could be very useful for the revolutionary movement. On one occasion, Gavrilov invited Chernov to attend a meeting of all the leading *Molokane* of the district, at which Gavrilov preached a sermon on a text from Isaiah concerning land organisation among the Jews. Chernov was most gratified to observe that the relevance of this topic to the contemporary agrarian problem in Russia escaped none of those present, as Timofey Fedorovich skilfully introduced into his sermon some of the ideas he had been discussing with Chernov for the egalitarian distribution of the land to the peasantry.[8]

Chernov tried to persuade his new friends that the *Molokane* should play a greater rôle in village politics. (As a rule, they took no part in the village gatherings because of the drunkenness which usually accompanied these meetings.) Chernov's arguments had some effect, and Timofey Fedorovich came to exert considerable influence in the commune. Another *Molokanin*, Erofey Fedotovich Firsin, organised an active campaign for the establishment of a *zemstvo* school in his village, in opposition to the local priest who was supported by the *zemskii nachal'nik*, a local official in charge of peasant affairs, who insisted that the new school should be a church institution. The peasants' wishes were disregarded, and the church school was built. Firsin organised a boycott of the school by the villagers, and when this action led to police reprisals, the peasants burned the school to the ground.[9]

In spite of these partial successes in mobilising the *Molokane*, Chernov was obliged to conclude that it was impossible to utilise the sect as a whole as an instrument of revolution: 'It was too heterogeneous, its rationalism was too petty, its general trend was too one-sidedly religious. In spite of the democratic structure, in which they were formally indistinguishable from the laymen, the leaders were imbued with the peculiar professional conservatism of a rudimentary ecclesiastical hierarchy.'[10] At the same time, however, contact with the sectarians facilitated the spread of revolutionary

[8] *ibid*, pp 283–92.

[9] *ibid*, pp 292–6.

[10] *ibid*, p 302.

influence in the countryside: 'the sect presented us with a ready-made organisation, with a wide network of local contacts, a developed system of conspiratorial practices, and a tradition of opposition to the authorities'.[11] The contacts which Chernov established through his friend the pedlar enabled the Socialist-Revolutionaries to get in touch not only with other *Molokane* in Tambov province, but also with members of other sects, such as the Baptists, in other parts of Russia.

The reception he received from *Molokane*, such as Timofey Fedorovich, taught Chernov a lesson which was to remain with him: the need to present socialism to the peasants 'not just as a dry doctrine concerning the most rational organisation of agriculture and the national economy, but also as an elevated moral philosophy'.[12] In the peasant mind – both for the Orthodox and for those who rejected Orthodoxy – moral, religious, social and political issues were inextricably intertwined. For the peasantry, as for the intelligentsia, socialism had to become a new secular religion, with a moral justification: 'otherwise the revolutionary movement in the countryside was in danger of assuming a petty class and egoistical character, of being morally stripped of its wings'.[13] Throughout his career, Chernov was to insist that the revolutionary peasant movement was more than a class struggle derived from a conflict of economic interests; it was guided by an ideal of social justice which the peasantry shared with the socialist intelligentsia. The peasants saw the intellectuals 'not merely as social teachers, but as apostles. They needed new saints for their new secular religion.'[14] It was the mission of the revolutionary, therefore, to emphasise the moral basis of socialism and to ensure that those peasants who had rejected the old values did not rebel from purely selfish economic motives. This concern with the moral aspect of socialism, in addition to its economic determinants, placed Chernov in the mainstream of Russian Populist thought.

The work of the former members of the Tambov student circles proved to be more fruitful than the contacts Chernov had established with the sectarians. P. A. Dobronravov had been one of Chernov's most devoted disciples among the Tambov students, and Chernov used his influence in the *zemstvo* to have his protégé, upon his

[11] *ibid*, pp 301–2.
[12] *ibid*, p 305.
[13] *ibid*, p 305.
[14] *ibid*, p 305.

graduation, appointed to a school in the area where his contacts with the *Molokane* were strongest. In his first two teaching posts, however, Dobronravov's impetuosity soon brought him into conflict with the local authorities as a troublemaker. 'For the good of his health', Chernov secured his transfer to the large village of Pavlodar, where he was put in charge of the local *zemstvo* school.[15]

Dobronravov set off for Pavlodar, taking with him one of the mobile libraries compiled by the Tambov students. In Pavlodar, he soon struck up an alliance with Shcherbinin, a landless peasant who had made an amateur study of the law and who earned a living by offering legal advice to his fellow-villagers. This Shcherbinin was a major thorn in the flesh of the local 'bosses' – the volost′ clerk, the volost′ elder and several rich peasants – who operated a racket, to which the local *zemskii nachal′nik* turned a blind eye, for extorting money illegally from the peasantry. Shcherbinin and Dobronravov decided to launch a campaign to break up the racket by having the clerk and elder removed from their positions of power. To this end they enlisted the support of a handful of the most reliable and intelligent villagers.

The office of volost′ elder was an elective one, and as the result of intensive canvassing of the peasant electors in the villages, the corrupt elder, Peresypkin, failed to be re-elected, in spite of attempts by the *zemskii nachal′nik* to influence the outcome. The unseating of the clerk, Kachalin, was more difficult, as his post was by appointment rather than election. Complaints against him got nowhere because he was backed by the *zemskii nachal′nik* and the local police chief. The peasants resorted to threats, informing the *zemskii* that the clerk would be killed if he were not speedily removed from office. The *zemskii*'s response was to call in troops. Several peasants were arrested, much to the rage of their fellow villagers, several of whom planned to release them by force.

At this point, Dobronravov and Shcherbinin assembled their small group of seven trusty peasants and made them swear a solemn oath that they would stand by one another to the end and would not desert their cause or betray their comrades: 'they decided to form a secret society which none had the right to leave, with death the penalty for betrayal.' This was the situation when Dobronravov decided to seek Chernov's advice on tactics for the planned rising.[16]

Chernov was naturally excited by Dobronravov's story. He felt

[15] *ibid*, pp 310–11.

[16] *ibid*, pp 311–15.

that the 'Society of brotherly love', as Shcherbinin had entitled the organisation, was exactly the type of peasant union that he himself had been dreaming about: 'His account left me in no doubt that a very valuable, extremely cohesive active nucleus, capable of leading the entire district, had been formed in Pavlodar. I was delighted that the peasants themselves had conceived of a regular secret organisation.' But this very fact led immediately to apprehension: 'I was afraid that it might all perish before its example could affect other areas. So I took it upon myself to calm Dobronravov down, and advised him to find some way out that would avoid staking the entire existence of the first revolutionary Peasant Union on a single card.'[17]

It was agreed that Chernov should return with Dobronravov to Pavlodar and there hold a 'council of war'. Chernov also proposed to rewrite the constitution of the organisation, which had been drafted by Shcherbinin, in order to 'define its aims clearly, so that its distribution in other places might have propaganda significance'. In Pavlodar, Chernov met Shcherbinin and the other members of the society and learned of the organisation's latest moral victory. The rich peasant, Ivan Trofimovich Popov (an erstwhile accomplice of the clerk and the elder), had been converted to the aims of the society, and, after burning the promissory notes which constituted his hold over the poorer peasants (a test of his sincerity), he had been accepted as a member. Popov's desertion soon led to the downfall of the rest of the 'bosses' and averted the need for the society to take any desperate action. Popov was prepared to give evidence against the racketeers, and Shcherbinin was able to draw up an indictment on the basis of the dossier of information which Popov supplied. An enquiry was held, with Popov as the chief witness, which led to the dismissal of the clerk and an official reprimand for the *zemskii nachal'nik*.[18]

Elated by the success of their campaign against the elder, the clerk and the *zemskii nachal'nik*, the Pavlodar peasants decided to turn their attention next to their other major enemy – the local landowner. They planned to drive him from his estate and divide his land among themselves. On this issue, a split developed between the members of the Brotherhood (on Chernov's suggestion, the society had been renamed the 'Brotherhood for the defence of the people's rights') and the rest of the villagers:

[17] *ibid*, pp 315–16.

[18] *ibid*, pp 316–21, 324–5.

The weakest and most ignorant peasants impetuously demanded this step. 'You yourselves stirred us up, and now that it's come to the crunch, you're chickening out', they cried to the more cautious and restrained 'Brothers'. 'Isn't that so? Who said that the land was not made by human hands, and that therefore no-one can appropriate it? Who said that the land is our common mother, the supplier of our needs, and that it should not be subject to speculation, and that the children of the land, the peasants who work the land, should not have their access to their mother barred? If the *pomeshchik*'s ownership of the land is unjust, then down with the *pomeshchik*, let's get rid of him, like we got rid of Peresypkin and Kachalin.'[19]

Here for the first time Chernov was faced with the problem of peasant spontaneity – a problem which was to bedevil the SR party throughout its history:

The immature ingenuous minds of the ignorant masses leapt from the general idea straight into action, without evaluating ends and means, without weighing up the difficulties, but with a naive faith in the possibility of 'the Tsar's command' being implemented wherever they had justice on their side.[20]

The Brothers were painfully aware of the dilemma:

On the one hand it was clear that agrarian disorders would result in repression, which would destroy all the fruits of the recent victory. On the other hand, the transformation was not very pleasant from being the foremost leaders of the crowd to acting as a brake on the movement, cooling things down and appealing for patience and restraint.[21]

Within the Brotherhood itself, opinions were divided. Ivan Trofimovich, the converted kulak, was the most outspoken advocate of land seizure; whereas Shcherbinin, backed by Dobronravov and Chernov, argued that such action, before the creation of a broader peasant organisation which could coordinate a simultaneous movement in other regions, would be premature and counter-productive. The view of the united leadership ultimately prevailed.

Meanwhile, the work of propaganda continued, and Dobronravov soon formed a second Pavlodar Brotherhood of younger peasants who had been influenced by the mobile library. Chernov continued to work among the Tambov peasants but without any further successes on the same scale. In 1898 he attempted to popularise the idea of the May Day celebration among the peasantry, but this project misfired, somewhat, as rumours spread rapidly through the

[19] *ibid*, p 326.
[20] *ibid*, p 326.
[21] *ibid*, p 326.

villages that 1 May was the 'appointed' day on which all the landowners' land could be seized by the peasants and redistributed among them.[22]

At the end of 1898, Chernov convened a small revolutionary peasant congress to which he invited eight peasants from five different districts of Tambov guberniya, as well as a member of the Tambov workers' and artisans' circle and, as a representative of the intelligentsia, Stepan Sletov, Sletova's brother. At this congress, future plans for the extension of propaganda and organisation in the countryside were discussed in some detail, and the problem of providing literature on an adequate scale for the purposes of peasant propaganda emerged as the major obstacle to the expansion of revolutionary activity in the villages. This task was felt to be beyond the resources of a single provincial group, and Chernov undertook to seek the cooperation of other Socialist-Revolutionary groups in Russia in order to establish a nationwide organisation for the coordination of work among the peasantry.[23]

From 1898, Chernov devoted himself to the creation of such a national organisation, leaving the conduct of peasant propaganda in Tambov to Sletov and other members of the local intelligentsia. Between November 1899 and March 1900, however, a series of arrests removed the leaders of the operation. Altogether 31 persons were arrested, one of the first being Sletov himself.[24]

[22] *ibid*, pp 327–9. [23] *ibid*, pp 329–32.
[24] *Revolyutsionnaya Rossiya*, no. 1 (1900), p 13.

3
The Agrarian-Socialist League

In his search for assistance from other Socialist-Revolutionary groups, Chernov soon realised just how isolated he was from the prevailing mood of these groups, which were at that time primarily engaged in negotiations with one another to find a common programmatic base for unification. Ideological innovation, in the form of proposals for a renewed emphasis on the revolutionary and socialist potential of the peasantry, was therefore doubly inappropriate to the existing spirit of the Socialist-Revolutionary movement.

Chernov visited Saratov, the major revolutionary centre on the Volga, but received no support there from either of the more influential circles, those of the Rakitnikovs and Argunov. Neither did he receive any encouragement from his contacts with the newly-formed 'Southern Party' of Socialist-Revolutionaries, or with the St Petersburg 'Group of *narodovol'tsy*'.[1]

In 1899, Chernov's period of administrative exile in Tambov came to an end, and he decided to take the opportunity of going abroad, to study at first hand the latest developments in the Western European socialist movement – which was at that time being racked by the revisionist controversies – and also to seek, in the émigré Populist circles, support for his plans to create an organisation which would coordinate and supply with suitable propaganda literature the groups and individuals working among the peasantry in Russia. En route to Switzerland, he first stopped off in St Petersburg to consult with Mikhaylovskii and the editorial board of his 'Legal Populist' journal, *Russkoe Bogatstvo* ('Russian wealth'), to which Chernov was beginning to contribute articles. Mikhaylovskii was sympathetic towards Chernov's plans for assimilating the latest ideas of Western European socialism into Russian Populist thought, but, to his disciple's chagrin, the master was very sceptical of his claims concerning the revolutionary potential of the contemporary countryside.[2]

[1] Chernov, *Zapiski Sotsialista-Revolyutsionera*, pp 332–5.
[2] *ibid*, pp 337–9.

In Zurich, Chernov found the emigration split into two squabbling factions: the 'elders' of the 'Liberation of labour' group, Plekhanov and Aksel′rod, against the entire younger generation of Social-Democrats. Both groups proved equally hostile to Chernov's vision of an imminent peasant revolution. The elders accused Chernov of resurrecting outworn Populist illusions, and the younger generation shared this view. Aksel′rod at first showed some interest in Chernov's schemes, but Chernov and Plekhanov soon established such acrimonious personal relations that Chernov became finally alienated from the entire émigré colony in Zurich.[3]

Another émigré group in Switzerland, however, took a much greater interest in Chernov's ideas. This was Zhitlovskii's 'Union of Russian Socialist-Revolutionaries', based in Berne and connected with the 'Northern Union' of Socialist-Revolutionaries in Russia. Chernov met Zhitlovskii in Zurich and found in him, for the first time, a member of the older generation who was prepared to take him seriously. Zhitlovskii promised to publish the Constitution which Chernov had drafted for the Pavlodar Brotherhood in the next issue of *Russkii Rabochii* ('Russian worker') the small journal which he edited, and he also gave Chernov an undertaking that his Union would launch a campaign to redirect the attention of Russian socialists towards the peasantry.[4]

Full of hope, Chernov set off for Berne with Zhitlovskii and remained there for about a year. He was soon to be disillusioned concerning the Union's ability to further his cause. The extent of Chernov's split with Zhitlovskii and his Union, and the reasons for it, are somewhat obscure. Although in his autobiography he describes the year in Berne as the 'honeymoon' of his friendship with Zhitlovskii, Chernov also suggests that there were serious differences of opinion between them[5] and implies that he left the Union because of the delays in the publication of the Constitution of the 'Brotherhood for the defence of the people's rights'.[6] Be that as it may, the Constitution was published by the Union in Geneva in October 1899 – a fact which Chernov's autobiography fails to mention. It was published, not in the journal *Russkii Rabochii*, but as a separate pamphlet, along with an appeal, 'A letter to the entire Russian peasantry', purporting to come from the Brotherhood. It was prefaced by a short introduction, 'From the publishers', which welcomed the formation of the Brotherhood and indicated broad

[3] Chernov, *Pered burey*, pp 102–3.
[4] *ibid*, pp 103–4.
[5] *ibid*, pp 105–6.
[6] *ibid*, p 112.

perspectives for a revolutionary union of peasants and workers, whose interests, it claimed, were basically the same. 'The publishers' also outlined their plans for the creation of a special revolutionary journal for the peasantry and requested contributions, both literary and financial, for such a journal.[7]

The Constitution of the original Pavlodar 'Society of brotherly love' had been drawn up by Shcherbinin, but Chernov had altered it, as he had altered the name of the organisation, to fit better his plans for wider propaganda among the peasantry. In Shcherbinin's Constitution, according to Chernov:

> The aims of the society were mentioned very briefly and diffusely. The main content of the Constitution consisted in indicating the obligations of each member towards the whole, and in defining what would happen if these were not fulfilled and he failed in his duty. In this respect the Constitution was more than strict. One kept reading: 'is liable to be deprived of his life'.[8]

The original Constitution saw as the main aim of the society the struggle 'against the *pomeshchiki* and other oppressors of the people who stand between the people and the Tsar'. This formulation of the traditional peasant view – that their misfortunes came, not from the Tsar himself, but from the gentry and officials who screened him from the people – had been adopted by Shcherbinin, Chernov tells us, in order to avert possible suspicion from the authorities, should the document happen to fall into their hands. Chernov, however, suggested that this device be abandoned, 'so that we should not confuse the people, instead of the authorities (who would not have been fooled in any case)'.[9] The published Constitution of the Brotherhood contained no explicit mention of the Tsar, but the accompanying 'Letter to the entire Russian peasantry' contained a direct attack on the peasant view that the Tsar himself was innocent of the oppression which was practised in his name.[10] Chernov's other proposals for amending the Constitution by expanding its social and political aims were accepted unanimously by the Pavlodar peasants.

The published Constitution fell into three parts: the aims, activity and rules for members of the Brotherhood. The aims of the Brotherhood, which for the benefit of the peasantry were explained in simple

[7] *Ustav 'bratstva dlya zashchity narodnykh prav'* (Geneva, 1899), pp 3–8.
[8] Chernov, *Zapiski Sotsialista-Revolyutsionera*, p 315.
[9] *ibid*, p 322.
[10] *Ustav 'bratstva dlya zashchity narodnykh prav'*, pp 9–12.

rhetorical terms, consisted in 'defending the legal rights of the people wherever these are trampled underfoot by the powerful of this world', by ensuring true self-government for the peasants without interference in the affairs of the commune by the state bureaucracy. The Brotherhood also aimed at the replacement of autocratic government by a legislative assembly elected by the people.[11] In the 'Letter to the entire Russian peasantry', this was described as an 'Assembly of the land' (*Zemskii sobor*),[12] but the Constitution of the Brotherhood explained its political demands more simply: 'To ensure that no new laws are passed without the consent of permanent delegates [*khodoki*] elected especially for that purpose by all the peasants and all the working people; so that no-one can impose levies, taxes or obligations on the people without their consent'.[13]

The aims of the Brotherhood also included a very important point which had not been present in Shcherbinin's original Constitution: a demand for land reform, which represented in embryo the SR programme for the 'socialisation' of the land: 'To ensure that the land ceases to be the property of the *pomeshchiki* and other private landowners, and is handed over to all the peasants who work on it, because the land was not created by human hands and labour, and therefore cannot belong to any individual, but should be the common possession of all who earn their livelihood by agricultural labour'.[14]

The activity of the Brotherhood was envisaged as wide-ranging, developing from local to national level. The first six points covered the campaign which could be conducted in each village on the basis of the peasants' immediate interests: propaganda, education and the organisation of strikes and boycotts directed against the *pomeshchiki*. Action against 'the oppressors and exploiters of the peasants' was to be conducted 'as far as possible by legal means', but 'in extreme cases they will be threatened with stiff penalties, as laid down in the secret agreement of the Brotherhood'. The three remaining points envisaged the formation of a network of Brotherhoods, which would ultimately unite to form a single large union. The section concluded: 'This Union must eventually achieve all the aims laid down in the Constitutions of the Brotherhoods: if necessary, it will use force to launch a coordinated attack on the enemies and oppressors of the people.'[15]

[11] *ibid*, pp 13–14.
[12] *ibid*, p 11.
[13] *ibid*, p 14.
[14] *ibid*, p 14.
[15] *ibid*, pp 14–16.

The final section of the Constitution, the 'rules for members', preserved many of the features of Shcherbinin's original, although the repeated invocation of the death penalty for disciplinary infringements was somewhat reduced. A solemn oath of secrecy was required from every member, and 'in case of treason, betrayal, or other such offence against the cause of the people, the Brotherhood may pass judgment on its former or present member, and pass sentence which may even affect his life'.[16]

The publication by Zhitlovskii's Union of the Constitution, with its perspectives for the formation of a union of peasant Brotherhoods served by a propaganda journal issued abroad, would seem to represent a fairly creditable if modest attempt to realise Chernov's aspirations. The beginning of 1900 found Chernov in Paris in the company of a different and more prestigious set of émigrés, who were to take over the tasks which had been outlined by the publishers of the Constitution. In Switzerland, Chernov had been approached by Semen Akimovich An-skii (Solomon Rappoport), a veteran of the 'movement to the people', former protégé of Gleb Uspenskii and now Lavrov's personal secretary in Paris. Lavrov's 'Group of old *narodovol'tsy*' was one of the few émigré Populist groups to have preserved its faith in the revolutionary and socialist potential of the peasantry, and news of Chernov's arrival in Switzerland, and of the nature of his mission, was for them an event of major significance. In Paris, he was to be hailed by them as 'the first swallow of Russia's coming revolutionary spring'.[17] On Lavrov's behalf, An-skii unfolded to Chernov an ambitious scheme for an organisation to direct the peasant movement from abroad, which would be completely independent of the existing émigré factions.[18] In Chernov's eyes, this prospect must undoubtedly have been more attractive than anything Zhitlovskii could offer. Lavrov was a giant of the Populist movement, whereas Zhitlovskii represented no more than one out of a dozen squabbling émigré circles.

In January 1900, therefore, Chernov left Berne for Paris to meet Lavrov's group. Shortly after his arrival, Lavrov fell fatally ill and died on 6 February. Lavrov's death, however, did not impede the realisation of his plan for the formation of an 'Agrarian-Socialist League'; rather the reverse. The assembly of Russian Populist

[16] *ibid*, p 16.
[17] Chernov, *Pered burey*, p 191.
[18] *ibid*, pp 111–18

émigrés from all over Europe, in Paris for Lavrov's funeral, proved very receptive to the idea. In Chernov's words: 'Lavrov's funeral became the christening party of our Agrarian-Socialist League: the dear departed was its invisible godfather, and Semen Akimovich An-skii was, as it were, the executor of his will concerning the League.'[19] Founder members of the League, apart from Chernov and An-skii, were Leonid Shishko, Feliks Volkhovskoy and Egor Lazarev, all veteran Populists associated with the 'Fund of the free Russian press' in London.[20]

It is not clear how far Chernov's departure from Switzerland for Paris represented a break with Zhitlovskii. Chernov's own autobiography suggests that there was a split,[21] but Spiridovich's history of the party presents rather a different account of the founding of the Agrarian-Socialist League. According to Spiridovich, Chernov first campaigned for the creation of a peasant literature in Zhitlovskii's circle, then he and Zhitlovskii, in an attempt to unite a broader spectrum of Populist opinion in the cause, held a conference to which members of the older generation, such as Shishko and Volkhovskoy, were invited. At this meeting a pamphlet, 'How the Minister takes care of the peasants', brought from Russia by Stepan Sletov, was read as an example of the sort of material the League might publish. The assembly of émigrés in Paris for the funeral of Lavrov concluded the negotiations already begun at the conference, by officially founding the League.[22] Zhitlovskii, in fact, subsequently became a leading member of the League.

The newly founded Agrarian-Socialist League began its publishing career by issuing a booklet containing an appeal 'To comrades in thought and deed', and an essay on the policy of the League – 'The immediate question of the revolutionary cause'. The appeal set out the fundamental aim of the League as follows:

> In view of the need to broaden the course of the revolutionary movement in general, and of the workers' movement in particular, by attracting to it the working masses of the countryside, the Agrarian-Socialist League has been formed abroad with the aim of aiding all comrades working directly or indirectly in this direction in Russia.

The tasks which the League would undertake to achieve this end were then laid down:

[19] *ibid*, pp 124–5.
[20] *ibid*, pp 125–7.
[21] *ibid*, p 112.
[22] Spiridovitch, p 111.

I. The publication and distribution of popular revolutionary literature, suitable for the peasants as well as the urban factory and craft workers, especially those who have links with the countryside.
II. Familiarising Russian comrades with the methods of socialist propaganda employed in the West among the working peasant masses (*trudovye krest'yanskie massy*), and with the forms of their organisation for the agrarian class struggle; assessing the historical experience of the 'movement to the people' by the Russian revolutionaries; studying all manifestations of socio-political unrest among the contemporary peasantry; the theoretical development of general problems of agrarian socialism.
III. Practical and immediate aid of all kinds to Russian comrades whose activity corresponds to the programme of the Agrarian-Socialist League.

The final part of the appeal was the most controversial, stating as it did the League's faith in the socialist potential of the 'working peasant masses' in Russia. Members of the League had to accept:

The ability of the Russian working peasant masses to take part in the active movement and in the struggle which will contribute to the evolution of Russian life in the direction indicated by the principles of international socialism.

Members also had to agree about:

The necessity and timeliness of conducting suitable social-revolutionary propaganda and agitation among this mass, to organise its advanced elements for a systematic struggle against economic exploitation and political oppression.

The appeal concluded with an exhortation to 'all comrades in ideas and sentiment' to help the cause by contributing literary works for publication and financial resources.[23]

The essay, 'The immediate question of the revolutionary cause', expanded on the points made in the appeal and constituted a justification, on both theoretical and practical grounds, of the need for revolutionary activity in the towns to be accompanied by widespread propaganda and agitation among the peasantry. The authors[24] attacked the Marxist view that the peasantry was essentially a reactionary force, whose sole aim was to 'turn back the wheel of history', and that a force for socialism could only be created in the countryside by the proletarianisation of the peasantry. They pointed out that this view of the peasantry, which had been developed

[23] *Ocherednoy vopros revolyutsionnago dela* (London, 1900), p 2.
[24] The essay was anonymous, although the appeal 'To comrades in thought and deed' appeared over the names of Rubanovich, Volkhovskoy, Lazarev, Zhitlovskii and Tereshkovich. The similarity in style and content between this essay and his later articles suggests that Chernov must have had a hand in its composition.

in Western Europe on the basis of the experience of 1848 and the Paris commune, was now being widely criticised by socialist leaders, such as Lafargue and Vandervelde. Capitalism in agriculture, they argued, had not played the positive rôle it had played in industry; there was no historical law which said that in all forms of production socialism must be preceded by capitalism; nor was there a law which said that all producers must pass through the purgatory of proletarianisation before they could enter the socialist heaven. It followed that Russian agriculture could indeed, as the Populists had always claimed it would, avoid the stage of capitalist development and proceed directly from communal agriculture to socialism: 'For a certain group of direct producers, for certain sectors of production, a more direct transition is also possible, through the development of various forms of communal property – including the village commune – to the nationalisation of the land, and through cooperation to socialism.'[25]

The essay then discussed – and dismissed – the various practical objections which could be made to their policy of drawing the peasantry into the general revolutionary movement which had revived in Russia at the end of the nineties. They stressed the social and cultural changes which had taken place in the countryside since the seventies, and also the changed attitude of the revolutionaries themselves. The Populists of the seventies had expected too much of the peasantry; they had imagined that militant appeals would immediately rouse the latent revolutionary spirit of the peasants. Now the revolutionaries looked more coolly at the peasantry; they realised that what was needed was a gradual programme of cultural and educational activity, with the aim of preparing the most active and intelligent individuals among the peasantry as revolutionary leaders. This new 'peasant intelligentsia' would constitute a permanent link between town and countryside; eventually, it was hoped, the revolutionary movement in the countryside would be completely taken over by the peasants themselves. For the immediate future, even a small contingent of energetic revolutionaries among the peasants could tip the scales in the event of a confrontation with the government in the towns. 'We are deeply convinced', the Agrarian Socialists continued,

> that the future in Russia can belong only to a party which can find a base for its struggle not only in the towns, but also in the countryside; which can in its

[25] *Ocherednoy vopros revolyutsionnago dela*, pp 6–8.

programme harmonise the representation and defence of the interests of the industrial working class and those of the mass of the working peasantry. Without any support from the peasantry – and even more so *against its will* – no revolutionary party in Russia can inflict a serious and decisive blow on the bourgeois-capitalist regime which in our country manages to co-exist peacefully with the remnants of the epoch of gentry-dominated serfdom under the wing of Russian absolutism.[26]

The activity of the League would have to follow two parallel lines. Firstly, they should arrange the publication and distribution of propaganda literature especially designed for the peasantry. Secondly, they should encourage the peasants to organise on the basis of their immediate local interests – the economic struggle against the *pomeshchiki* and kulaks and the political conflict with the *zemskie nachal'niki* and the local authorities. The actual methods and tactics to be employed would be decided by experience and would vary according to circumstances. It was the duty of the intelligentsia to inform the peasants of the most effective means devised 'by the collective historical experience of Russia and Western Europe':

To acquaint the activists in the countryside with this experience is the immediate task of the intelligentsia engaged in revolutionary and cultural work. Such a union of the intelligentsia and the people – and it alone – can turn the contemporary spontaneous popular movements into conscious ones and direct them along rational lines. And only a union of the working people of the town and the countryside will represent a sufficiently powerful force to smash the might of the existing order and prepare for the triumph of the ideals of socialism and revolution.[27]

The second edition of the pamphlet, which was published in 1901, elaborated on the theoretical justification for conducting socialist propaganda in the countryside. The analogy drawn by earlier writers between industrial and agricultural capitalism, it claimed, had proved to be misleading. The Western European experience had shown that the economy of the small peasant producer was far more capable of survival in the face of capitalist competition than had been predicted; rural capitalism exploited the small producers without necessarily turning them into an organised proletariat concentrated in large-scale production units, as in the case of industry. Moreover, the Russian Social-Democrats' classification of the 'working peasantry' (*trudovoe krest'yanstvo* – those who support themselves exclusively by their own labour) as 'petty bourgeois' was

[26] *ibid*, p 23. (Emphasis in the original)
[27] *ibid*, pp 26–7.

'both theoretically and practically incorrect', implying as it did that the small peasant producer lay on the same socio-economic continuum as the big bourgeoisie. In fact, the Agrarian Socialists argued that there was a qualitative and not just a quantitative difference between the economy of the working peasantry and that of the bourgeois capitalist:

> The latter [bourgeois capitalism] is a means of extracting surplus value: the former [peasant economy] is simply a mode of production. The latter guarantees its owner an unearned income: the former does not guarantee its owner against becoming a tributary of capitalism. The great majority of peasants comprise a particular class of independent agricultural producers, the source of whose income is labour – but only labour which is still not alienated from the means of production . . . In essence, therefore, the working peasantry is an economic category sharply distinct from the bourgeoisie and more closely approximating to the proletariat.[28]

The category of the working peasantry, the authors explained, was distinct from both the rural bourgeoisie and the agricultural proletariat, although it had some features in common with both. Like the bourgeoisie, the peasantry owned its own means of production; but unlike the bourgeoisie, it did not exploit the labour of others. Like the proletariat, its only source of income was personal labour; and again like the proletariat, this labour could be exploited by the privileged classes, through rents, taxes, etc. Therefore the working peasantry belonged, the Agrarian-Socialists insisted, not on the same continuum as the bourgeoisie, but on the continuum of the proletariat; and in practice the peasantry had always produced a joint movement with the rural proletariat, rather than with the bourgeoisie.[29] Many of these ideas, which appeared in 'The immediate question' in rather a haphazard and unsystematic form, were later to be developed by Chernov on the pages of *Revolyutsionnaya Rossiya* ('Revolutionary Russia'), the SR party journal, in a more sophisticated analysis of the political sociology of the peasantry.

[28] *Ocherednoy vopros revolyutsionnago dela*, 2nd edn (Geneva, 1901), pp 9–10.
[29] *ibid*, pp 42–3, 10.

4
Rural propaganda in Saratov guberniya

In the first two years of its existence, the Agrarian-Socialist League issued two editions, of 1,000 copies each, of 'The immediate question of the revolutionary cause'; also five propaganda pamphlets for the peasantry: 'How the Minister takes care of the peasants' and 'How the Hungarian peasants are fighting for their rights', each in editions of 1,000 copies; 'Peasant unions in Sicily', 'Sketches from Russian history' and 'Conversations about the land', each in editions of 2,000 copies.[1] The first copies of these pamphlets to reach the propagandists working in Russia evoked such a favourable response that the League was soon overwhelmed by requests for more literature than its slender finances could afford to publish. The problem of supply was exacerbated by the hazards of smuggling the illegal literature into Russia. At the end of 1901 the League discovered that N. K. Pauli, who had been in charge of transportation, was an *agent provocateur* in the pay of the secret police, who had thus intercepted most of the literature at the frontier.[2]

The arrival in Russia of the first publications of the Agrarian-Socialist League was particularly welcomed by a group of Socialist-Revolutionary intellectuals in Saratov, on the Volga. Throughout the 1890s, Saratov had been a major stronghold of neo-Populism; like Tambov, it was one of those provincial towns on the periphery of European Russia in which political exiles were allowed to reside, under police supervision, after their return from Siberia. Another similarity with Tambov was the existence of a relatively liberal and enlightened *zemstvo*, which promoted educational and cultural activities which could be utilised for purposes of political discussion. By the middle of the decade, Argunov tells us, the freedom and the flourishing of intellectual life in Saratov had earned the town

[1] 'Kassovyi otchet Agrarno-Sotsialisticheskoy Ligi', *Revolyutsionnaya Rossiya*, no. 8 (June 1902), p 28.

[2] Breshkovskaya, *Sotsialist-Revolyutsioner*, no. 4 (1912), pp 104–5, 112–13.

the title of 'the Athens of the Volga'.[3] Natanson's 'Party of the people's rights' had been based in Saratov, and the town was also the original centre of Argunov's 'Union of Socialist-Revolutionaries'. As Chernov had discovered in 1898, the Saratov groups of the nineties paid little attention to the peasantry, being more concerned with general theoretical discussion among themselves. Argunov's Union accepted the Social-Democratic thesis concerning the inevitability of capitalist development in the countryside, and the attitude towards the peasantry expressed in its programme was, in Chernov's words, 'complete scepticism for the present, and a theoretical defence for the future, when access to the countryside would be facilitated by political freedom, won without the aid, and without the participation of the peasantry'.[4]

After the departure of Argunov's Union to Moscow, a group of intellectuals came together in Saratov who were more sympathetic towards the idea of an immediate Socialist-Revolutionary campaign in the countryside. This group included the Rakitnikovs, whose views had changed since Chernov's visit; L. P. Bulanov, a former member of *Zemlya i volya*; and P. P. Kraft, an old *narodovolets* who had tried to organise propaganda activity among the peasantry in Penza guberniya between 1895 and 1899.[5] There still existed, however, a considerable gulf between theory and practice – a gulf which was not bridged until the arrival in Saratov in 1900 of Ekaterina Breshko-Breshkovskaya.

Breshkovskaya was at that time 56 years old. The daughter of a liberal landowner from the province of Chernigov, she had taken part in the 'movement to the people' of 1874 and had been exiled to Siberia in the 'trial of the 193' in 1878.[6] In September 1896 she returned to European Russia, eager to take up where she had left off twenty years before. For the next few years, Breshkovskaya travelled the length and breadth of European Russia, preaching the gospel of peasant socialism and trying to convince the Populist intelligentsia of the need to create a new propaganda literature for

[3] A. A. Argunov, 'Iz proshlago Partii Sotsialistov-Revolyutsionerov', *Byloe*, no. 10/22 (October 1907), p 103.

[4] Chernov, *Zapiski Sotsialista-Revolyutsionera*, p 333.

[5] I. Rakitnikova, 'Revolyutsionnaya rabota v krest'yanstve v Saratovskoy gubernii v 1900–1902 gg.', *Katorga i Ssylka*, kn 47 (1928), p 7.

[6] For Breshkovskaya's early career, see K. Breshkovskaia, *Hidden springs of the Russian revolution* (Stanford, 1931); A. S. Blackwell, ed, *The little grandmother of the Russian revolution* (London, 1918).

the countryside. The task was a thankless one, and Breshkovskaya found herself totally isolated from the younger generation, whose views on the peasantry reflected the current Social-Democratic teaching. This was all the more frustrating for Breshkovskaya because such contacts as she had established with the peasants since her return from Siberia had convinced her that the peasantry was now much more receptive to revolutionary ideas than it had been in the seventies, largely as a result of the spread of education in the countryside in the intervening twenty years.[7]

In Saratov, Breshkovskaya was delighted to find that her ideas met with a sympathetic response, not only from the Rakitnikovs and their circle, but also from a considerable section of the students in the various secondary schools and colleges in the town. Breshkovskaya explained, in terms of their social origin, the particular receptivity of the Saratov students to the idea of agrarian socialism. The liberal *zemstvo* of the province pursued a policy of encouraging the sons of peasants to receive a secondary vocational education by providing them with maintenance grants and by making more places available for this type of education than did most other guberniyas. The colleges run by the *zemstvo* also contained a considerable proportion of students 'whose healthy natures had been unable to tolerate the barracks-type régime of the purely state-run institutions, and who had been expelled "for rudeness" from the classical and practical high schools. In general', she concluded, 'these were the freshest and most determined element of the Russian student body'.[8]

A particularly promising base for the launching of a propaganda campaign in the countryside was provided by the Mariinskoe agricultural college in the village of Nikolaev (*Nikolaevskii gorodok*), about twenty miles from Saratov, where most of the pupils were the sons of peasants from the neighbouring villages. Breshkovskaya succeeded in persuading these lads to conduct propaganda in the villages, starting with general educational activity, and later moving over to the advocacy of socialist ideas. The peasants' responsiveness and interest encouraged the students, and small study circles were formed in a number of villages.[9]

The creation of a peasant demand for literature, through the formation of these circles, soon raised the same supply problem for the Saratov Populists as had been faced by Chernov a few years

[7] Breshkovskaya, *Sotsialist-Revolyutsioner*, no. 4 (1912), pp 122–3.
[8] E. Breshkovskaya, 'Pis'ma starago druga; pis'mo pyatoe', *Revolyutsionnaya Rossiya*, no. 67 (May 1905), p 5.
[9] *ibid*, pp 5–6; Breshkovskaya, *Sotsialist-Revolyutsioner*, no. 4 (1912), p 125.

earlier in Tambov. They managed to unearth a few copies of pamphlets for the peasantry which dated from the 'movement to the people', and set about revising them and bringing them up to date. Several leaflets which Tolstoy had written for the peasants were also found to be suitable. This material was supplemented by new works composed by the Saratov intellectuals themselves and by the first publications of the Agrarian-Socialist League. Having collected a number of copies of printed pamphlets and manuscripts suitable for peasant propaganda, the group set about organising the duplication of this material for distribution to the countryside. In the absence of a printing press or any other sophisticated means of copying, they had to use the most primitive method available, hectographing. The advantage of hectographing was that it required no complex or expensive equipment; its disadvantage was that it was highly labour-intensive. Labour, however, was readily available, in the form of nearly one hundred young volunteers from the various schools and colleges in Saratov. They took over several sheds and attics in the homes of sympathetic intellectuals and set them up as hectographing workshops. Both Breshkovskaya and Rakitnikova provide vivid pictures of the feverish activity that was conducted in these workshops.[10] The girls copied out page after page of the original pamphlets in hectographing ink, in their neatest printing so that the peasants would not find the duplicated booklets too difficult to read. Sometimes they copied directly from the original; sometimes they would take it in turns to dictate aloud, so that several master-copies of the same original could be produced simultaneously. The boys were in charge of the copying process itself, making the hectograph gels and running off copies from the imprints. The freshly printed pages were hung up on lines to dry, before being collated and sewn together into booklets. A further relay of schoolgirls checked and corrected the finished products. In order to allay the suspicions of the authorities, the illegal pamphlets were issued in a 'legal' form, disguised in false covers either as students' exercise books or as official publications. Rakitnikova recalls that the League's pamphlet 'Conversations about the land' was distributed in a cover marked 'Issued by the St Petersburg Joint Stock Company', and 'How the Minister takes care of the peasants' was entitled 'Circular of the Ministry of Internal Affairs'.

The students devoted most of their spare time to these hecto-

[10] Breshkovskaya, *Revolyutsionnaya Rossiya*, no. 67 (May 1905), p 6; *Sotsialist-Revolyutsioner*, no. 4 (1912), pp 125–6; Rakitnikova, 'Revolyutsionnaya rabota v krest'yanstve . . .', pp 7–8.

graphing activities, Sundays and school holidays being times of particularly intensive work. Breshkovskaya estimated that several thousand pamphlets were produced by hectograph in the first year of literary activity, but that even this quantity failed to satisfy more than a fraction of the demand. This demand soon came not only from within the guberniya of Saratov itself and the neighbouring Volga guberniyas of Penza, Tambov, Samara and Voronezh, but also from more distant places such as Tula, Ufa, Vyatka, Perm', Nizhnii Novgorod, Chernigov, Khar'kov and Poltava, where revolutionary agitation in the countryside was beginning to become respectable and even popular.[11]

In the middle of 1901 the Saratov group embarked on a more ambitious project, which promised to realise a long-cherished dream of Breshkovskaya's – the creation of a newspaper specially written for the peasants. The first number of *Krest'yanskoe Delo* ('The peasant cause') was issued in a mimeographed edition of 400–500 copies. It was a thick journal of over fifty pages, and its authors included Rakitnikov, Bulanov and other Saratov intellectuals. A long editorial explained the Socialist-Revolutionary programme in simple language: the poverty of the peasants was a consequence of their exploitation by the *pomeshchiki* and government; a just social order could only be established in the countryside as a result of the socialisation of the land; to this end a union of peasants and workers was necessary – together they could fight for the implementation of the political demands of the SRs. Other articles dealt with historical and topical issues of relevance to the position of the peasantry, such as the Emancipation Act and its consequences, current legislation about migration to Siberia, and the causes of famine. In all of these articles the point was repeatedly stressed that government policy, approved personally by the Tsar, was to favour the interests of the gentry at the expense of the peasants, and that the only way to alter this situation was to overthrow the autocracy and introduce democratic government. The first paragraph of the editorial explained, in somewhat timid and apologetic tones, why a group of urban intellectuals should presume to tell the peasants what to do. It would be difficult to find a clearer or more eloquent statement of

[11] Breshkovskaya notes bitterly that none of these other groups had enough initiative to set up duplicating activities of their own; they relied on the Saratov SRs and complained angrily if they were unable to cope with the demand. Eventually the Saratov group had to send experienced hectographers to other towns to demonstrate the process. *Revolyutsionnaya Rossiya*, no. 67 (May 1905), p 6.

the Populist concept of the moral responsibility of the intelligentsia towards the peasantry:

As we begin to publish *Krest'yanskoe Delo*, we ought to tell you who we are and what we want. First of all – we are town dwellers and know village life only from the sidelines. And yet we have taken it upon ourselves to discuss peasant needs and peasant affairs. Whether we are capable of this task, our village readers will decide for themselves. We ourselves see the matter like this: perhaps we shall make mistakes in little things, in details; perhaps we shall not express ourselves the way the peasants are used to talking; perhaps as a result of this the peasants will fail to understand some of the things in our newspaper, or will not understand them in the way we intended. But we are convinced that we have a more correct understanding of the causes of peasant poverty than have the peasants themselves, and that we know better than they do how they can escape from their unhappy position. And this being so, it would be a sin for us to keep silent. [12]

Although this first number of *Krest'yanskoe Delo* was enormously popular among the peasants, the Saratov group was unable to follow it up with a second number, partly because of technical difficulties and partly as a result of a series of arrests of members of the Saratov organisation in 1902. By the end of 1901, it had become clear that the efforts of the volunteer hectographers were not sufficient to satisfy the rapidly expanding demand, and the Saratov group began seriously to consider the establishment of a printing press. In 1902, as a result of negotiations conducted by Kraft on behalf of the Saratov SRs, a press was set up in Penza to supplement the task of the Saratov hectographers by publishing propaganda literature for the peasantry. This press, however, survived only a few months, before being seized by the police in the autumn of 1902. The small group in charge of it were arrested. During its brief existence, the Penza press managed to publish revised editions of two of the most popular pamphlets, 'A cunning ploy' and 'Surely it need not be so', as well as several revolutionary proclamations. [13]

The literature which was produced by the Saratov students, or received in Saratov from the Agrarian-Socialist League abroad, was distributed to the countryside by members of the rural intelligentsia – teachers, doctors and medical assistants; by the students themselves; by workers who had been recruited into the revolutionary circles in Saratov; and by some of the more 'developed' peasants.

[12] *Krest'yanskoe Delo*, no. 1 (Saratov, 1901), p 1.

[13] Rakitnikova, 'Revolyutsionnaya rabota v krest'yanstve . . .', p 10; Breshkovskaya, *Revolyutsionnaya Rossiya,* no 67 (May 1905), p 6.

Two villages in particular became focal points for propaganda. The first of these was Nikolaev, in Saratov uezd, where the Mariinskoe agricultural college was situated. The second was Turki, in Balashov uezd, which throughout the nineties had been a centre of cultural and educational work conducted among the peasantry by the rural intelligentsia – in particular by the doctor, V. D. Chenykaev; the medical assistant, Mariya Obukhova; and the teacher, Viktorin Aref′ev, himself the son of a peasant.[14]

The agricultural students, whose leader was Mikhail Ivanovich Sokolov, later to achieve notoriety as an SR Maximalist and terrorist under his nickname 'The Bear' (*Medved′*), were in close contact with the central group in Saratov, from whom they received supplies of literature which they distributed and even reduplicated themselves by hectograph. The students had contacts not only in the region of Nikolaev, but also throughout various uezds in Saratov guberniya and also in more distant areas – the guberniyas of Samara, Penza, Nizhnii Novgorod and Ufa, as well as St Petersburg and Siberia. The literature was distributed by various means. When the students went home for the holidays, they would take with them bundles of pamphlets to distribute to the local peasantry. The sphere of influence of the college was further extended as the students graduated and took up posts as district agronomists, often in other guberniyas. One student continued his propaganda activity in Perm′ guberniya, another in Tver′. Sokolov also dispatched literature by post to contacts in *zemstvo* offices, bookstores and other cultural and educational establishments. These contacts, too, extended beyond Saratov guberniya; in Menzelinsk, in Ufa guberniya, literature from Nikolaev enjoyed great popularity with the soldiers of the garrison.

In addition to this extensive distribution of literature, the Mariinskoe students also conducted an intensive oral propaganda in Nikolaev itself and in the neighbouring villages and hamlets. Secret meetings were held at night in peasant huts, and soon a small group was formed of the most 'conscious' peasants, who in turn assumed the rôle of propagandists and distributed literature to their fellow-villagers.

Similar activity was carried on in Balashov uezd by the group headed by Chenykaev and Viktorin Aref′ev. The propaganda literature which was obtained by the intelligentsia through their contacts

[14] Rakitnikova, 'Revolyutsionnaya rabota v krest′yanstve . . .', p 9.

in Saratov was distributed throughout the district by the peasants themselves. Meetings were organised in the villages at which the 'little books' were read aloud and discussed, and money was collected for the financing of further publications. In general, the peasant response to the message conveyed in the propaganda pamphlets was very favourable, and the widespread distribution of revolutionary literature in Saratov guberniya appears to have been a major factor in the disturbances which took place there in 1902.[15]

[15] *ibid*, pp 10–17.

5
The party and the League

By the end of the 1890s, attempts at the unification of the various Socialist-Revolutionary circles in Russia had resulted in two major groupings: the 'Union of Socialist-Revolutionaries' (or 'Northern Union'), which was founded by Argunov in Saratov in 1896, and in 1897 transferred its headquarters to Moscow; and the 'Party of Socialist-Revolutionaries' (or 'Southern Party'), which was formed at Voronezh in 1897. In the course of 1901, the 'Northern Union' and the 'Southern Party' combined to form a united 'Party of Socialist-Revolutionaries'. Other, smaller Socialist-Revolutionary groupings in Russia, such as Gershuni's predominantly Jewish 'Workers' party for the political liberation of Russia' and the independent Saratov circles, also adhered to the new party at this period.[1]

The discordant emigration, however, proved less amenable to unification than the Russian organisations. Towards the end of 1901 Gershuni went abroad, fully empowered by the leadership of the united party, whose headquarters were now in Saratov, to enter into negotiations with the émigrés. Some, including Chernov and Mikhail Gots, were highly enthusiastic about the formation of a united party, and Chernov and Gots undertook the publication abroad of *Revolyutsionnaya Rossiya*, the Union's newspaper, whose secret press in Tomsk had recently been seized by the Tsarist police. *Revolyutsionnaya Rossiya* was to become the official organ of the united party. Other émigrés were somewhat more sceptical concerning the stability of the newly-formed party, and some had reservations concerning its programme. Eventually, however, a measure of agreement was reached and published in the third number of *Revolyutsionnaya Rossiya*: a Central Committee was to be formed to head the party and to supervise the editing of the official organ; the theoretical organ of the party was to be *Vestnik Russkoy Revolyutsii* ('Herald of the Russian revolution'), a journal edited in Paris by K. Tarasov (N. S. Rusanov); and Zhitlovskii's 'Union of Russian Socialist-Revolutionaries' was to be transformed into the

[1] Sletov, pp 67–106; Spiridovitch, pp 61–101.

'PSR Organisation Abroad', which was also to include the editorial boards of the two party organs.[2]

The Agrarian-Socialist League at first remained significantly aloof from the united SR party. There were several reasons why the old Populists in the League (for it was principally the veterans of the seventies who held out for autonomy) were reluctant to surrender their independence. In the first place, they were afraid that the formation of the new party might prove to be only a flash in the pan, and many were unwilling to commit themselves until they were sure that the party was a stable and reputable body. Others felt strongly that the League should remain a non-party organisation, with membership open to Social-Democrats as well as to Socialist-Revolutionaries. A single SD, David Soskice, had joined the League; and Volkhovskoy, in particular, who had recruited Soskice, was convinced that the latter would leave the League if it abandoned its non-party status, thus closing the door to any further enlistment of Social-Democrats. Volkhovskoy and Shishko also cherished the dream of creating an independent peasant socialist party in Russia and saw the Agrarian-Socialist League abroad as the nucleus from which such a party could be organised. All of these prospects would be threatened if the League were to merge with the SR party.[3] The reluctance of the veteran Populists to relinquish their autonomy may also be explained in psychological terms. For them the message brought from Russia by Chernov was, as An-skii told Chernov, 'a justification of the past and a promise for the future'.[4] After two decades in the revolutionary wilderness, their stubborn faith in the promised land of agrarian socialism seemed at last to be on the point of realisation, through the League which they had founded. They were understandably reluctant to entrust the fulfilment of their most cherished vision to a group of unknown youths in Russia – a group, moreover, which did not seem to share their view of the significance of the peasantry for the revolutionary cause.[5]

At the time of its formation, the range of views within the new SR party concerning the rôle of the peasantry in the revolution was very wide. Of the two major component bodies of the party, the 'Northern

[2] *Revolyutsionnaya Rossiya*, no. 3 (January 1902), p 1. For accounts of the negotiations with the émigrés, see Sletov, pp 107–8; Spiridovitch, pp 101–7; Chernov, *Pered burey*, pp 133–61.
[3] A. Kubov, 'S. N. Sletov', in *Pamyati S. N. Sletova* (Paris, 1916), pp 10–11; Chernov, *Pered burey*, pp 158–9.
[4] *ibid*, p 117.
[5] *ibid*, pp 158–9.

Union' had been less sympathetic towards the peasantry than the 'Southern Party'. The programme of the Union, as expressed in its pamphlet 'Our tasks', represented a curious combination of SD views on the capitalist development of Russia (in agriculture as well as industry), together with the *narodovol'cheskii* emphasis on terrorism as the principal means of gaining political freedom. In the struggle for political liberty, the two main social forces on which the party should rely were the socialist intelligentsia and the industrial proletariat. (This point, with its significant exclusion of the peasantry, was emphasised several times in the programme.) Unlike the SDs, however, the Union did not exclude the peasantry from the socialist movement on the grounds that they were a petty bourgeois class. On the contrary, although they claimed that the development of capitalism in agriculture was dividing the old patriarchal peasantry into classes of exploiters and exploited, they referred to the mass of the contemporary peasantry as comprising part of the exploited 'working class'. Since their class position, therefore, did not prevent the peasantry from sharing the socialist interests of the urban proletariat, the Union was prepared to concede that it was possible for 'persons standing close to them' to conduct propaganda among 'the most developed section' of the peasantry, and even to organise them on the basis of their immediate economic and political interests. On the whole, however, the Union considered that the involvement of the peasantry in the current struggle for political freedom was both unnecessary and premature:

> The peasantry, representing as it does the overwhelming majority of the working population of Russia, is destined to play an important part in our economic and political future. But while assigning the peasantry such a rôle in the future, the social-revolutionary party cannot *at present* consider it to be a major support for the achievement of political freedom, nor a suitable soil for social-revolutionary propaganda.
>
> Because of its political subjection, its poverty, its ignorance, and its dispersal over the vast territory of Russia, the peasantry is relatively inaccessible to social-revolutionary propaganda, and a conscious *mass revolutionary* movement of the peasantry is at present impossible.[6]

The 'Manifesto' of the 'Southern Party', in contrast to the programme of the Union, made no mention of terrorism, placing its major emphasis on the economic struggle of the working classes.

[6] *Nashi zadachi*, 2nd edn (1900); reprinted in A. I. Spiridovich, *Partiya Sotsialistov-Revolyutsionerov i ee predshestvenniki, 1886–1916*, 2nd edn (Petrograd, 1918), pp 552–62. The Russian editions contain documentary appendices which do not appear in the French translation. (Emphasis in the original).

It rejected the Union's view that there was no immediate need for peasant participation in the movement for constitutional reform:

> We are convinced that without the sympathy and support of the peasantry the class of factory and industrial workers is incapable of destroying the power of the Russian government and obtaining even political freedom, not to mention the economic transformation of society. And we must recognise that revolutionary activity among the peasantry is completely possible at the present time, since within the peasant estate [*soslovie*] numerous groups have already formed who are as interested in the abolition of the existing economic and political structure as is the industrial proletariat.[7]

The Party accepted that social differentiation had been taking place in the countryside since Emancipation. They distinguished three main social groups within the contemporary peasantry: the rural, petty bourgeoisie, who exploited hired labour on their farms; the rural proletariat, who lived exclusively by hiring out their labour; and the 'land-short' (*malozemel'noe*) peasantry, who occupied an intermediate position between the first two groups and comprised the great majority of the peasantry. Although the members of this last category still possessed land of their own and were independent farmers, they were becoming progressively impoverished and were increasingly forced to hire themselves out as labourers. To this extent, their economic interests, as well as their political and legal interests, were identical to those of the proletariat: 'From this it follows that revolutionary propaganda of the ideas of political freedom, the nationalisation of the land, and the organisation of all social life on socialist principles, is essential and completely possible, both among the rural proletariat and among the "land-short" peasantry.'[8]

The Party also rejected the Union's view that the low cultural level of the contemporary peasantry was a major impediment to the spread of Socialist-Revolutionary propaganda in the countryside. They pointed to the spread of education, the emergence of greater independence among the peasantry as a result of the development of off-farm employment, and the growth of rationalist sects as factors which made the peasantry now 'more capable of conscious protest than in the seventies'. They also considered the existence of the commune to have positive significance: it enabled the peasants to grasp the concept of the nationalisation of the land and also created an

[7] *Manifest Partii Sotsialistov-Revolyutsionerov* (1900); reprinted in Spiridovich, pp 566–7.

[8] *ibid*, p 567.

awareness of common interests among its members. The Party saw the decades since Emancipation as a period of intensifying conflict in the countryside between the mass of the peasantry, on the one hand, and the gentry and the local administration, on the other. It was the revolutionaries' task to divert the spontaneous outbursts of peasant unrest – which had been occurring with greater frequency in recent years – into more organised and constructive channels.

The Party, however, envisaged the struggle for political freedom as a gradual and long-term process, which was still only in its initial stages. For the immediate future, priority should be given to the organisation of the urban workers: 'However important and essential revolutionary activity in the countryside may be, we shall at present, from purely tactical considerations, aim to concentrate our existing forces in the towns – mainly because of the higher cultural level of the urban working population, compared with the rural, and the greater productivity of work in this milieu.'[9] Propaganda and agitation in the countryside, by those whose utilisation there would in no way weaken the urban effort, was welcomed, however. Members of the rural intelligentsia and urban workers who moved to factories in rural locations, or who frequently visited relatives in the villages, were to be encouraged to join the Party, which undertook to supply them with literature and other assistance.

Thus, albeit for rather different reasons, neither the 'Northern Union' nor the 'Southern Party' had been prepared to launch the sort of immediate campaign among the peasantry which was advocated by the founders of the Agrarian-Socialist League. Similar caution was expressed by the united party. Although the SRs were not to agree on a common programme acceptable to the membership as a whole until the First Congress in January 1906, by the beginning of 1902 both *Revolyutsionnaya Rossiya* and *Vestnik Russkoy Revolyutsii* had published provisional programmatic statements which were intended as a basis for the unification of the movement. An article, 'The urgent task', in the third number of *Revolyutsionnaya Rossiya*, proposed a 'minimum practical programme' for all Russian socialists. This programme, which involved no theoretical content, simply listed the social groups from which the socialists could hope to gain support in the immediate struggle for political freedom. Perhaps because of the proposals it contained for the formation of a united front of all revolutionary parties for the political battle with autocracy, the programme put its major emphasis on the rôle of the

[9] *ibid*, p 568.

workers and the intelligentsia:

The party devotes its attention primarily to work among two strata of the population, the industrial workers in large centres, and the intelligentsia . . . The working class, especially its more advanced sector, concentrated in large towns and industrial centres, constitutes the main support of the party.

Concerning the peasantry, the programme was more circumspect – probably in order to avoid antagonising the Social-Democrats:

Among the peasant masses, the aforementioned revolutionary work of the party is conducted to the extent which the party's existing connections with the countryside permit. In any case, the party will not lose a single opportunity of attracting to the revolutionary movement individuals and groups from among the peasantry, and of extending, through them, its influence on the rest of the peasant mass. Therefore the party is fully prepared to cooperate with individuals and groups from the intelligentsia and the peasantry who already have as their aim revolutionary activity in the countryside.[10]

An even more negative attitude towards revolutionary activity among the peasantry had been revealed in the editorial 'Our programme' in the first number of Rusanov's journal *Vestnik Russkoy Revolyutsii*, which served as the basis of agreement among the Paris 'Group of old *narodovol'tsy*', the 'Northern Union' of Socialist-Revolutionaries, and Gershuni's 'Workers' party for the political liberation of Russia'. This programme claimed to follow the ideological tradition of *Narodnaya volya*, revised to take into account more recent developments, of which the growth of capitalism under the protective aegis of the autocracy was the most significant. The influence of *Narodnaya volya* was clearly evident in the emphasis 'Our Programme' placed on the primacy of the political struggle over the economic and on the necessity of terrorism. The journal assigned the major rôle in the fight against autocracy to the socialist intelligentsia and the urban proletariat; these two groups alone, they thought, might be capable of overthrowing the existing political system. It followed, therefore, that the peasantry constituted only a broad area of secondary support for the democratic revolution, which would be won primarily in the urban centres.

In this analysis, as elsewhere, the editors of the *Vestnik* claimed to be the heirs of *Narodnaya volya*. On the basis of the experience of the 'movements to the people', *Narodnaya volya* had rejected the earlier Populist view that the peasantry could provide the initiative for revolution in Russia. The authors of 'Our programme' recognised the significance of developments which had taken place in the

[10] 'Neotlozhnaya zadacha', *Revolyutsionnaya Rossiya*, no. 3 (January 1902), p 8.

countryside since the seventies: the spread of education, leading to the creation of a peasant intelligentsia; the growth of urban influence on the peasantry through the recruitment of industrial workers who still retained their links with the villages; and the increasing peasant unrest as a consequence of intensified economic and political conflicts in the countryside. They considered none of these changes, however, to be sufficiently important to cause them to reject *Narodnaya volya*'s assessment of the revolutionary potential of the peasantry; their main value was that the contemporary peasantry was more likely to be sympathetic to the idea of political freedom than the peasantry of the seventies had been. Since the peasants were destined to play only an ancillary rôle in the democratic revolution, 'Our programme' considered it unnecessary to devote any particular propaganda effort towards the countryside:

> The revolutionaries' regard for the commune and their demands for the extension of peasant landholding in one form or another are sufficient motives to make the peasants sympathetic towards the democratic revolution. But to attempt to go further and, for example, to delegate a section of our forces working in the towns to spread socialist propaganda in the countryside, seems to us to be an exceedingly non-advantageous exercise, likely to divert the rapid advance of the revolutionary army against autocracy. It goes without saying, however, that we extend a warm welcome to propaganda in the countryside by those elements whose occupation, so to speak, ties them there.[11]

The relegation of the peasantry to such a secondary position in the revolutionary movement by the editors of what was to become the official theoretical journal of the new SR party infuriated the Agrarian-Socialist League. An-skii for a time refused to cooperate at all with Rusanov. Chernov, however, persuaded him that their best tactic would be to go along with the *Vestnik* in a united front, hoping that in the course of time their opponents would be converted to the League's point of view.[12] A certain degree of compromise was reached when the second number of *Vestnik*, which appeared in February 1902, contained an article by Stepan Sletov, 'On the land', which argued the League's case for the involvement of the peasantry in the contemporary revolutionary movement. In a footnote dissociating themselves from Sletov's conclusions, the editors of the journal declared:

> Although the views of the author of 'On the land' differ from those which we put forward in the programme of *Vestnik Russkoy Revolyutsii*, we are pleased

[11] 'Nasha programma', *Vestnik Russkoy Revolyutsii*, no. 1 (July 1901), pp 12–13.
[12] Chernov, *Pered burey*, pp 160–61.

to publish this article, in view of the interesting information which it contains concerning the contemporary countryside, which has been so little studied, and is so unfamiliar to revolutionaries. Only a whole series of factual investigations and personal observations covering a wide area will enable us to judge how far the conclusions drawn by our comrade on the basis of his own observations may be applied to the whole of peasant Russia. We do not conceal from ourselves all the difficulties involved in reaching a correct formulation of the peasant problem. The more familiar we are with the contemporary Russian countryside, the more easily shall we avoid both the unfounded optimism which leads to old errors and the dangers of pessimism, which may exclude a very major and important area for revolutionary work.[13]

Stepan Nikolaevich Sletov, the author of 'On the land', was born in Tambov in 1876, the son of a liberal landowner who was a respected local public figure. As a schoolboy, Sletov was influenced by the ideas of the Populist political exiles in Tambov; whilst a student in Moscow in the mid-nineties, however, he became more attracted to Marxism. In 1896, he was arrested for membership of the illegal 'Union council' of students in Moscow and for organising a demonstration. He was sentenced to three years' administrative exile in Ufa guberniya, but in 1897 his father succeeded in having his son's place of exile transferred to Tambov. There, under the influence of his sister and Chernov, Sletov came to reject his Social-Democratic views, especially those concerning the peasantry. When Chernov left Tambov in 1899, it was to Sletov that he entrusted the continuation of his work among the peasants. In 1901 Sletov, too, went abroad, to Switzerland, where he joined the Agrarian-Socialist League.[14]

Sletov's article 'On the land' was based on a pamphlet, 'On the question of revolutionary activity among the peasantry', which had been published in a hectographed edition by the Tambov circle in 1901. The evidence it cited was largely drawn from Sletov's personal experiences in Tambov. On the basis of these observations, Sletov challenged the Social-Democratic view of the peasantry which, by implication, was shared by many SRs:

Unfortunately, in our opinion, the majority of existing revolutionary programmes suffer from inattention to actual conditions in the countryside. In speaking of the countryside, these programmes usually place in the forefront its stratification into a bourgeoisie and a proletariat, and place great hopes on the revolutionisation of the countryside by the urban proletariat. But in our opinion, in talking about the assessment of the revolutionary significance of the peasantry it is essential to take into account that which is characteristic of

[13] Nechetnyi, *Vestnik Russkoy Revolyutsii*, no. 2 (1902), p 37.
[14] Kubov, *Pamyati S. N. Sletova*, pp 5–9; Chernov, *Zapiski Sotsialista-Revolyutsionera*, pp 330–32.

the countryside and distinguishes it from the town: namely, the mass of the working peasantry directly connected with the land. It is the interests and aspirations of this mass which determine the attitude of the countryside towards social revolution. And it is they, therefore, whom the revolutionary who wishes to influence the peasantry must bear in mind.

Sletov continued, in a direct attack on the views expressed in 'Our programme':

To leave the mass of the peasantry outside its sphere of influence would mean political suicide for any political party. The urban movement, given even the *passivity* of the peasantry, is doomed to certain defeat. For this there are Western European analogies.[15]

It was the mass of the undifferentiated peasantry, Sletov claimed, who were at the present time manifesting the most militant and revolutionary attitudes in the countryside; the impoverished agricultural proletariat, by contrast, on whom the Social-Democrats placed their major hopes, were the most passive and downtrodden sector of rural society. There was an obvious sociological explanation for this, as Sletov pointed out: it was in the less differentiated communes that the greatest solidarity of peasant interests existed, and this was expressed in common action against the gentry landowners and the local administration.[16]

Sletov's article concluded with an impassioned plea to the younger generation of revolutionaries in Russia: 'Comrades! Pay greater attention to Russian reality: the multi-million mass of the Russian peasantry cannot wait until the process of capitalist development unites them with the proletariat. They are suffering and struggling, but in their struggle they are fumbling their way in the darkness. Bring to this struggle the light of your knowledge!'[17]

Sletov's words were to prove prophetic. Within a few weeks of the publication of his article, while the young SR party was still divided on its attitude towards the peasantry, widespread agrarian disturbances broke out in the south of Russia.

[15] Nechetnyi, *Vestnik Russkoy Revolyutsii*, no. 2 (1902), pp 79–80. (Emphasis in the original).

[16] *ibid*, pp 80–82.

[17] *ibid*, p 82.

Part II

THE CAMPAIGN FOR THE PEASANTRY (1902–1904)

6
The peasant movement of 1902

The beginning of the twentieth century ushered in a period of widespread social unrest in Russia. From the end of the 1890s there was a steady increase in student disorders in the universities, a growing strike movement in the industrial centres, and peasant disturbances in the countryside. All of these trends were to culminate in the revolutionary upheavals of 1905.

The underlying causes of the peasant movement which broke out in 1902 were economic. By the provisions of the Emancipation Act of 1861, the peasants received less land than they had previously used under serfdom, and an unprecedented increase in the size of the rural population in the second half of the nineteenth century intensified the problem of 'land-hunger'. Heavy redemption payments on their communal holdings, in addition to an onerous burden of direct and indirect taxation, increased the impoverishment of the peasantry. The inadequacy of his allotment to meet his obligations forced the peasant either to rent or to purchase land from the gentry, or to seek off-farm wage-labour in agriculture or industry. The pressure of population increase, however, pushed land prices and rents up, and kept wages low. The economic dependence of the peasantry on the gentry landowners was therefore on the increase in the decades after Emancipation. Those of the gentry who retained their land at the end of the century either rented their estates to the neighbouring peasantry or went over to more capitalistic methods of farming. Although in many areas the system was a mixed one, forms of renting, including money-rent, labour-rent and share-cropping, predominated in the central agricultural areas of the Black Earth and Volga; whereas capitalist agriculture, with the estates being worked for money-wages by a landless or near-landless agricultural proletariat, was developing mainly on the Western periphery – the Baltic provinces, Belorussia, the Ukraine and Novorossiya. In areas where this transition to capitalist agriculture was taking place, the peasants were deprived not only of the opportunity of renting land, but also, in many cases, of their traditional rights of access to resources such as forest and pasture. Conflicts over land, rents and wages between the peasantry and the large landowners intensified towards the end of the century.[1]

The increase in peasant militancy at the turn of the century, however, cannot be explained solely in terms of the worsening economic situation in the countryside. (The famine years of 1891–2, after all, did not produce the sort of movement which erupted ten years later.) It was a combination of material and non-material factors which caused the peasants from the end of the 1890s to respond to their situation by direct action, contrasting with the passivity they had displayed, with few exceptions, for over a century. Sletov, in his article 'On the land', listed what he saw as the major developments which were contributing to the rising tide of peasant unrest.

Since Emancipation, Sletov claimed, a new generation of peasants had grown up in the countryside who were aware not only that they had rights as free men, but also that these rights were being denied them by their former masters, the gentry, and by the authorities. Traditional peasant attitudes had dissociated the Tsar from the actions of his servants, but the consistently pro-gentry policies of Alexander III and Nicholas II had caused the peasants to question the rôle of the Tsar as the 'little father' of his people. At the same time, the peasants' attachment to the Orthodox religion had declined, resulting in the development of secular scepticism, and in the growth of mystical and rationalist sects. This erosion of peasant faith in the two pillars of patriarchal Russian society – autocracy and Orthodoxy – had led, in Sletov's experience, to the creation of a new group of 'conscious fighters against the existing political and social order'. These men had developed their critique of the status quo quite independently of any influence from the intelligentsia, but they proved most responsive to revolutionary ideas when they encountered them.[2]

A similar account of the changes which were occurring in peasant attitudes towards the end of the century is provided by Breshkov-

[1] The classic English-language study of the pre-revolutionary peasantry is G. T. Robinson, *Rural Russia under the old régime* (London, 1932). For the economic position of the peasantry at the beginning of the century, see also S. M. Dubrovskii, *Krest'yanskoe dvizhenie v revolyutsii 1905–1907 gg.* (Moscow, 1956), pp 7–35.

[2] Nechetnyi, *Vestnik Russkoy Revolyutsii,* no. 2 (1902), pp 46–78. Sletov's contemporary account (1901) does not mention names and places, but is clearly based on his experiences in Tambov, and the 'types' of peasant revolutionaries he lists correspond quite closely with the character sketches of the members of the Pavlodar Brotherhood drawn by Chernov in his *Zapiski Sotsialista-Revolyutsionera* (1922).

skaya. When she returned to European Russia after twenty years of Siberian exile, she was struck by the transformation:

The first thing that sprang to my attention was the significantly greater extent of literacy and the desire of the more literate to read serious books in the hope of finding answers to their insoluble problems . . . Next, one could not help noticing a greater independence of behaviour and, among the younger peasants, a deliberate ignoring of the gentry and the state officials . . . On entering the churches I noticed a complete absence of candles where previously there had been so many that the sacristan had to remove them before they were half-burnt. The only worshippers were the old people and the little children. There was a complete absence of young and middle-aged attenders. Moreover, there was hardly a single teenage girl, not to mention the lads, who had not been working away from home, travelling hundreds of miles to the south of Russia at harvest time, or to the sugar refineries in Kiev and elsewhere.

The former fanatical attitude towards the Tsar was no longer in evidence, but hatred of the landowners and officials had grown, and had become more acute and more conscious. The peasants of their own accord discussed the evils of these two institutions, although often from an incorrect point of view, and they already had a faint realisation that in other countries the laws were the same for all citizens, and that the authorities there were elected, and not appointed from above.[3]

All of these economic and non-economic factors contributed to the militant mood of the peasantry at the beginning of the twentieth century. The exact timing and location of the movement which broke out in the spring of 1902, however, must be explained in terms of more specific causes: famine and the distribution of revolutionary propaganda. In the areas affected by peasant unrest in 1902, the harvest of 1901 had been poor, and severe hardships had been suffered by the poorer peasants in the winter of 1901–2. In an atmosphere of acute economic crisis, the peasants placed greater credence in rumours which suggested that the solution to their problems lay in the dispossession of the large landowners.[4]

Ever since their disappointment with the terms of the Emancipation Act of 1861, rumours had been rife among the Russian peasantry concerning the imminence of a 'second freedom', in which all the land would be redistributed among them. At the time of the Russo-Turkish war, especially, expectations of the 'Tsar's favour concerning the land' were heightened.[5] At the turn of the century, according

[3] Breshkovskaya, *Sotsialist-Revolyutsioner*, no. 4 (1912), pp 118–19.

[4] P. Maslov, *Agrarnyi vopros v Rossii* (2 vols, St Petersburg, 1905–8), vol 2, p 107; V. Gorn, 'Krest'yanskoe dvizhenie do 1905 g.', in *Obshchestvennoe dvizhenie . . .*, vol 1, p 246.

[5] *ibid*, p 234.

to Sletov, alongside the millenarian hopes of a new 'manifesto' from the Tsar there also existed the belief that land and liberty could only be achieved from below, by a general peasant rising such as that which had occurred under Pugachev.[6] The discontented peasants responded to revolutionary propaganda with varying degrees of sophistication: some interpreted it as sanctioning the use of direct action; in other cases, peasant unrest was reported to have been precipitated by the distribution of revolutionary proclamations which the peasants interpreted as copies of a manifesto from the Tsar granting a redistribution of the land.

The peasant movement of 1902 assumed its greatest dimensions in the Ukrainian guberniyas of Poltava and Khar′kov. The troubles began in March in Konstantinograd uezd, in Poltava guberniya, when the peasants raided the estate of the Duke of Mecklenburg, seizing the produce and livestock in the barns and burning the manor house and outbuildings, saying: 'We need the land, we shall clear it and plough it.' Thereafter, the movement spread rapidly to neighbouring uezds in Poltava and Khar′kov guberniyas. Altogether, about eighty estates were raided. Reports of the movement suggest that the peasants behaved in a calm and organised manner and that they seemed to feel that their actions were justified. Often the decision to raid an estate was taken openly at the village gathering, and the raiding party was headed by the village elder. The confiscated goods were divided fairly among the peasants, according to need, and also in many cases they took care to leave the *pomeshchik* sufficient food for himself and his family till the next harvest and enough seed for the next sowing. Cases of physical violence against the estate owners or their servants were rare.

In some instances the peasants were content to obtain sufficient food to satisfy their immediate needs; more frequently, however, their aims were more fundamental and were directed towards the general redistribution of the lands of the large estates. In such cases, the peasants sought to drive the gentry away – initially by polite requests that they should depart, then by threats and, as a last resort, by arson. Once the landowner had left, the peasants burned down the property, to ensure that 'the master' would not return. Sometimes the peasants justified their actions in terms of 'the Tsar's manifesto', and they referred to the revolutionary pamphlets and proclamations as evidence that it was now 'permitted' to seize the land. In other cases, however, it appears that the peasants saw their

[6] Nechetnyi, *Vestnik Russkoy Revolyutsii*, no. 2 (1902), pp 65–6.

justification in the principles of social justice: why should they starve, when the *pomeshchik*'s barns were full of grain and hay which they, the peasants, had laboured to produce; and why should the gentry claim the land, when they did not work it with their own hands? For those who still had faith in the Tsar, the two justifications were interrelated: if the Tsar were indeed the true benefactor of his people, he would wish to see social justice implemented through 'black repartition'. So convinced were some peasants that the Tsar supported their actions that even the arrival of troops to suppress the movement did not disillusion them: the Tsar had sent the soldiers, the peasants assumed, to supervise the orderly redistribution of the land. This belief sometimes had tragic consequences, as in an incident in the village of Kovalevka where a crowd of peasants refused to disperse when ordered to do so by an officer. 'You dare not fire', the peasants told the troops. 'The Tsar has not commanded it.' When several of their number lay dead or wounded, the peasants begged the troops to depart, saying that 'the officers will have to answer for this to His Majesty the Emperor'.[7]

The movement in Poltava and Khar'kov triggered off similar disturbances in the neighbouring Ukrainian guberniyas of Kherson, Ekaterinoslav and Bessarabia. At the same time, agrarian unrest flared up in the Volga provinces of Saratov and Tambov. By the middle of 1902 the whole of the south of Russia, from the Ukraine to the Urals, was affected by the movement. In most cases, the forms of the movement were similar – raids on estates and arson. However, the rumours of a manifesto from the Tsar, which played such an important part in Poltava and Khar'kov and which endowed the movement there with its peculiar mass psychology, were less in evidence elsewhere. On the Volga, conflicts with the gentry often arose from specific local grievances and were precipitated by the famine conditions, by the appearance of revolutionary propaganda, and by news of the disturbances in the Ukraine. Clashes between the peasants and the gentry were particularly acute in Saratov, where, in addition to destructive violence against estates, the movement also assumed the form of wage-strikes and rent boycotts.[8]

[7] Maslov, vol 2, pp 108–18. Maslov's account of the movement is based on newspaper reports, including those in *Revolyutsionnaya Rossiya.*

[8] *ibid*, pp 118–23; Gorn, *Obshchestvennoe dvizhenie* . . ., vol 1, pp 249–52.

7
The SR Peasant Union

In June 1902, *Revolyutsionnaya Rossiya* devoted an entire issue to the peasant movement in the south. The appearance of this issue marked the triumph of Chernov and his 'agrarian' faction over the *narodovol'tsy* in the SR party. The events in Poltava and Khar'kov were seen as a justification of the views of the Agrarian-Socialist League, and from 1902 onwards the party as a whole adopted a consistently pro-peasant policy.

In his editorial, 'The peasant movement', Chernov put forward an important claim, which he was later to develop in a series of theoretical articles in *Revolyutsionnaya Rossiya* – that the contemporary peasant movement was semi-socialist in character. He attacked the view of the movement expressed in the Social-Democratic journal *Iskra* ('The spark'). *Iskra* saw the peasant movement as an integral part of the bourgeois revolution – an attack on the remnants of feudalism in Tsarist society, which would clear the way for the development of capitalism in Russia. Chernov rejected the SD assumption that the forthcoming revolution would be bourgeois in character: bourgeois revolution 'from below' had, he claimed, been forestalled in Russia by bourgeois revolution 'from above'. The 'Great Reforms' of Alexander II in the 1860s had represented 'a metamorphosis of feudal autocracy into gentry–bourgeois bureaucratism' and had already cleared the way for capitalist development, under the protection of the Tsarist government. The bourgeoisie, therefore, had no direct interest in the political overthrow of autocracy. The forthcoming revolution would be primarily political, but it would go beyond the framework of bourgeois democracy and introduce far-reaching social and economic reforms which would pave the way to socialism. A guarantee of the progressive socio-economic character of the revolution lay in the fact that the peasantry had, as the current movement showed, 'already put forward a semi-socialist programme: the land should not be private property; it should only be held on a basis of just, egalitarian *utilisation* – utilisation, moreover, by those who work it personally and live from their labour; the product of labour should belong to the labourer'. The Socialist-Revolutionaries, in Chernov's view, 'need only provide a rational, scientific formulation of these completely correct principles to produce from them the pure idea of socialism'.[1]

The peasant movement in the South, the editorial continued, had justified the view of the commune expressed in the programme of the Agrarian-Socialist League. The peasants of Poltava and Khar'kov had not seized the gentry land and property on an individual basis, but had distributed them among the members of the commune according to need. Chernov attacked the Social-Democrats, who were advocating that the peasants be given the right of free exit from the commune, and the right of free disposal of their land, in order to create capitalist conditions in the countryside: 'They accused the peasant of individualism and a fanatical passion for private property. And now, when the peasantry is proclaiming the egalitarian principle for the utilisation of the land as a common good, the Social-Democrats are advocating a diametrically opposed demand.'

The SRs, Chernov protested, were 'far from idealising the contemporary commune, half-smothered in the clutches of administrative and fiscal oppression'. But it was clear that the tradition of communal control of the land would make it easier for the peasants to grasp the concept of socialisation – in which the control of the land was vested in 'the greater collective, the entire people'. The replacement of communal by individual ownership of land, as advocated by the SDs, would 'contradict the very spirit of socialism'; whereas socialisation, involving the development of collective property in land, was a progressive measure which the SR party advocated 'in full accord with international socialism'. Together with the development of collective forms of production, as in cooperatives, it would prepare the way for the socialisation of agricultural production.[2]

Although at this stage the concepts were not developed in any practical detail, Chernov in his editorial drew a clear distinction between the socialisation of the land, as a transitional measure under which the land would be held collectively but worked and utilised by individuals or households on an egalitarian basis, and the socialisa-

[1] 'Krest'yanskoe dvizhenie', *Revolyutsionnaya Rossiya*, no. 8 (June 1902), pp 3–4. The great majority of articles in *Revolyutsionnaya Rossiya* were published anonymously. Birmingham University Library, however, possesses a microfilm made in Prague of a copy of the journal in which the names of the authors of many of the anonymous articles have been added in Chernov's own handwriting.

[2] *ibid*, p 4.

tion of agricultural production, in which the land would be both held and worked collectively. The socialisation of the land, unlike the socialisation of agricultural production, was not in itself a socialist measure; but insofar as it was non-capitalist and non-individualist, it could be regarded as a 'semi-socialist' transitional aim. This aim, Chernov optimistically asserted, was implicit in the contemporary peasant movement; the SRs' task was simply to persuade the peasants that the party's demand for the socialisation of the land represented an effective programmatic expression of the peasant aspiration for 'black repartition'.

Chernov's editorial announced the formation of an 'SR Peasant Union' (*Krest'yanskii Soyuz Partii Sotsialistov-Revolyutsionerov*) to direct the party's activities in the countryside. An appeal from the Peasant Union, 'To all those working for revolutionary socialism in Russia', which set out the aims and tactics of the Union and which expanded upon some of the points made by Chernov in his editorial, was published in the same issue of *Revolyutsionnaya Rossiya.*[3] The time was now past, the authors of the appeal began, when Socialist-Revolutionaries could content themselves with paying only lip-service to the revolutionary potential of the peasantry. In the nineties the passivity of the peasants and the numerical weakness of the Socialist-Revolutionary groups might have constituted a valid justification for inactivity; recent events, however, had drastically altered these circumstances. Unrest in all sectors of society had intensified, and revolution was more imminent than could have been foreseen a decade earlier. The socialists of the nineties had imagined that by the time a revolutionary situation had matured in Russia the communal peasantry would have become largely proletarianised; now it was clear that the outcome of the revolution would be determined by the attitudes and aspirations of the mass of the undifferentiated peasantry. The intelligentsia and the proletariat could achieve nothing without the support of the countryside; even the passive neutrality of the peasants would not guarantee victory for the revolutionary forces. It was therefore essential that the peasantry should be drawn into the revolutionary movement.

How possible, at the present time, was a conscious revolutionary movement of the peasantry, acting in concert with the proletariat

[3] 'Ot Krest'yanskago Soyuza Partii Sotsialistov-Revolyutsionerov ko vsem rabotnikam revolyutsionnago sotsializma v Rossii', *R.R.* (*Revolyutsionnaya Rossiya*), no. 8 (June 1902), pp 5–14.

and intelligentsia? This was the 'major problem' to which the founders of the SR Peasant Union addressed themselves. The peasant's land-hunger, they pointed out, gave him an obvious interest in agrarian reform. As yet, however, the peasants had no clear idea of the form which such a transformation should assume:

> We are not blind to the fact that, in the peasants' aspirations for the transfer of the land from those who do not work it to those who do, the shining ideal of communalisation of the land [*obmirshchenie-obobshchestvlenie zemli*] has been obscured by the dark blot of hope in the Tsar and a lack of clarity as to whether the disposal of the land will pass into the hands of the entire people, or of individual communes, or even of individual peasants. We know that we shall have to put in a lot of hard work to clear the pure socialist principle of the *communalisation* [*obobshchestvlenie*] of the land from tradition and individualist views of the land, but then, if the idea of the *socialisation* [*sotsializatsiya*] of the land had been produced ready-made by the peasants, there would be nothing for us to do. [4]

The task of persuading the peasantry of the justice of the SR programme for the socialisation of the land, the Union continued, was made easier by the social and cultural developments which had taken place in the countryside in the last decades of the nineteenth century. The spread of literacy and urban influence since the time of the 'movement to the people' guaranteed that its failure would not be repeated. The appeal pointed out that 'in some respects, no class in Russia is as activated towards a purely political struggle as is the peasantry': the administrative structure of the post-Reform countryside was such that the peasantry enjoyed a greater degree of participation in their local organs of self-government – the village and volost' gatherings – than did any other sector of society. On the other hand, these bodies were subject to such a degree of interference from the government authorities, leading to so many conflicts, that the peasants' everyday experiences acquainted them with the political facts of life and imbued them with a strong class feeling of 'us' – the peasant world – against 'them' – the state bureaucracy. Recent government policy towards the peasantry – in particular, the introduction under Alexander III of the institution of *zemskie nachal'niki* – had only served to exacerbate this animosity. The experience of those isolated members of the rural intelligentsia who had engaged in revolutionary activity in the countryside in recent years confirmed that the peasantry was now more receptive to propaganda than ever before.[5]

[4] *ibid*, p 7.

[5] *ibid*, pp 8–9.

The present situation of widespread peasant unrest, the appeal continued, showed how urgent was the need for revolutionary influence on the countryside. The Peasant Union foresaw two probable developments in the agrarian situation in the immediate future.

Firstly, the movement which had begun in the Ukraine might spread to cover the whole of Russia. This would be a welcome development, which would increase the chances of victory for the movement for political liberation; but the very spontaneity of the peasant movement contained within it the danger of another Pugachev rebellion – Pushkin's anarchic 'Russian revolt, both senseless and ruthless' – which had simply flared up and died down again without achieving any substantial improvement in the condition of the peasantry. To prevent such an outcome, the party must ensure that peasant protest was governed not by 'any obscure rumour about the Tsar's favour, concealed by the officials', nor by 'various narrow and mystical sectarian revelations', but by the concepts of political liberty advocated by the revolutionary parties, which would ensure that the actions of the peasantry were coordinated with those of the workers and intelligentsia in the towns.

The second possibility was that the government might act to forestall peasant unrest by granting some minor and partial agrarian reforms. Intensive propaganda would be required to ensure that the peasants were not fooled by such reforms, which, if introduced, might prove a serious obstacle to the cause of revolution. These two considerations made essential a Socialist-Revolutionary campaign in the countryside. Those elements in the party who had been sceptical concerning the revolutionary potential of the peasantry had been confounded by the events of the spring of 1902, but it was not too late to harness the peasant movement to their cause:

> It would be tragic and shameful for us, under the influence of past failures and dogmas long ago refuted by life, to remain again aside from life – but this time not because we were unable to move it from the spot, but because life itself had already moved sooner than we, disillusioned and disheartened by reaction, had expected, and because it did not move along the paths which we had predicted for it in our theories . . . Insofar as conscious revolutionary work has lagged behind what has been happening within the peasantry – to which the majority had stubbornly closed their eyes in recent years – so must we now catch up with the movement of life . . . And our work among the peasantry in the next few years can and must make up for our virtually total inaction over the past few decades. [6]

[6] *ibid*, p 10.

What were to be the aims and tactics of the SR Peasant Union? The ultimate aim of the party was, of course, 'the realisation of the socialist ideal in all its fullness'. Socialism, however, could not be achieved in Russia in a single leap, and the party proposed a minimum economic programme of transitional reforms, as a first stage. A clear distinction was therefore drawn between the 'maximum' and 'minimum' programmes – a distinction which was to create considerable problems for the SRs throughout their history. The maximum agrarian programme involved the socialisation or collectivisation of agricultural production; the minimum programme envisaged, firstly, the socialisation of the land, which was defined as 'its conversion into the property of the whole of society, for utilisation by those who work it', and, secondly, the creation of cooperative associations among the peasantry, which would prepare the way for the collective agricultural production of the socialist future.

These economic measures, however, could only be implemented as the result of the achievement of political freedom. The democratic revolution, therefore, should be the immediate objective of the SR Peasant Union:

> Leaving open meanwhile the question as to what extent the peasantry is ready for a purely political struggle, we must at any rate do everything we can to draw the greatest possible section of it into this struggle, and to strengthen and extend the political element in every economic movement of the peasantry. Therefore, taking as its motto those most bright and glorious words, hallowed by tradition, 'land and liberty', the Peasant Union puts 'liberty' first and foremost.[7]

In view of the importance of the political struggle, the party's policy in the countryside should now move away from the previous practice of 'self-sufficient economic propaganda in narrow peasant circles' to '*general political and social-revolutionary agitation* among the broad masses of the peasantry'. The work should be extensive as well as intensive, and at this stage the emphasis should be on the former: broad sectors of the peasantry should be made aware of the party's aims, so that in the imminent revolutionary confrontation they would offer some degree of support to the intelligentsia and workers. To this end, written and oral propaganda addressed to the peasantry should always stress that social transformations could only come about as the result of a political revolution. The desirability of economic reform, which the peasants could appreciate

[7] *ibid*, p 11.

on the basis of their own personal, everyday experience, should serve as the argument for political freedom: '*We must appeal to the peasant through Land to Liberty, and lead him through Liberty to Land.*'[8]

In accordance with these new aims, new forms of propaganda should be developed. Until now, the party had relied on the distribution of 'thousands of copies of pamphlets which explained our programme more-or-less fully, and demanded a certain degree of effort if the peasants were to understand them fully'; now they should distribute 'tens and hundreds of thousands of small leaflets', which would explain party policy in the most general and simple terms, capable of being grasped by the 'broadest masses' of the peasantry. The mass distribution of such leaflets required the involvement of new forces in peasant propaganda. The intensive work of preparing 'conscious cadres of revolutionary socialism' among the peasantry, in circles organised by the rural intelligentsia in their own localities, should continue; but it should be supplemented by the extensive distribution of propaganda leaflets by more mobile elements, including urban intellectuals and workers.

The Peasant Union's proposal for the diversion of urban revolutionary forces into the countryside for a mass campaign of agitation marked a new departure for the agrarian-socialist movement, and the authors of the appeal considered it necessary to defend their views against possible accusations that they would thereby weaken the urban movement. The recent upsurge of interest in socialism among young people in the towns meant, they argued, that there was a surplus of revolutionaries in many places, especially in the urban centres, where there was only a small complement of industrial workers. The direction of some of this surplus to the countryside could only benefit the revolutionary movement as a whole. Among the social groups whose energies could usefully be employed in the villages without detriment to the urban movement, the authors listed: students during their summer vacation; administrative exiles in provincial towns; and, rather improbably, escaped political prisoners who, apparently, were roaming the Russian countryside in growing numbers, in order to avoid police vigilance in the towns. In general, however, the success of peasant propaganda, as exemplified by the experience of the past few years, was the most important argument in favour of a campaign in the countryside: 'At the

[8] *ibid*, pp 11–12. (Emphasis in the original).

present time the countryside gives the revolutionary perhaps no less return on the spiritual capital he expends than does the factory. To economise on our investment in such a profitable business, when the expenditure of one agitator from the intelligentsia produces dozens of agitators from the peasantry, would be more than improvident.'[9]

The appeal concluded by indicating the projected development of revolutionary activity by the peasantry once they had been influenced by propaganda. Here again the primacy of the political over the economic struggle was stressed. The first task was to organise the peasants into secret circles, to be known as 'Brotherhoods' or as 'committees of the Peasant Union of the party'; ultimately it was hoped that a network of these bodies would cover the whole of Russia. Apart from the recruitment of new members and the spreading of propaganda, the activity of the brotherhoods should consist, firstly, in gaining influence in the commune, by having their members elected to positions of responsibility in the organs of peasant self-government, where they could set an example to their fellow-villagers by taking a stand against the state bureaucracy. Secondly, they should encourage peaceful forms of the economic movement, such as agricultural strikes and boycotts, which, apart from their aim of material improvement, would serve the constructive purpose of uniting the peasantry in common solidarity against the *pomeshchiki* and kulaks, thus creating the basis for a future political movement. Finally, in addition to these essentially peaceful forms of action, the Peasant Union envisaged 'the possibility and perhaps the inevitability of a violent armed struggle'.

At this early stage of the movement, such violence would consist in acts of individual political terror: the examples cited were the killing of 'spies, traitors and informers' as acts of self-defence, and also the murder of members of the local administration who had particularly incurred the hatred of the peasantry. The next stage in the movement would be one of 'open, mass and purely political activity'. This would take the form of demonstrations, a campaign of petitions putting forward the political and economic demands of the SR party, and a mass refusal by the peasantry to pay taxes or provide recruits for the army until these demands were met. The Union recognised that it was rather optimistic to expect such a degree of political coordination from the peasantry in the immediate future, but it felt that even a partial realisation of these objectives might just

[9] *ibid*, p 13.

tip the scales in the coming confrontation between the revolutionary forces and the government;

> At such a decisive moment even a small but organised movement of only a part of the peasantry, given the sympathetic neutrality of the rest, would have great moral and material significance: when troops are required simultaneously both for the towns and for the villages, when, as may be hoped, the troops themselves refuse to serve absolutism against the people, then the autocracy will have to yield.[10]

In its first manifesto, therefore, the SR Peasant Union called for a revolutionary campaign in the countryside in a tone of much greater urgency than had the pamphlets of the Agrarian-Socialist League. The outbreak of the movement in the south had shown that the mood of the peasantry was even more militant than the Agrarians had realised. The spontaneity of the peasantry had in fact taken the SRs by surprise: the peasants had moved ahead of the party, and the task now was to catch up with the movement and harness it to the conscious political aims of the revolutionaries.

The same number of *Revolyutsionnaya Rossiya* that announced the formation of the SR Peasant Union also announced another important event in the organisation of activity among the peasantry: the establishment of a federative link between the party and the Agrarian-Socialist League.[11] The creation of the Peasant Union, and the publication of its manifesto, had brought SR policy into line with that of the Agrarian-Socialists and thus removed the final barrier to unification. But even before this, the eventual rapprochement of the League and the party was guaranteed, for purely practical considerations. The League was only a small group of émigrés, with no organisation in Russia to transport and distribute its publications. The party, on the other hand, had an existing organisational network in Russia which, in practice, served to distribute the League's publications there. Those who transported the pamphlets of the League into Russia met up with local SR groups and committees which had already begun work in the countryside.

If the League and the party, therefore, shared the same organisation in Russia, there seemed little point in the controlling bodies remaining separate. In terms of their personal composition, in fact, these two bodies were virtually identical, since many of the indi-

[10] *ibid*, p 14.
[11] 'Iz partiynoy deyatel'nosti', *R.R.*, no. 8 (June 1902), p 27.

viduals who worked on the writing and publication of League literature were also engaged in similar work for the party. Chernov and An-skii, who were among the first of the leading Agrarian-Socialists to join the united party and who held influential positions in both organisations, were strong advocates of amalgamation.[12]

The final agreement, approved at the First Congress of the League in August 1902, represented a compromise between those who sought complete integration and those who still held out for autonomy. Each body was to retain its complete internal independence, but each entered into a federative association with the other, based on a common acceptance of the programme for propaganda in the countryside laid out in the League's pamphlet 'The immediate question of the revolutionary cause', and in the appeal of the SR Peasant Union 'To all those working for revolutionary socialism in Russia'. The two organisations agreed to combine in the publication of pamphlets and booklets of a popular nature for peasants and workers; these would constitute a series to be known as the 'Popular revolutionary library' (*Narodno-revolyutsionnaya biblioteka*), issued as 'Publications of the Party of Socialist-Revolutionaries and the Agrarian-Socialist League'. The party undertook to organise the distribution of all the League's publications in Russia and to supply the League with all necessary information, literary works for publication, and – probably the most important – financial support.[13]

The impact of SR finance soon made itself felt on the publishing activity of the League. In the period from its formation to the end of 1901, the League had issued a total of 10,000 copies of publications (six titles, in editions of 1,000 and 2,000 copies). In the first six months of 1902, a further 15,000 copies were published (four titles in editions of 3,000 and 4,000 copies).[14] At the First Congress of the League, however, it was announced that the party had suggested that future editions be of 10,000 copies,[15] and in the second half of 1902 a further 65,000 publications were issued in the 'Popular revolutionary library' (seven titles in editions of 5,000 and 10,000).[16] In addition to these joint publications of the party and the League, the SR Peasant Union published its appeal 'To all those working for

[12] Chernov, *Pered burey*, pp 158–9; Spiridovitch, p 139.
[13] 'Federativnyi dogovor mezhdu PS-Rov i Agrarno-Sotsialisticheskoy Ligoy', *R.R.*, no. 9 (July 1902), p 18.
[14] 'Kassovyi otchet Agrarno-Sotsialisticheskoy Ligi', *R.R.*, no. 8 (June 1902), p 28.
[15] 'Pervyi s″ezd Agrarno-Sotsialisticheskoy Ligi', *R.R.*, no. 12 (October 1902), p 21.
[16] 'Iz partiynoy deyatel′nosti', *R.R.*, no. 16 (January 1903), p 18.

revolutionary socialism in Russia' (in an edition of 5,000 copies); an appeal 'To the entire Russian peasantry' (in an edition of 10,000 copies); and a propaganda pamphlet, 'The unjust organisation of the Russian state' (also in an edition of 10,000 copies). In 1902 also, the party began to issue a newspaper, *Narodnoe Delo* ('The people's cause'), intended for both workers and peasants, and an accompanying series of pamphlets, 'The library of the people's cause'. The first two numbers of *Narodnoe Delo* (in editions of 5,000 copies) and the first pamphlet in the series, 'Tsar Famine' (in an edition of 10,000 copies), appeared in 1902. Several other pamphlets published by the party, independently of the League, were suitable for the peasantry. Altogether 317,000 copies of SR publications were issued abroad in the course of 1902, and the weight of literature transported into Russia was 160 poods (about $2\frac{1}{2}$ tons).[17]

Breshkovskaya has provided us with a vivid picture of the transportation of the illegal literature into Russia from Switzerland in these early years. The treachery of Pauli had alerted the gendarmes on the Western frontier to the smuggling routes which were being used, and much of the literature entrusted to professional smugglers continued to fall into the hands of the police. Alternative methods were sought, such as concealing pamphlets in imported goods: 'They were packed into empty cupboards and other pieces of furniture being delivered into Russia from abroad, they were stuffed into barrels of fruit, vegetable oil and so on.' Students returning to Russia for the vacations carried pamphlets sewn into their clothing in what were nicknamed 'suits of armour'. The party also bribed sailors to smuggle literature into Russia by sea. Breshkovskaya complains that the party had to reckon not only with the Russian police, but also with the German and Austrian authorities, who were, she says, more hostile to SR publications than to those of the Social-Democrats, because of the party's reputation as a dangerous organisation of anarchists and terrorists. In spite of these obstacles, however, the illegal literature continued to get through, though never in sufficient quantity to satisfy the demand of the local committees.[18]

In 1903 the publishing situation was rather different. Local party committees were able to set up illegal presses in Russia itself, so that the émigré presses were no longer the exclusive source of supply. Only one new title, 'For land and liberty', was issued in the 'Popular

[17] *ibid*, pp 18–19.
[18] Breshkovskaya, *Sotsialist-Revolyutsioner*, no. 4 (1912), pp 104–6.

revolutionary library' (in an edition of 5,000). The remaining joint publications of the party and the League in 1903 were a third edition of 'How the Minister takes care of the peasants', a second edition of 'The will of the Tsar and the will of the people', and a Ukrainian edition of 'The tale of the unjust Tsar'. The total number of publications in the series was only 30,000 as compared with 80,000 in 1902. Many of the works published by the party press in 1903, in emigration or in Russia, were in fact reprints of pamphlets originally issued under the imprint of the League or the Peasant Union. Thus new editions were issued of 'To the entire Russian peasantry', 'Conversations about the land' and 'The will of the Tsar and the will of the people'. The total volume of SR publications for 1903 was greater than that for 1902 – 395,000 copies. In addition to these propaganda pamphlets and copies of party newspapers and journals, various proclamations and leaflets were issued by local party committees.[19]

[19] 'Iz partiynoy deyatel'nosti', *R.R.*, no. 40 (January 1904), p 23.

8
The problem of cadres

The initial appeal of the SR Peasant Union 'To all those working for revolutionary socialism in Russia' had raised the question of the creation of conscious party cadres among the peasantry; and from 1902 onwards this was the most important practical problem which faced the SRs in the countryside.

The urban intellectuals

The original announcement in No. 8 of *Revolyutsionnaya Rossiya* concerning the formation of the SR Peasant Union had given very little information about the structure of the Union, other than that it was to unite all party members working in the countryside. No. 13, however, provided greater detail concerning the organisation of the Union and the background to its formation. The creation of the SR Peasant Union as an ancillary organ of the party represented an institutional recognition of a situation which already existed, in reality, since:

> As long ago as the autumn of last year, several local groups had already allocated several of their members especially for the conduct of peasant affairs. They in their turn had drawn other people into the cause, people who did not belong to the local group, and thus they created a new group which had no name but was particularly engaged in supplying the countryside with propaganda.[1]

It was decided that a local committee of the Peasant Union could be formed only under the auspices of an existing party committee, if the committee felt that the expansion of its activity in the countryside required the recruitment of individuals especially for that purpose: 'Such an organisation would be a safeguard both against any one-sided enthusiasm for peasant affairs, to the detriment of other party work, and against any harmful separation of peasant work from the total complex of party activity.'[2]

[1] 'Iz partiynoy deyatel'nosti', *R.R.*, no. 13 (November 1902), p 22.
[2] *ibid*, p 22.

At the time of writing, two local committees of the Peasant Union had issued proclamations to the peasantry – those of Saratov and Khar'kov. It is not clear how many local committees of the Peasant Union were formed in the course of 1902 and 1903, nor how far their activity extended to the organisation of peasant Brotherhoods, as well as the distribution of literature. The work of the committee of the Peasant Union of Ekaterinoslav guberniya, reported in *Revolyutsionnaya Rossiya* in October 1903, appears to have been particularly intensive. Contacts had been formed with peasants in twenty villages throughout the guberniya; in twelve of these, 'groups of the committee of the Ekaterinoslav Peasant Union' had been formed, each of which was supplied with a small library consisting of twenty to thirty publications of the party and the Agrarian-Socialist League. The committee itself had also issued three hectographed pamphlets, two of which dealt with local issues.[3]

From 1902 onwards a steady stream of reports from the countryside on the progress of revolutionary activity among the peasants began to appear in *Revolyutsionnaya Rossiya.* At first these reports concentrated on the peasants' favourable response to propaganda. In September 1902 the Peasant Union claimed that its first steps had encountered 'soil prepared for the reception of socialist ideas; wherever it began its activities it met with sympathy and a readiness actively to help it'.[4] From Saratov guberniya it was reported that:

> The conscious elements of the peasantry are mainly occupied in distributing illegal literature, and there are complaints from all sides concerning the shortage of such literature. The most popular are books of a fictional character . . . The peasants say, 'If we had more of such books, we could raise the entire district.' Some villages order a hundred copies of one title, so that it is impossible to satisfy the demand. In some places, they try to hectograph their own proclamations, and organise regional committees. (I know of only one, covering five or six villages.) To obtain funds to pay for the illegal books they collect money from the readers, or form cooperatives to do agricultural work. The books are widely distributed, and a pamphlet reaching the village passes through a dozen hands . . .[5]

Another correspondent wrote:

> A year's activity by the SRs in the villages of Penza guberniya has convinced them that the peasants are completely receptive to the propaganda of Socialist-Revolutionary ideas. They avidly read the literature distributed among them, sometimes at a complete gathering of the village, and are totally sympathetic towards it. At the same time a considerable number of peasant propagandists

[3] 'Iz partiynoy deyatel'nosti', *R.R.*, no. 34 (October 1903), p 21.
[4] 'Iz partiynoy deyatel'nosti', *R.R.*, no. 11 (September 1902), p 23.
[5] 'Chto delaetsya v krest'yanstve', *R.R.*, no. 17 (February 1903), p 19.

have emerged from their midst who, in terms of their energy, their serious approach to the business and their propensity to act in a conspiratorial manner, compare most favourably with the intelligentsia and the urban workers . . .[6]

Yet another reporter provided further details concerning the rôle of the 'conscious' elements of the peasantry – the 'village intelligentsia', as he called them, because they were better educated than their fellows. This stratum consisted mainly of the village artisans, such as joiners and blacksmiths, and the estate stewards. Other 'conscious' elements were urban workers and their families who had returned home to their native villages. This peasant intelligentsia played a crucial rôle in the task of conveying revolutionary ideas to the other peasants, since they were able to read the 'little books' and interpret them to their fellows. This had a double advantage: oral propaganda was less dangerous, since the authorities could have no tangible evidence of it; and also the process of interpretation by a fellow-villager made political ideas more comprehensible to the average illiterate peasant, since the peasant propagandist tended to use everyday graphic illustrations of his point. The same correspondent found that many sectarians became propagandists, because literacy was higher among the rationalist sects than among the Orthodox peasantry. Also, he pointed out, every sectarian was by definition a 'man of ideas' (*ideynyi chelovek*), fully aware of the political implications of his religious beliefs.[7]

In some villages, the two-stage process of dissemination of revolutionary ideas took rather a different form and followed a more traditional pattern of influence. It was reported from Saratov guberniya that when a new pamphlet reached a village, the village gathering of heads of households would meet in a hut to consider it. The young men were sent away. Then the village elder, who was in charge of the pamphlet, would hand it to the clerk – often the only literate person in the village – to read aloud. If the pamphlet was considered 'suitable' by the gathering, its contents were communicated to the young men and other non-voting members of the village. If any member objected to the contents of the pamphlet, he was forced to take an oath of secrecy not to betray his fellows to the authorities.[8]

[6] 'Iz partiynoy deyatel'nosti', *R.R.*, no. 17 (February 1903), p 20.
[7] 'Iz nablyudenii propagandista', *R.R.*, no. 18 (February 1903), p 16.
[8] 'Chto delaetsya v krest'yanstve', *R.R.*, no. 19 (March 1903), p 15.

Gratifying as these reports from the countryside must have been for the party, a few shadows soon fell on the initial glowing picture of success. The Peasant Union's policy of dispatching urban *intelligenty* to the countryside was, it seems, in some places having the counter-productive effect of making the peasants suspicious of the intelligentsia and their motives. In March 1903 *Revolyutsionnaya Rossiya* published a letter from a peasant revolutionary, in which he attacked the dilettante nature of much propaganda by the intelligentsia:

To work among the peasantry, it's best to be a peasant yourself, or to have studied properly the life of the peasants, and to live among them not as a master but as a peasant. Only then will they understand you and trust you fully. I know from experience of several examples of unsuccessful work among the peasants by students and *pomeshchiki.* And no wonder. The student, living in the countryside, gives the peasants literature and talks to them about liberty, equality, fraternity and so on. At the same time he himself is frittering away thirty to fifty roubles a month on trifles. Meanwhile the peasants, to whom he's explaining that each of them should help the needy with their last crumb, and sacrifice themselves for the benefit of others, are shivering with cold, and their children are dying of hunger . . . How can the peasants trust such people? . . . The work shouldn't be done by students and *pomeshchiki*, who very rarely succeed in attracting the peasants, but by the peasants themselves. To this end we should first of all cultivate the most outstanding of the more conscious peasants, who could work themselves and serve as an example to the others.[9]

This peasant correspondent saw the rôle of the intelligentsia in the countryside as essentially an ancillary one, their most useful task being that of advising and obtaining literature from the towns to supply the peasant propagandists.

It may be that the writer was overstating the case against the urban intelligentsia as propagandists, as the editors of *Revolyutsionnaya Rossiya* hastened to point out in a footnote to the letter:

The author of this manuscript is of course correct insofar as he affirms that, all other things being equal, peasant propagandists have many advantages over *intelligenty*. Being of the same flesh and blood as the village masses, they have every opportunity to find the quickest path to the hearts of their brother peasants. But the author exaggerates the intelligentsia's chances of failure. We know of a number of *intelligent* propagandists who had only to appear in the countryside to start up immediately a process of unrest and revolutionary crystallisation.[10]

[9] 'Golosa iz derevni', *R.R.*, no. 20 (March 1903), p 13.
[10] *ibid*, p 13.

Nevertheless, the sort of considerations raised by this letter may partly have been behind the introduction, later in the same year, of a new party policy of greater emphasis on the rôle of the rural intelligentsia, especially the village schoolteachers, in the task of spreading propaganda to the countryside. The teachers were, after all, the type of *intelligent* approved of by the peasant correspondent quoted above, living in the villages 'not as masters, but as peasants', and capable of fulfilling an intermediary rôle between the peasants themselves and the urban party organisation.

The kulaks

If peasant hostility towards certain elements of the urban intelligentsia represented the first major snag in the implementation of the policies of the Peasant Union, then the second followed close upon its heels, in the form of a report in the very next number of *Revolyutsionnaya Rossiya* from a correspondent in Elisavetgrad uezd in the guberniya of Kherson. The problem which he outlined concerned the rôle of the more prosperous peasantry in spreading revolutionary propaganda in the countryside. The prosperous peasants were among the most receptive elements in the villages to new political ideas; but the correspondent was concerned that the critical references to kulaks in the SR pamphlets threatened to alienate these men from the party, and he raised the whole issue of the definition of a kulak.

The strata he was describing, the correspondent said, derived their prosperity from their use of modern techniques, and not from exploitation of the labour of others. The old kulaks in the district, who had gained their wealth through speculating in land, had gradually been dying out in the last few years of famine and crop-failure, and had been replaced as the most influential men in the village by a new generation of young and literate peasants with a progressive approach both to agriculture and to life in general. They read farming journals, consulted the local agronomist, and introduced new methods, such as crop rotation. The correspondent made a point of noting that these peasants made little use of hired labour, except at harvest time, and relied mainly on family labour. They encouraged their own children, however, to stay on at school, and often hired a lad for the winter to compensate for the labour of sons who were studying. If they or their animals fell ill, they turned to the *zemstvo* doctor or veterinary surgeon rather than to the village 'wise woman'. Being literate, they made a point of acquainting themselves with the legislation dealing with peasant affairs and actively criticised the conduct of the local authorities. They were also critical of many of the traditions of peasant life and were frequently disrespectful of the old men. They rejected religion as superstition and criticised the priests. The attitude of the other peasants towards these 'new men' was somewhat ambivalent: many of the younger men admired and respected them for their economic success and for their constant championship of the peasants' rights; but the older men resented them as 'freethinkers' who undermined the traditional life of the village.[11]

The correspondent pointed out that it was the very prosperity of these peasants which brought them into conflict with the local authorities. The uezd was, in general, greatly impoverished and had accumulated an enormous debt of tax arrears. Because of the principle of collective responsibility of the commune for taxes, the burden of payment lay most heavily on the richer peasants, and the authorities had recently issued orders to the *zemskie nachal'niki* that the arrears should be paid by confiscating and selling the 'excess' livestock of the more prosperous peasants.[12] The 'new men' were obviously Stolypin's 'sturdy and strong' peasants, who found the restrictions on free enterprise imposed by existing legislation extremely onerous, to such an extent that they had become the leading oppositional element in the villages. Before the advent of the revolutionaries, however, their opposition had lacked any positive direction or formulation.

These peasants had proved avid and highly receptive readers of revolutionary propaganda. The correspondent reported that 'the idea that the land, being a gift of nature, and not a commodity, should belong to those who work it, made a particularly strong impression on them, and soon it was shared by quite a wide circle of peasants'. They volunteered to become propagandists, to raise the level of consciousness of their fellows, as a preliminary to organisational activity. One aspect of the content of the revolutionary literature, however, was proving an obstacle to the recruitment of these 'thrifty' peasants – namely, the attacks it contained on the kulaks. 'In concluding', the correspondent wrote:

I cannot remain silent concerning the distress caused to our readers by various sections of the afore-mentioned pamphlets. Misconstruing the word 'kulak', they understand it to refer to the more prosperous villagers, and those who

[11] 'Chto delaetsya v krest'yanstve', *R.R.*, no. 21 (April 1903), pp 12–13.
[12] *ibid*, p 12.

exert any kind of pressure on the commune. For this reason, they took the warnings against the kulaks, scattered in various passages of the pamphlets, to refer to themselves, and they consider that although in exceptional circumstances these warnings may be justified, they are tactless, and harm the interests of our cause. They are tactless because at first, at least, propaganda must inevitably be channelled through these very 'intellectual peasants', as the most energetic, influential and developed persons in the village. They are firmly convinced that the *intelligent* is unsuitable as a propagandist for the village, and in fact has so far shown little sign of appearing as such. If in the course of time the intelligentsia do decide to assume this rôle, they will not be able to withstand pressure from the police, and the final result will be that these same prosperous peasant-farmers will become the agitators. We tried to convince them that they misunderstood the use of the term 'kulak' – and indeed, in our opinion, no economic theory could include these people in that category. But our argument was only partly successful, and so when we returned to town on a temporary absence they all begged us to convey to 'them' that 'they' should either 'write differently' or give a more accurate definition of the expression 'kulak'.[13]

This first major indication of the rôle of the more prosperous peasants in the task of spreading revolutionary ideas in the countryside,[14] and the issue it raised of the party's attitude towards, or definition of, the rich peasant or kulak, involved serious theoretical and tactical problems for the leadership. The editorial reply to the correspondent from Kherson guberniya is therefore particularly interesting. It began by recognising the significance of these 'new men', who differed from the traditional kulaks by their independence of, and opposition to, the local authorities. This stratum lay on the border-line between the 'working peasantry' and the rural bourgeoisie, and shared some of the characteristics of each of these groups. The editors accepted that these men were often the most intelligent and independent characters in the village and were therefore most likely to lead peasant opposition to the authorities. They compared this new group with the 'labour aristocracy' in industry, who shared some of the interests of the mass of the workers and were in a good position to lead them – while at the same time, on the basis of interests peculiar to themselves, they might constitute a separate group with different interests from those of the masses. As with the labour aristocracy, propaganda directed towards the 'peasant aristocracy' should lay more emphasis on the wider moral

[13] *ibid*, p 14.

[14] Confirmation soon followed in reports from other regions. For example, it was reported from Tula that: 'There are villages where the leaders are the richest peasants, which may partly be explained by the fact that they have the most frequent contact with the urban and rural intelligentsia', *R.R.*, no. 30 (August 1903), p 16.

aspects of socialism than on narrow economic self-interest. There was, however, an important difference between the class position of the labour aristocracy and that of the peasant aristocracy. Whereas the skilled worker was still a proletarian, the prosperous peasant was in fact a member of the developing rural bourgeoisie and shared some of its interests. For the leadership of the peasant movement to fall into the hands of a stratum which had so much in common with the kulaks, constituted, in the view of the SR leaders, 'a considerable danger for the future'.[15]

They recalled that Engelhardt, in his famous 'Letters from the countryside', written in the 1870s and 1880s, had observed that the most rabid 'liberals' and 'freethinkers' in the villages were the richest peasants, who found themselves in conflict both with the authorities and with the *pomeshchiki* and who were ardent advocates of 'black repartition'. Their motives for desiring the redistribution of the land of the large estates were, however, rather different from those expressed by the Populist intelligentsia. Engelhardt had quoted one of these kulaks as saying: 'See how the *pomeshchik* lets his lands go to waste: if only us peasants could get our hands on it, what an income it would give!' The editors of *Revolyutsionnaya Rossiya* commented:

> It is not difficult to appreciate that by 'us peasants' here they meant not the ordinary ploughman-farmer, but the peasant-merchant, the businessman, the kulak. His enmity towards the gentry landowner is purely a conflict between legal estates, not between classes. It is not a form of the conflict of labour against capital, but rather a conflict of capital against land-rent and the monopolies of the feudal serf-owner.[16]

They also recalled that although Sletov, in his article 'On the land', had listed the more prosperous peasants, alienated from the local authorities, among the elements most receptive to revolutionary propaganda, he had also pointed out that in conditions of political freedom such peasants would constitute a class of conservative individual farmers. They concluded that from the point of view of tactics the party could utilise those of the more prosperous peasants who were prepared to sacrifice their own material interests as a separate group in favour of the moral ideal of egalitarian communal peasant landholding. The kulak who was concerned primarily with his own economic self-interest, however, should be treated with grave suspicion. It was only in the first stage of the revolution – the

[15] 'Chto delaetsya v krest'yanstve', *R.R.*, no. 21 (April 1903), p 14.
[16] *ibid*, p 14.

overthrow of the autocratic government – that the interests of the peasant bourgeoisie coincided with those of the working peasantry: it was the SRs' task to ensure that the leadership of the peasant movement should not fall into the hands of the kulaks:

We cannot forgo our duty to explain to the peasants the contradictions between their interests and those of the kulaks, simply in order to gain the support of the latter for the present. We must not conceal this inevitable clash of interests, but prepare the working peasantry in advance for the moment when it will appear sharply and distinctly. Otherwise the horny hands of the peasant masses will only be plucking chestnuts from the fire for the village bourgeoisie.[17]

The editorial comment concluded by emphasising the theoretical implications of this issue. It was pointed out that it was the policy of the SDs – which the SRs had always condemned – to encourage the development of peasant agriculture along capitalist lines by demanding the abolition of the estate privileges of the gentry and the removal of legal restrictions on peasant landowning, such as the legislation governing withdrawal from the commune. The SDs saw the immediate task of socialists in the countryside to be the making of the bourgeois revolution, which would clear the way for capitalist development by abolishing the 'remnants of feudalism' in agriculture. Only then, on the basis of capitalist relationships, could the socialist stage of the revolution be carried through by the rural proletariat. In the first, anti-feudal stage, the peasantry as a whole would unite against the privileges of the gentry landowners. The demands of the SDs for this stage of the agrarian revolution were designed to encompass the common interests of the working peasantry and the rural bourgeoisie; but many of these demands, in the view of the SRs – for example, the right of free disposal of communal land – were more in the interests of the kulaks than the poorer peasantry.

The SRs, on the other hand, saw the contemporary peasant movement as essentially a class conflict of labour against capital in all its forms, regardless of legal estate. Unlike the SD programme, which would primarily benefit the rural bourgeoisie, the SR programme for the socialisation of the land was designed to benefit the mass of the working peasantry at the expense of both the gentry and the kulaks:

Thus our minimum agrarian programme contains the slogan of the socialisation of the land, which necessarily divides the kulak elements of the village

[17] *ibid*, p 15.

from the working peasantry. To the extent that this slogan becomes popular in the countryside, the working peasantry is putting forward its own programme, essentially hostile to the kulak and bourgeois strata. The war-cry 'land to those who work it, for communal egalitarian utilisation', is aimed both against *pomeshchik* landownership and against the bourgeois landownership of the stronger peasants.[18]

Thus both the SRs and the SDs saw the socialist transformation of Russian agriculture as a two-stage process; but they disagreed over the alignment of the groups within the peasantry at the different stages of the movement. Both agreed that the peasantry as a whole had an interest in abolishing the privileges of gentry landownership; but whereas the SDs believed that only the agricultural proletariat could overthrow the capitalist farming of the peasant bourgeoisie, the SRs held that the 'working peasantry' – the rural proletariat plus the small independent producers – were opposed to the development of capitalism in agriculture. In other words, the anti-feudal bourgeois-democratic interests which the SDs attributed to the movement of the peasantry as a whole, the SRs attributed solely to the kulaks; the anti-capitalist, pro-socialist interests which the SRs attributed to the 'working peasantry' (excluding the kulaks), the SDs attributed solely to the rural proletariat.

The SR view of the alignments within the peasantry was derived from their entire theory of class and the class struggle, as it was developed by Chernov in a series of articles in *Revolyutsionnaya Rossiya* in 1902 and 1903, which elaborated the views expressed in 'The immediate question of the revolutionary cause'. The starting point for Chernov's analysis was a critique of the SD view that the peasantry 'as a whole' belonged to the petty bourgeoisie.[19] The SDs' justification for this classification was that the peasants owned their means of production; and, according to Marx, class position was determined by relationship to the means of production. This

[18] *ibid*, p 15.

[19] Chernov's critique of the SDs' agrarian policy at this period was mainly directed against articles published in *Iskra* and *Zarya* in 1901–2, which preceded the adoption of the party's agrarian programme at the Second SD Congress in the summer of 1903. Many of these articles were by Lenin, and can be found in his complete works, e.g. 'Rabochaya partiya i krest'yanstvo' (*Iskra*, 1901), *Polnoe Sobranie Sochinenii*, 5th edn (55 vols, Moscow, 1958–65), vol 4, pp 429–37; 'Agrarnaya programma russkoy sotsial-demokratii' (*Zarya*, 1902), *ibid*, vol 6, pp 303–48; 'Revolyutsionnyi avantyurizm' (*Iskra*, 1902), *ibid*, vol 6, pp 377–98. This last article, directed against the SRs, contained the statements to which Chernov most objected: that the peasantry as a whole belonged to the petty bourgeoisie (p 390), and that the peasant movement of 1902 was bourgeois in character (p 392).

view, Chernov claimed, represented an oversimplification of Marx's thought. Class position was determined, not by relationship to the means of production, but by relationship to the means of distribution, that is, by source of income. This had been Marx's position in the famous unfinished final section of the third volume of *Capital*, in which he distinguished the three great classes of modern society as labourers, capitalists and landowners, who derived their income from wages, profit and rent respectively. The question then arose: why was it these three sources of income which were the primary determinants of class? Marx's manuscript had broken off before he had answered his own question, but the solution, Chernov believed, was implicit in Marx's other writings, and indeed could be found also in the writings of other social scientists as diverse as Adam Smith, Chernyshevskii and Kautsky: 'According to this theory, the division of contemporary bourgeois society into social classes is functionally related to the division of the common national income into those basic forms which, at a given level of national income, can only be increased one at the expense of the other.'[20] The wages of labour could be increased only at the expense of the profit of the capitalist, and the profit of the capitalist at the expense of the rent of the landowner. The conflicts between labour and capital, and between capital and landed property, were therefore the basic class conflicts in modern society.

There was also another way in which the Russian SDs oversimplified and distorted Marx's class theory, in Chernov's view: by confusing the concept of 'means of production' with that of 'capital'. The bourgeoisie, for Marx, were the representatives of capital, and capital was the means of production *alienated* from the producer, increasing in value from the unpaid labour of the hired worker. Ownership of his means of production by the small producer did not, in itself, make him a bourgeois.[21]

If these theoretical considerations were applied to the determination of the class position of the contemporary Russian peasantry, then, Chernov asserted, it was self-evident that the peasantry as a whole belonged, not to the spheres of capital or land-rent, but to the army of labour. The mass of peasants, far from enjoying the economic benefits of the capitalist farmer or landowner, were, on the contrary, cruelly exploited by capital in all its forms – directly through money-lending and land-rent, and indirectly through fiscal

[20] 'K teorii klassovoy bor′by', *R.R.*, no. 27 (July 1903), p 14.
[21] *ibid*, p 15.

pressure from the state, which represented the interests of the gentry landowners and the industrial bourgeoisie. The small peasant producers, therefore, shared the anti-capitalist class antagonism of the agricultural and industrial proletariat, with whom they were allied in the concept of a single 'working class' of 'the labouring and exploited people'.[22]

The SDs, because they erroneously considered ownership of the means of production to be the basic criterion of class allegiance, saw the mass of the small peasant producers in the Russian countryside as petty bourgeois. This view the SRs decisively rejected. To call the peasantry 'petty' bourgeois implied that there was only a quantitative difference between the peasants and the 'middle' or 'big' bourgeoisie. The SRs could not accept this, because 'within the "peasantry as a whole" we distinguish a number of strata not only with quantitatively different, but also with qualitatively opposed, interests'.[23] The distinguishing feature of the bourgeoisie was that they derived their income from surplus value, by exploiting, directly or indirectly, the labour of others. On the basis of this criterion, the peasantry 'as a whole' could not even be considered 'petty' bourgeois.

The SRs divided the peasantry into two major categories. The first was 'the working peasanty [*trudovoe krest'yanstvo*], living by the exploitation of their own labour'. The other was 'the rural bourgeoisie – middle and petty – living to a greater or lesser extent by the exploitation of the labour of others'. The working peasantry could be further divided into two sub-categories: the agricultural proletariat – 'peasants living exclusively or mainly by the *sale* of their labour, and totally, or almost totally, deprived of possession of the means of production' – and the class of independent agricultural producers (*klass samostoyatel'nykh zemledel'tsev*), 'living exclusively or mainly by the application of their own labour, on their personal responsibility, to the means of production (individual, communal or rented)'. The only real difference between the agricultural proletariat and the independent producers was that the latter owned or controlled their means of production; this, however, did not constitute a class barrier and was, in any case, overridden by the basic similarities between them. These similarities were twofold. In the first place, the source of existence of both was 'labour, as a distinct politico-economic category'; and secondly, both were pitilessly exploited,

[22] 'K teorii klassovoy bor'by', *R.R.*, no. 34 (October 1903), pp 5–9.
[23] 'Klassovaya bor'ba v derevne', *R.R.*, no. 11 (September 1902), p 7.

directly or indirectly, by capital. It followed that these two groups within the working peasantry shared common interests in antagonism to the bourgeois capitalists, and that these interests could be utilised by a revolutionary socialist party.

In contrast to the theorists of *Iskra*, who considered the agricultural proletariat to be the only rural class with an interest in socialism, the SRs viewed the working peasantry, as a whole, as a potential revolutionary force for socialism. This view was derived not only from theory, but also from empirical evidence: it was their own experience in Russia, as well as the experience of many Western European socialists, that the independent peasant producer was often more receptive to socialist teaching than was the landless agricultural labourer. There was therefore no need for Russian socialists to wait for the proletarianisation of the peasantry to produce a rural class responsive to their teaching. This view was based on a false analogy with the proletarianisation of the artisan class in the towns – a process which had created a more cohesive and revolutionary class in the industrial workers. Those who drew this parallel had failed to observe that 'in the sphere of agriculture the creative, organising rôle of capitalism is completely overshadowed by its destructive, disorganising rôle'. Marx himself had noted that the distribution of agricultural workers over a wide area weakened their ability to resist; whereas the urban workers were strengthened by their geographical concentration.[24] Western European experience had produced no evidence of an independent revolutionary movement of the agricultural proletariat. In Russia, a revolutionary-socialist movement in the countryside would represent the interests not only of hired labour, as the SDs assumed, but of '*labour in general*, whether it is put by its owner onto the market, or applied independently to the means of production'. Socialism, after all, was the 'kingdom of labour', whereas capitalism was the 'kingdom of the exploitation of labour'.[25]

Because of their different theoretical views on the nature of classes and the class struggle, the SRs and SDs held divergent opinions on the socio-political nature of the peasant movement of 1902. For the SDs, the movement was 'an echo of the past, the last outbreak of those peasant revolts which have been directed and are

[24] *ibid*, pp 7–9.
[25] 'Proletarii-batraki v russkoy derevne', *R.R.*, no. 12 (October 1902), pp 5–7. (Emphasis in the original)

universally directed against the bonds of feudal servitude, and whose rôle is played out as soon as these bonds are destroyed and bourgeois "freedom" is established in their place'.[26]

The SRs did not claim that the peasant movement was consciously socialist in character, but they held that it was anti-capitalist as well as anti-feudal. Even the reports in *Iskra* had contained evidence of sharp conflicts between the working peasantry and the rural bourgeoisie. The peasant movement was a movement 'of the poor against the rich, of those who labour against those who do not, of the exploited against those who extort surplus value'; it was 'the embryo of that future movement of the labouring strata of the countryside which will provide a firm basis of support for a socialist party among the peasantry'. It was the SRs' task, therefore, to ensure that the movement was led, not by the rural bourgeoisie, who sought to promote their own economic interests under the guise of a democratic attack on gentry landownership, but by a socialist party which represented the aspirations of the great mass of the working peasantry for a guarantee of their rights to the land.[27]

The rural intelligentsia

By the middle of 1903, two major problems had developed in the implementation of the policies of the SR Peasant Union: firstly, there was evidence of the unsuitability of certain members of the urban intelligentsia for propaganda activity in the villages; and, secondly, it appeared that at the village level the richer peasants threatened to exert an influence which was, in the eyes of the party leadership, undesirable from the ideological point of view. It is in this light that one must interpret the renewed emphasis, from the summer of 1903, which the party laid on the rôle of the rural intelligentsia – especially the village schoolteachers – in the task of spreading party influence in the countryside. We have already drawn attention to the rôle of the rural intelligentsia in the countryside, before 1902, when they constituted virtually the only revolutionary cadres in the villages. Even after the appeal of the Peasant Union in 1902 to other sectors of society to participate in raising the political consciousness of the peasantry, the rural intelligentsia continued

[26] 'Kharakter sovremennago krest'yanskago dvizheniya', *R.R.*, no. 13 (November 1902), p 4.

[27] *ibid*, pp 4–5.

to play a major part. The advantages of using the rural intelligentsia in this way were twofold. In the first place, unlike the urban intelligentsia and students, they were close to the peasants, sharing their way of life and enjoying their confidence. And in the second place, unlike the kulaks, they did not, and could not, have any class interests which might run counter to the ideological interests of the party.

The first evidence of the party's new emphasis on the rôle of the village intelligentsia came in July 1903, when *Revolyutsionnaya Rossiya* published a highly emotional and rhetorical appeal from Breshkovskaya, 'To the rural intelligentsia', in which she reiterated the Populist view of the leading rôle of the intelligentsia in the revolutionary movement, and she called upon them to undertake propaganda activity in the countryside. Far too many intellectuals, she claimed, were dragging out a passive existence in the countryside, apparently indifferent to the misery of the peasants who surrounded them. This was especially reprehensible in that the intelligentsia had gained their education at the expense of the people; they were morally bound to put their knowledge to the service of the people, by acting as the bearers of consciousness and organisation to the masses:

> You are the salt of the Russian earth, crystallised at the expense of the people among whom life has scattered you in tiny grains; and woe to you, if you refuse to dissolve into the medium which surrounds you, if you stand aside from life without repaying with interest what she has given you. Remember that perhaps only one worker out of every ten thousand enjoys the benefits of knowledge which you possess; remember, too, that he who possesses such knowledge cannot be truly happy unless his best thoughts and feelings enter the life which surrounds him and serve his great ideal.[28]

The SRs sought their support mainly from the humbler strata of the rural intelligentsia – such as the teachers and medical auxiliaries – who were closer to the peasants, in many respects, than the professional men with higher education – such as the doctors and lawyers. The teachers, in particular, because of their numerical preponderance and their unique status as educators in the village, were the objects of SR attention.

In August 1903 *Revolyutsionnaya Rossiya* announced that the previously non-party Union of Primary Teachers (*Soyuz narodnykh uchiteley*), founded a few months earlier, had joined the SR party, and it published an appeal from the committee of the new SR

[28] E. Breshkovskaya, 'K sel′skoy intelligentsii', *R.R.*, no. 28 (July 1903), p 6.

Teachers' Union, 'To all primary teachers in Russia'.[29] Whereas Breshkovskaya's appeal to the rural intelligentsia had stressed mainly the subjective factors which should motivate them to propagandise and organise the peasantry, the appeal by the Teachers' Union laid more emphasis on objective factors, such as the strategic position occupied by the teacher in the countryside, and his crucial rôle as a contact between rural and urban society and culture:

> We, who have in our hands the schools, books, contacts with the urban intelligentsia, are virtually the only people in the countryside to whom the peasant can unburden his troubled soul, from whom he can hear sincere words of justice. On us, as virtually the only representatives in the countryside of the fighting intelligentsia, there lies an historic responsibility to our consciences and to our motherland – the profound task of aiding this multimillion army of the peasantry oppressed by the government.[30]

From discussions in later issues of *Revolyutsionnaya Rossiya*, it is clear that the initial announcement concerning the formation of the SR Teachers' Union was somewhat inaccurate: the non-party Union had not joined the PSR, but rather the SR Union had split off from the non-party Union as a result of disagreements with the SD members concerning the content of the propaganda with which the Union was to supply its members for distribution to the peasantry.[31] From 1903, the non-party Union existed in parallel with the SR Union, although the former was severely weakened by the schism of the SRs and tried in vain to persuade them to return to the fold.[32]

The formation of a separate SR Teachers' Union was attacked not only by the non-party teachers, but also by certain elements within the party itself. They pointed out that the aims of the Teachers' Union, as set out in its initial appeal, were identical with those of the party's Peasant Union – the political organisation and education of the peasantry – and they questioned the need for a separate

[29] 'Iz partiynoy deyatel'nosti', *R.R.*, no. 30 (August 1903), p 20. The term 'primary teacher' (*narodnyi uchitel'*) does not refer specifically to rural (*sel'skii*) teachers, but it was obvious from the content of the appeal that the main aim of the Union was to recruit rural teachers for propaganda activity among the peasantry. A later article stated that while the Union was originally intended to unite rural teachers, it would welcome as members not only urban teachers, but also representatives of the provincial intelligentsia other than teachers. 'K voprosu o roli narodnykh uchiteley v sotsial'no-revolyutsionnom dvizhenii', *R.R.*, no. 40 (January 1904), p. 8.

[30] 'Iz partiynoy deyatel'nosti', *R.R.*, no. 30 (August 1903), p 20.

[31] 'K voprosu o roli narodnykh uchiteley v sotsial'no-revolyutsionnom dvizhenii', *R.R.*, no. 40 (January 1904), p 6.

[32] 'Ob"edinitel'naya popytka', *R.R.*, no. 37 (December 1903), pp 3–4.

Teachers' Union to perform the same functions. Sletov, in a letter to the editors of *Revolyutsionnaya Rossiya*, recognised the significance of the rôle of the teachers in organising the countryside, but he insisted that members of many other social groups and professions played an equally important rôle in the spreading of SR ideas among the peasantry. There were ideological dangers, he asserted, in the claim of the Teachers' Union that one professional group could assume the leadership of another entire class: only the party as a whole could make such a claim.[33] The offending passage in the appeal of the Teachers' Union had read:

Comrades, let us now unite to form a single mighty family, a single mighty union of the primary teachers of Russia, which will put forward as its slogan the fight for political freedom and socialism; a union which will openly adhere to the party and march forward proudly under its banner, leading the conscious army of the peasantry which has already been established.[34]

The editors of the journal, in a footnote to Sletov's article, claimed that he had misinterpreted the significance of this passage:

The Committee of the Teachers' Union had no intention of resolving the general issue as to which organisation should lead the peasant movement, but was simply calling on the primary teachers to assume the leadership rôle of which they are capable. Thus they did not intend to imply that teachers occupy any monopoly position in the movement.[35]

A letter from the Committee of the Teachers' Union, published in a subsequent issue, confirmed this interpretation:

Basing ourselves on the socialist point of view, we first of all bear in mind that the liberation of the working masses must be accomplished by their own efforts. Our appeal to the primary teachers to take up the leadership rôle of which they are capable in this struggle of the workers for their liberation has, of course, nothing in common with a claim that the teachers have any kind of monopoly or privilege for leadership.[36]

The question still remained as to what the distinction should be between the sphere of activity of the Teachers' Union and that of the Peasant Union. Sletov, in his article, suggested that the paramount aim of the Teachers' Union should be to organise the teachers themselves, to provide them with a forum for discussion, and to

[33] S. Nechetnyi, 'K voprosu o postanovke raboty v derevne; pis'mo v redaktsiyu', *R.R.*, no. 35 (November 1903), p 9.
[34] 'Iz partiynoy deyatel'nosti', *R.R.*, no. 30 (August 1903), p 20.
[35] Nechetnyi, 'K voprosu o postanovke raboty v derevne . . .', *R.R.*, no. 35 (November 1903), p 9.
[36] 'Pis'mo v redaktsiyu', *R.R.*, no. 37 (December 1903), p 24.

supply them with theoretical literature. Revolutionary activity among the peasantry, however, should come under the jurisdiction, not of the Teachers' Union, but of the local party organisation, through the Peasant Union in areas where it existed.[37] The party's definitive statement on this issue, the article 'On the problem of the rôle of the primary teacher in the social-revolutionary movement', confirmed Sletov's view, and it distinguished the relative scope of the two organisations according to the following formula: 'Insofar as the teacher directs his activity towards work among the teaching profession, it is natural for him to be a member of the SR Teachers' Union; but when he works among the peasants, in the spirit of the SR Peasant Union, he thereby becomes in fact a member of that union, and may enter, with full rights, into peasant Brotherhoods, committees, etc.'[38]

The first report of the Committee of the Teachers' Union confirmed that in practice the Union confined itself to propagandising and organising the teachers themselves, enabling them to overcome the disadvantages of their social isolation in the countryside. The founders of the Union had recruited members at various summer courses for teachers in June and July 1903. By the end of the year, they had managed to establish contacts in ten guberniyas, mainly in central Russia. Members were supplied with revolutionary literature – theoretical works to further their own political education, and libraries of popular works, legal and illegal, for the peasantry. In the first six months of its existence, the Union had distributed about ten poods (3 cwt) of revolutionary literature and 1,500 copies of the appeal 'To all the primary teachers in Russia'. Contacts with the teachers were maintained through the supply of publications, correspondence, personal visits, meetings at which discussion papers were read, and regular congresses of teachers' representatives.[39]

In essence, the formation of the SR Teachers' Union represented an institutional recognition of the rôle already played by the rural teachers, and also an attempt to unite these isolated revolutionaries by providing a communication network parallel and supplementary to that already supplied by the existing party organisation. Its formation also marked, as we have already noted, a renewed em-

[37] Nechetnyi, 'K voprosu o postanovke raboty v derevne . . .', *R.R.*, no. 35 (November 1903), pp 10–11.

[38] 'K voprosu o roli narodnykh uchiteley . . .', *R.R.*, no. 40 (January 1904), p 8.

[39] 'Otchet Komiteta Soyuza Narodnykh Uchiteley Partii Sotsialistov-Revolyutsionerov', *R.R.*, no. 40 (January 1904), p 22.

phasis in party tactics on the rôle of the rural intelligentsia, as compared with the previous advocacy of a new movement to the people from the towns.

The urban workers

After the brutal suppression of the movement in Poltava and Khar'kov in 1902, peasant unrest continued on a more muted scale throughout 1903. In 1903, the forefront of the revolutionary stage was occupied by the working class movement, culminating in the general strike in the South in the summer. The militancy of the industrial workers appears to have redirected the attention of the SRs to the need to consolidate the links between the movement of the urban proletariat and that of the peasantry. This consideration lay behind Sletov's attack on what he saw as the exclusive claims of the rural teachers concerning their rôle as propagandists among the peasantry.

Breshkovskaya, too, was concerned about the need to strengthen contacts between the workers and the peasants. In an article in *Revolyutsionnaya Rossiya* in September 1903, in which she assessed the achievement of SR activity in the countryside since the formation of the Peasant Union a year earlier, she admitted that in terms of the total peasant population of Russia only a very small proportion had as yet been affected by revolutionary propaganda. In view of the small number of propagandists who were initially at the party's disposal, however, she felt that the SRs could claim to have had remarkable success in influencing large numbers of peasants in many different guberniyas. This had proved that 'the intensiveness of our work in the peasantry can be rewarded by the broadly extensive dissemination of our ideas'.[40] A measure of the party's success lay in the fact that the areas affected by peasant disturbances in 1902 had been those in which SR propaganda was most widely distributed – the Ukraine, the Volga and the Central Black Earth belt. In these areas, she claimed, propaganda was mainly carried on by the rural intelligentsia, those who 'are linked to the countryside by their own mode of life'. It was a matter for regret, in Breshkovskaya's opinion, that there had as yet been little evidence of revol-

[40] E. Breshkovskaya, 'Rabota Sotsialistov-Revolyutsionerov sredi krest'yan i voprosy vremeni', *R.R.*, no. 31 (September 1903), p 4.

utionary influence on the peasantry by the urban workers. This could be explained by the predominance of SD influence in the major industrial centres: the SDs failed in their propaganda to emphasise the common interests of the workers and peasants, and therefore the workers they influenced did not utilise their links with the villages for revolutionary purposes. There was no other explanation, Breshkovskaya felt, for the fact that there had been few signs of peasant unrest in the guberniyas of Moscow and St Petersburg. At the same time, SR experience in Saratov, Kiev and Ekaterinoslav, where the party had been engaged for some time in activity among the industrial workers, showed that the latter could be successfully utilised as propagandists in the countryside. Similar results could be achieved elsewhere, if the urban revolutionaries took care to make the workers aware of the links which existed between town and countryside. Such contacts would benefit both the workers and the peasantry, by creating conscious channels of communication and coordination between the urban and rural movements: 'There is no doubt that, for example, the workers' disturbances in St Petersburg and Moscow and elsewhere would have had incomparably greater force and significance if the surrounding provinces had manifested some kind of revolutionary mood; if they had at least known why the workers were protesting.'[41]

Sletov's article, 'On the question of the organisation of work in the countryside', written in July and published in *Revolyutsionnaya Rossiya* in November 1903, made a similar point, although he presented a more optimistic picture than Breshkovskaya of the extent to which urban workers were already influencing the peasantry. It was only in the non-industrial provinces, especially in the South-East (i.e. the Volga region and the Central Black Earth), Sletov claimed, that the rural intelligentsia played the major rôle as conductors of SR propaganda. Around the major industrial centres, mainly those in the South – such as Odessa, Kiev and Ekaterinoslav – where the SRs had already consolidated their position, the most important propagandists among the peasantry were the urban workers who had some kind of contact with the countryside. These contacts could be of three main kinds: firstly, the urban workers, mainly artisans such as painters and joiners, who sought seasonal work in the villages in summer; secondly, those who still had family ties with the countryside; and thirdly, peasant

[41] *ibid*, p 6.

artisans who found seasonal work in the towns in summer, but who wintered in their native villages.[42]

In the South, Sletov claimed, there already existed that contact between the urban and rural movements which Breshkovskaya considered so desirable. After the failure of a May Day demonstration, for example, the workers, instead of relapsing into apathy and disillusionment, had directed their revolutionary energies towards the countryside. This fact, in Sletov's opinion, justified the SRs' policy of extending their activity to the peasantry, and showed how groundless were any fears that such an extension might weaken the urban movement. Provided the local party organisations were able to regulate and control the propaganda activity of the workers in the countryside, 'the town would not only not suffer any loss, but moreover would receive broad and mighty support from the revolutionised countryside'.[43]

By the end of 1903, the SRs had made some considerable progress in their campaign for the peasantry, and the party's first report to the Socialist International, in 1904, presented an optimistic picture of the development of its propaganda effort in the countryside.[44] Problems had arisen, but the leadership proved flexible in its adaptations to meet them. But, before the SRs had time to consolidate these propaganda successes, events themselves took another leap forward – precipitated, this time, by the disastrous course of the Russo-Japanese war.

42 Nechetnyi, 'K voprosu o postanovke raboty v derevne . . .', *R.R.*, no. 35 (November 1903), pp 9–10.

43 *ibid*, p 10.

44 *Rapport du parti socialiste révolutionnaire de russie au congrès socialiste international d'Amsterdam* (Paris, 1904), pp 35–46.

9
Agrarian terrorism

The outbreak of the Russo-Japanese war at the beginning of 1904 was greeted by the revolutionary parties as an opportunity to launch a further attack on the autocracy. A new campaign of political terror was undertaken by the SRs, which achieved its most spectacular success in the assassination of Plehve, the hated Minister of the Interior, on 15 July 1904. At this time, a group was formed within the party who felt that its terrorist activities were too exclusively political and should be more closely integrated into the mass movement by the sanctioning of economic terror. The most outspoken advocates of this view were the faction of 'agrarian terrorists' which formed in Geneva in 1904, led by a group of Breshkovskaya's disciples – including Evgenii Lozinskii (Ustinov) and Mikhail Sokolov, the former student of the Mariinskoe agricultural college near Saratov and a future Maximalist leader. Their supporters were drawn mainly from the youngest and most recent contingent of émigrés.[1]

The term 'agrarian terror' was used to describe the measures of destructive violence which were traditionally adopted by the peasantry in the course of their local conflicts with the gentry landowners. These measures included murder, arson, the destruction of crops, the killing of livestock, etc. Before 1904, the attitude of both the SR Peasant Union and the Agrarian-Socialist League towards the peasants' use of 'agrarian terror' had been an ambivalent one. The initial appeal of the SR Peasant Union 'To all those working for revolutionary socialism in Russia' had essentially avoided the issue of 'agrarian terror'. For the economic struggle, it had advocated the use of constructive and organised means, such as strikes and boycotts, and the examples it gave of violent tactics – attacks on spies and informers, and on hated local officials – belonged to the realm

[1] V. Chernov, 'K kharakteristike maksimalizma', *Sotsialist-Revolyutsioner*, no. 1 (1910), pp 184–9.

of political terror as practised by the urban terrorists.[2] The Peasant Union's first pamphlet, 'To the entire Russian peasantry', was more specific in its recommendation of tactics to the peasantry. They should launch a campaign of wage- and rent-strikes and boycotts against the landowners. Thereafter:

If this doesn't work . . . , you will have to adopt your own means, even stronger than these. You can agree not only to boycott this man, but also to do everything you can to harm his economy. This end may be served by letting your cattle trample his fields, by chopping down his forest, by fires 'from unknown causes' and other such means. And it happens nowadays in some villages that 'from an unknown cause' a bridge over a ravine or over a river may collapse just at the time when an unloved *zemskii nachal'nik* or police chief happens to be riding over it; and there are all sorts of other such cases, especially on quiet roads on dark nights . . .[3]

Having drawn the peasants' attention to such tactics, the Peasant Union quickly retreated to a more cautious position on 'agrarian terror':

The peasant Brotherhood will not rouse the peasants to bloodshed senselessly and indiscriminately. On the contrary, wherever possible it will restrain the commune to peaceful and legal means. But these means do not always work. It may happen that the commune will lose faith in them, that it is unable to restrain its own hotheads, and decides to resort either to the 'red cock' [arson] or to some other means of its own. Then the Brotherhood must certainly assist the villagers to bring the project to a successful conclusion, or take over the entire responsibility for the whole affair, ensuring that the proposed punishment is a just one, and concealing all traces from the authorities.[4]

The question of 'agrarian terror' was raised at the First Congress of the Agrarian-Socialist League in August 1902. The main achievement of the Congress was the working out and approval of a 'Programme of revolutionary activity in the countryside'. In many respects, this programme corresponded to that of the SR Peasant Union. A similar distinction was drawn between intensive and extensive activity, between 'propaganda' and 'agitation'. The aim of 'propaganda' was to prepare cadres of conscious revolutionaries among the peasantry; the aim of 'agitation' was to 'revolutionise the entire peasant mass'. Like the Peasant Union, the League advocated the organisation of the peasantry into local Brotherhoods and unions; it also envisaged a similar range of activities for these bodies,

[2] 'Ot Krest'yanskago Soyuza Partii Sotsialistov-Revolyutsionerov ko vsem rabotnikam revolyutsionnago sotsializma v Rossii', *R.R.*, no. 8 (June 1902), pp 11–14.

[3] *Ko vsemu russkomu krest'yanstvu ot Krest'yanskago Soyuza Partii Sotsialistov-Revolyutsionerov* (n.p., 1902), p 24. [4] *ibid*, pp 25–6.

and a similar transition from local political and economic action to a mass political campaign for a democratic revolution and the socialisation of the land.[5] The League, however, dealt with the issue of tactics in the countryside in rather more detail than had the Peasant Union in its manifesto. The speaker who introduced the debate on this point emphasised the desirability of constructive forms of economic protest such as strikes and boycotts. He recognised that the peasants themselves often resorted to destructive violence, but he felt that the party could not advocate a programme of 'agrarian terror', because of the difficulties involved in controlling such acts and accepting responsibility for them. The initiative and responsibility for 'agrarian terror' must rest with the local peasant organisations, but the party 'can only advise them to observe the greatest restraint and caution, and to move from peaceful means to violence only when such a move is *absolutely* necessary'.[6]

In the 'Programme of revolutionary activity' itself, the League's attitude towards 'agrarian terror' was explained even more cautiously, in terms similar to those of the Peasant Union's pamphlet 'To the entire Russian peasantry': the Brotherhoods should always recommend peaceful means, but if the peasants themselves resorted to violence, the Brotherhood should support this action:

> They should aim to confine the peasant struggle as far as possible to peaceful means; but in cases where the peasants have lost faith in the efficacy of peaceful means and resort to violent actions against the property or life of their oppressor, whether he be a private individual or a member of the administration (such actions would include: the trampling of crops by cattle; illicit woodcutting; arson; beatings up; armed attacks, etc.), the local secret society should assist the villagers to bring the project to a successful conclusion, or take over the responsibility for the entire affair, ensuring that the proposed punishment is a just one, and concealing all traces of the crime.[7]

The issue of 'agrarian terror' remained one on which opinions within the movement were divided, and the ambivalent attitudes expressed in these early publications appear to represent a shifting compromise between the advocates of 'agrarian terror' and its opponents. At the Second Congress of the League, in August 1903, a resolution was passed, after 'lengthy debates', that:

> The popular editions of the Agrarian-Socialist League should provide the reader, in the most objective form possible, with all the information necessary

[5] 'Pervyi s"ezd Agrarno-Sotsialisticheskoy Ligi', *R.R.*, no. 12 (October 1902) pp 22–3.

[6] *ibid*, p 22.

[7] *ibid*, p 23.

for a comparative assessment of 'agrarian terror' together with other means of struggle of the working peasantry, both from the moral and from the political angle; but they should avoid even any indirect incitement to 'agrarian terror'.[8]

In the course of 1904, as the possibility of a revolutionary confrontation in Russia became more imminent, the young 'agrarian terrorists' in Geneva presented a direct challenge to the official party leadership's ambivalent attitude towards 'agrarian terror'. A resolution composed by Ustinov, and issued by the Geneva group, argued that the party should organise combat detachments (*boevye druzhiny*) in the countryside, whose purpose should be to organise and to accomplish acts of both political terror and 'agrarian terror' at the local level, 'with the aim of scaring and disorganising all the direct representatives and agents of the contemporary ruling classes'. 'Agrarian terror' was defined as the use of violence against the lives and property of the economic oppressors of the people, and included such measures as: illicit cattle grazing and woodcutting on the landowner's estate; the seizure of his property by the peasant communes, arson and other destruction of property; the murder of *pomeshchiki*; and armed attacks. The local combat detachments should try to introduce an element of organisation into spontaneous acts undertaken by the peasantry, but any attempt at control by higher party organisations would be unnecessary and even harmful, since it was likely to 'paralyse the revolutionary energy of the masses and impede the action of the local combat groups'. The resolution concluded by demanding that the party should launch a propaganda campaign of leaflets and proclamations, calling on the peasantry to organise their own combat detachments.

At a meeting of the Geneva émigrés, Ustinov defended his resolution. It was beyond the physical resources of the party, he claimed, to organise a peasant rising; all they could hope to do was to exert an ideological influence on the peasantry by flooding the countryside with propaganda for 'agrarian terror'. In a speech in support of Ustinov, Sokolov argued that 'agrarian terror' was the traditional means of peasant revolt since the time of Sten′ka Razin and Pugachev; the party should not reject these tactics which had been developed by the peasants as their 'own means'.[9]

8 'Kratkii otchet o vtorom s″ezde Agrarno-Sotsialisticheskoy Ligi', *R.R.*, no. 31 (September 1903), p 24.
9 Chernov, *Sotsialist-Revolyutsioner*, no. 1 (1910), pp 189–91.

The 'old guard' of the party, on the suggestion of Osip Minor, composed its own counter-resolution, 'On work in the countryside and on "agrarian terror" ', which constituted the most unequivocal rejection to date of the inclusion of 'agrarian terror' in the party's tactics. They saw the dangers to lie in:

> The local uncoordinated character of acts of 'agrarian terror', which makes their regulation and control by the party difficult, and, consequently, cannot prevent unwarranted excesses which may be harmful to the moral prestige of the movement; and the danger of the degeneration in the movement if the spread of an 'agrarian-terrorist' mood should outstrip the development of the social-revolutionary consciousness and organisation of the masses and turn the movement from a collective struggle for the socialisation of the land into a guerrilla struggle by individual groups for the immediate improvement of their own economic position.[10]

The official leadership then presented their own 'plan of campaign' for the countryside. This plan was largely a restatement of the policies which the SR Peasant Union had announced in 1902, but it was more specific about the party's attitude towards violence. It envisaged the organisation of a network of peasant unions which would coordinate their activities with those of the urban party organisations and prepare for a single coordinated movement. As a preparation for this rising, the peasants should back up their political and economic demands by a boycott of the landowners and the authorities. Such a boycott would, of course, provoke repressions, and the peasants would then meet violence with violence. At this stage, the local peasant organisations would act as 'combat detachments' and lead the peasants' opposition. A series of such conflicts would amount to a partial or general uprising, supporting or supported by a similar movement in the towns.[11]

In contrast to the resolution of the 'agrarian terrorists', which had 25 signatures, the resolution of the official leadership was signed by only 16 persons. These 16 names, however, included the most senior and respected leaders of the party: Chernov, Shishko, Volkhovskoy and Minor. Other leaders who were absent from Geneva at the time of the debate, but who supported the resolution, were Mikhail Gots and Stepan Sletov. Breshkovskaya, who, when the issue came to a head, was touring the United States on a highly successful fund-raising trip, disowned her former protégés upon her return. In 1905, her series of articles in *Revolyutsionnaya Rossiya*, 'Letters from an

[10] *ibid*, pp 191–2.

[11] *ibid*, p 192.

old friend', explicitly denounced 'agrarian terrorism'.[12] The only member of the older generation to support Ustinov was the former Tolstoyan, Prince Khilkov, who was soon to leave the party.[13]

The SR Central Committee adopted rather an indulgent attitude towards the young 'agrarian terrorists'. They were given complete freedom to advocate their views within the party, but they were warned that as long as the official leadership continued to reject 'agrarian terror', they could not preach their beliefs to the peasantry and still remain within the party. After a long period of hesitation, they agreed to accept party discipline. Thus when members of the group decided to return to Russia, the Central Committee gave them every assistance, supplying them with false passports and money.

The leaders' trust in the agrarians' good faith was soon to be rudely shattered. Reports began to reach Geneva that Sokolov and his followers were openly advocating not only 'agrarian terror', but also industrial sabotage and financial expropriations, and that these policies had met with support from the party committee in Ekaterinoslav, and from the regional committee of the North-West. A proclamation addressed 'To the workers and peasants', issued by Sokolov in Minsk in November 1904, which roused the masses to violence in an ultra-demagogic style – calling on them to 'Beat up the Tsarist officials, the capitalists and the landowners!' – caused particular consternation in Geneva, and Sokolov was summoned abroad to explain his actions. Again he was allowed to remain within the party, after repeating the undertakings to observe party discipline which, it appeared, he had no intention of keeping. In fact, the Central Committee had no means of exerting control over the actions of the 'agrarian terrorists' in Russia. Both Breshkovskaya and Sletov, who had a certain degree of sympathy with the agrarians' aims, if not with their methods, had volunteered to go to Russia to attempt a reconciliation. However, Breshkovskaya's American trip had intervened, and Sletov was arrested on the Russian border on 3 September 1904, having been betrayed to the police by Azef, the notorious *agent provocateur* on the SR Central Committee, with whom he had quarrelled on the issue of the autonomy of the party's Terrorist Organisation.[14]

After this, no further attempts were made by the leadership to

[12] In particular, her sixth letter, 'V otvet nekotorym molodym tovarishcham', *R.R.*, no. 69 (June 1905), pp 5–7.

[13] Chernov, *Sotsialist-Revolyutsioner*, no. 1 (1910), pp 193–4.

[14] *ibid*, pp 194–201.

exercise control over the agrarians' activities in Russia. Throughout the winter of 1904–5 Sokolov continued his attempts to turn the SR Peasant Union into an 'agrarian-terrorist' organisation. At the beginning of April 1905, the police raided a congress of the Peasant Union in Kursk which was attended by all the leading agrarians.[15] The arrest of Sokolov and his followers virtually destroyed the 'agrarian terrorist' movement. Some of those who remained free accepted party discipline; others joined the allied Maximalist faction which, in the course of 1905, was primarily concerned with economic terror in an urban rather than a rural context. The tolerance which the party leadership displayed towards the 'agrarian terrorists', however, meant that the SRs launched themselves into the revolution of 1905 with this major tactical issue still very much open and unresolved, and with the Peasant Union severely split and weakened.

[15] Spiridovitch, p 224.

Part III

THE REVOLUTION OF 1905

10
The party, the peasantry and the revolution

The disastrous progress of the Russo-Japanese war inspired a rising tide of protest against the incompetence of the government from liberal opinion throughout 1904, and demands intensified for political freedom. It was not until the end of the year, however, that the masses were drawn into the liberation movement, with the revival of strike activity by the workers in December. The appearance of the masses on the scene provided the revolutionary parties with an opportunity to wrest from the liberals the leadership of the struggle against the autocracy, and in the course of 1905 both the SRs and the SDs sought to organise and extend their influence over the workers and peasants.

The SRs' agrarian tactics

The 'Bloody Sunday' events in St Petersburg on 9 January 1905, which triggered off a series of sympathetic strikes and demonstrations throughout the country, were greeted by the SRs as the beginning of the long-awaited revolution which would topple the autocracy, and the party called for a national armed uprising which would draw the countryside as well as the towns into the revolutionary movement.[1] Indeed, peasant disturbances followed quickly on the heels of the urban unrest, starting in Kursk guberniya in February, and spreading to Chernigov, Orel and other provinces. In Kursk guberniya the movement was precipitated by the appearance in the village of Sal′noe, in Dmitrievsk uezd, of an SR proclamation entitled 'Brother peasants!', accompanied by rumours that in the spring, when the troops were expected to return from Manchuria, there would be a general redistribution of the land. The peasants declared that the land was now theirs, and a series of raids began on the neighbouring estates.[2]

[1] 'Preddverie revolyutsii', *R.R.*, no. 58 (January 1905), pp 1–2.
[2] Maslov, vol 2, pp 147–58.

In March 1905 a leading article in *Revolyutsionnaya Rossiya* welcomed these outbursts of peasant unrest as the forerunners of an imminent agrarian revolution. In many respects, the article pointed out, the movement appeared similar in character to that of 1902 in Poltava and Khar′kov. Eyewitness reports suggested that there was the same concern on the part of the peasants to avoid unnecessary bloodshed; the same desire to divide up what they had seized on a just and egalitarian basis; and the same strong conviction that their actions were justified. There was, however, no evidence of the rumours concerning the 'Tsar's manifesto', which had played such an important part in the movement of 1902; instead, 'revolutionary manifestoes have replaced those of the Tsar'.[3] The report from Kursk in the following issue of *Revolyutsionnaya Rossiya* reinforced the party's optimism concerning the nature and aims of the peasant movement. The majority of the peasants, the correspondent wrote, regarded the seizure of land and property only as a temporary measure, by means of which it would be possible to achieve a 'general redistribution'.[4]

As the agrarian movement spread, SR enthusiasm for peasant spontaneity came increasingly to be tempered by concern that the movement be guided by socialist consciousness. This concern was particularly evoked by news of peasant land seizures, and by the fear that the spontaneous movement, far from socialising the land of the confiscated estates, was simply appropriating it as the possession of the individual peasant communes.

Initially, the SRs had adopted an attitude of cautious approval of spontaneous land seizures. In 1902 they had welcomed the movement in the south as semi-socialist, although the first manifesto of the SR Peasant Union stressed the need for political organisation and political means of struggle. In May 1904 the editors of *Revolyutsionnaya Rossiya* pointed out that revolutionary seizures of the land, such as those which had occurred in Poltava and Khar′kov in 1902, were an inevitable response by the peasants to conditions of land-hunger, and that the land seizures should be supported and even advocated by the party. They added the proviso, however, that: 'as socialists we must try to guide this seizure in the direction of our ideals. The only way to do this is by the socialisation of the land.'[5] They were quite hopeful that this guidance of the peasants would be acceptable:

[3] 'Predvestiya agrarnoy revolyutsii', *R.R.*, no. 61 (March 1905), p 13.
[4] 'Rabochee dvizhenie v gorodakh i derevnyakh', *R.R.*, no. 62 (March 1905), p 13.
[5] 'Dnevnik chitatelya', *R.R.*, no. 47 (May 1904), p 7.

Because the peasants who rose acted not like robbers seizing as much as they could of another's property, because they were guided not only by their need, but also by *the principle of justice* – that is, the realisation that everyone who wishes to work has a right to the land – then they will understand the legal consequence and the only possible form of implementing this principle, that is, the transfer of all the land to public possession and its egalitarian utilisation.[6]

Later in 1904, with the emergence of the 'agrarian terrorists' who advocated all forms of spontaneous peasant action, destructive as well as constructive, the party felt obliged to define its attitude towards land seizures more carefully. The 'plan of campaign' advanced by the SR leadership in their counter-resolution against 'agrarian terrorism' envisaged an organised revolutionary peasant movement, in which:

Insofar as the party slogan for this movement should be the gaining of the land, this should consist not in the seizure of particular plots by particular individuals or even small groups, but in the abolition of the boundaries and borders of private ownership, in the declaration of the land to be *common* property, and in the demand for its general, egalitarian and universal distribution for the use of those who work it.[7]

These views were restated by Chernov in May 1905 in an editorial in *Revolyutsionnaya Rossiya*, in which he stressed the need for the party to instil organisation and consciousness into the peasant movement. The SRs, he said, welcomed all spontaneous expressions of discontent, insofar as they revealed the growth of a revolutionary mood in the countryside. It would be pure demagogy, however, if they were actually to advocate the use of traditional peasant tactics, such as 'agrarian terror'; instead, they should urge organisation and coordination with the urban movement. Similarly, their slogan was not simply 'take the land', but involved the concept of socialisation. This could be achieved by direct action as part of the revolutionary peasant movement. The peasants should:

seize the fields and have them ploughed by the commune; use the pastures and forests on the state and appanage lands and on the gentry estates, in an organised manner; and then *drive out* the authorities and *take possession* of the land. This possession of the land, however, should consist not in the arbitrary seizure of particular plots by particular individuals, but in the abolition of the boundaries and borders of private ownership, in the declaration of the land to be common property, and in the demand for its general, egalitarian and universal distribution for the use of those who work it.[8]

6 *ibid*, p 7. (Emphasis in the original)
7 Chernov, *Sotsialist-Revolyutsioner*, no. 1 (1910), p 192.
8 'Reaktsionnaya demagogiya i revolyutsionnyi sotsializm', *R.R.*, no. 67 (May 1905), p 3.

Temporary measures for the distribution of the land which was seized should be taken by the elected representatives of the peasantry; but the final decision was to be left to the Constituent Assembly.[9]

A further impetus to SR criticism of 'revolutionary demagogy' in the form of indiscriminate appeals for land seizures was provided by the agrarian policy adopted by the Bolsheviks in 1905. The Second SD Congress in 1903 had advocated the return to the peasantry of the lands they had lost at Emancipation, and the removal of all legal and fiscal discrimination against the peasants.[10] In 1905, Lenin persuaded his faction to adopt a more radical policy. The Third (Bolshevik) Congress, meeting in April 1905, resolved 'That Social-Democracy set itself the task of supporting energetically all revolutionary measures undertaken by the peasantry to improve their position, including the confiscation of the gentry, state, church, monastery and appanage lands.'[11] The SRs – and some SDs as well – attacked this resolution as opportunistic.[12] Mikhail Gots accused the Bolsheviks of abandoning socialist principles by failing to specify what should be done with the confiscated lands. Simply to support any measure of land seizure, Gots alleged, without attempting to exert a socialist influence on its outcome, was pure demagogy:

> It is clear that any socialist who 'lends support' to a transfer of land from the hands of the *pomeshchiki* to the hands of the peasant kulak is playing a very sorry part. No less sorry is the part he plays when he restricts himself simply to supporting any seizure of land by the peasants, without doing everything he can to ensure that such a major revolution in property relations brings the people as close as possible to the socialist order.[13]

If the peasants simply seized the land as the property of the individual village, Gots pointed out, injustice and inequality of distribution would still remain. It was the socialists' task to explain to the peasants that only socialisation would ensure egalitarian distribution, not only for themselves, but also for future generations.[14]

In the summer of 1905, various local peasant congresses were

[9] *ibid*, p 3.
[10] *Vtoroy s"ezd RSDRP; protokoly* (Moscow, 1959), pp 423–4.
[11] *Tretii s"ezd RSDRP; protokoly* (Moscow, 1959), p 454.
[12] See Lenin's defence of the resolution against the charge of opportunism: 'Otnoshenie sotsial-demokratii k krest'yanskomu dvizheniyu', *Polnoe Sobranie Sochinenii*, vol 11, pp 215–24.
[13] 'Iz dnevnika chitatelya', *R.R.*, no. 70 (July 1905), p 12.
[14] *ibid*, p 12.

organised by the party, especially in its strongholds in the Central Black Earth region, the Volga and the South.[15] At the beginning of June, a congress of party workers in the countryside, representing the North-West, Central and Volga regions, met 'in one of the central towns of Russia' to discuss the organisation and tactics of SR activity in the countryside.[16] A major task of the congress, in view of the recent attempt by the 'agrarian terrorists' at a takeover, was to restructure the SR Peasant Union as an active revolutionary force in the countryside. Local reports from the delegates showed that the party had so far made little progress towards the realisation of its aim of creating a nationwide organisation of the peasantry. Activity was most intensive on the Volga and in the North-West, where special agents attached to several urban committees travelled from village to village, holding public meetings and organising brotherhoods. In the Central region no systematic organisational work had been achieved, but the urban committees distributed literature to the peasantry through a number of contacts in the villages. There was, however, a general shortage of literature and of organisers.[17]

In order to deal with this problem, it was decided that the Central Committee should form a central controlling body for the Union. This Central Peasant Union was to have at its disposal a number of 'travelling agents', whose task was to supervise the organisation of work among the peasantry in the local party committees. Peasant unions should be formed at oblast′, guberniya and uezd levels, and peasant Brotherhoods in the volost′s and villages. To alleviate the difficulty of obtaining propaganda literature from abroad, it was resolved to set up a Russian Technical Bureau of the Peasant Union, which was to be entrusted with setting up local printing presses in Russia. The Bureau was also to publish a newspaper for the peasants which would deal with general aspects of the party programme, and a series of leaflets on specific political and economic topics.[18] The first number of the peasant newspaper, entitled *Zemlya i Volya!* ('Land and liberty!'), was issued in an edition of 20,000 copies in August 1905.[19]

The most important decision of the Congress was to call for a general economic and political strike in the countryside during the

[15] 'Iz partiynoy deyatel′nosti', *R.R.*, no. 67 (May 1905), p 14.
[16] 'Iz partiynoy deyatel′nosti', *R.R.*, no. 72 (August 1905), p 20.
[17] 'Iz partiynoy deyatel′nosti', *R.R.*, no. 76 (October 1905), p 24.
[18] *ibid*, pp 24–5.
[19] 'Iz partiynoy deyatel′nosti', *R.R.*, no. 73 (August 1905), p 27.

harvest period. A proclamation to this effect, headed 'Brother peasants!', was drawn up and distributed in 'tens of thousands' of copies by the Peasant Union. The proclamation explained to the peasants that the fiasco of the Russo-Japanese war showed the utter bankruptcy of the Tsarist government. The people should stage a national uprising to seize land and liberty, but, as a preparatory measure, they should first organise a general strike, which was to begin on St Elijah's day – 20 July, the day on which harvesting traditionally began. The form which this strike should take was to be decided in accordance with local conditions; the important thing was that it should happen simultaneously all over the country. The proclamation made detailed suggestions for the course of the movement. First the agricultural labourers should stop work and demand an improvement of 50% in their wage rates, and better conditions; and those peasants who rented land from the gentry should ask for a reduction of a third or a half in their rents. If these demands were not promptly met, the commune should carry off the landowners' grain and hay; if the peasants were short of pasture and woodland, they should graze their animals in the gentry's meadows and chop firewood in their forests – taking care, however, not to cause unnecessary damage. Bad elders and clerks should be dismissed and replaced by the election of 'reliable and conscientious' men. Local government institutions, such as the volost′ courts, should be boycotted, and the policemen and officials driven out and 'dealt with according to their deserts'; similar treatment should be afforded to corrupt priests. No taxes should be paid, and the peasants were advised to 'try hard' not to drink the liquor sold in the state vodka shops. If troops were brought in to pacify the peasants, the latter should try to reason with the soldiers and persuade them to surrender their arms; but they should show no mercy to the officers and the authorities. Finally, the peasants should assemble in their village gatherings and discuss the reorganisation of the state on a just basis. Resolutions should be passed on these issues, and neighbouring villages should be kept informed. The congress also decided to launch a campaign of political terror in the countryside, parallel with the strike movement. Combat detachments should be organised in the villages to lead this campaign. The detachments would also act as a popular militia, and obtain arms in preparation for the uprising.[20]

[20] 'Iz partiynoy deyatel′nosti', *R.R.*, no. 72 (August 1905), pp 20–21. The text of the proclamation, and a brief report of the congress, were published in no. 72; the more detailed report appeared in no. 76.

The fate of this call for a general agricultural strike is a significant indicator of the extent of SR influence on the peasantry in the summer of 1905. In fact, as might have been predicted from the evidence of the local reports at the congress, the party did not possess an adequate organisation in the countryside to ensure the realisation of its plan. The same number of the *Revolyutsionnaya Rossiya* that published the text of the proclamation to the peasants had to admit that the party could claim to have had only a partial success. Nevertheless, it continued, 'If the creation of a coordinated general strike was not fully achieved, we must still derive great satisfaction from the fact that the vast peasant movement which covered Russia in June and July nonetheless followed the plan described in this proclamation.'[21]

Here the party was being disingenuous. Spontaneity remained the keynote of the peasant movement throughout 1905, and if its course sometimes corresponded to the blueprint set out for it by the SRs, this was due more to coincidence than to design. Moreover, the summer of 1905 saw the creation of a body which was to rival the revolutionary parties in their claims to represent the interests of the peasantry – the All-Russia Peasant Union. The congresses of the Peasant Union, which met in July and November 1905, provided an opportunity for the SRs to compare their programme and tactics with the aspirations of the peasant delegates, who represented the most politically conscious element in the countryside.

The first Peasant Congress

The initiative for the formation of the All-Russia Peasant Union came in May 1905 from a group of liberals in Moscow guberniya, who sought to involve the peasantry in the campaign for the formation of professional unions, which was playing such an important part in the development of the revolutionary movement at that time. The SRs' attitude towards these unions was defined by Chernov in an article in *Revolyutsionnaya Rossiya* in June 1905. The party, he said, welcomed the movement as a means of drawing into the political struggle broader strata of society than would be attracted to purely party organisations. SRs were encouraged to join the unions in order to exert an influence on their aims and tactics, and thus to ensure that the party gained the greatest possible advantage from their formation. To this end, Chernov welcomed the extension of the 'Union of

[21] 'Iz partiynoy deyatel'nosti', *R.R.*, no. 72 (August 1905), p 21.

unions' to include trade unions of workers and peasants, as well as the unions of professional men which had originated the movement.[22]

The founding congress of the All-Russia Peasant Union, held in Moscow at the end of July, was attended by over a hundred peasants from 28 provinces of European Russia, and by about 25 intellectuals, and it soon developed into a contest among the liberals, the SRs and the SDs, for influence over the decisions of the peasant delegates. The discussion of the Union's programme began with its political demands. The Congress unanimously passed resolutions demanding full civil liberties and the convocation of a Constituent Assembly elected on the basis of universal, direct, equal and secret suffrage for men and women over the age of twenty. No specific mention was made of the form of state which would replace the autocracy, but, since the proposal by the official SD representative that the Congress should demand a democratic republic was rejected, a constitutional monarchy was apparently envisaged.[23]

The item of the programme which held the greatest interest for the peasant delegates was, of course, the land question. The chairman announced that more than thirty members had put their names down to speak on this issue, and the intensity of the peasants' feelings was reflected in their impassioned addresses on the floor of the Congress. All were agreed that private property in land should be abolished; but sharp differences existed on the way in which this should be achieved. On the question of the form of landholding which should replace private property, there was little disagreement; only one delegate voted against the resolution that: 'The land should be considered the common property of the entire people'.[24] In the debate, the only speaker to dissent from this view was the SD representative, who argued that the time was ripe only for political reforms, and not for 'such a socialist measure as the confiscation of the land', which, like the alienation of the factories, could be accomplished only after the further development of capitalism and class consciousness.[25]

The peasant delegates themselves expressed their views with varying degrees of sophistication. Some used religious phraseology:

[22] 'Organizatsionnyi vopros', *R.R.*, no. 69 (June 1905), pp 2–5.

[23] *Protokol uchreditel'nago s"ezda Vserossiyskago Krest'yanskago Soyuza* (St Petersburg, 1905), pp 23–6.

[24] *ibid*, p 38.

[25] *ibid*, pp 33–4.

The people see the land as the gift of God, like air and water. Those who need it should receive it.[26]

God gave the land to all alike, the land provides us with food and drink . . . The land should be given to all who can work it.[27]

The land is the true mother of us all. She was not made by human hands, she was created by the Holy Spirit, and therefore ought not to be bought and sold.[28]

Others used more secular terms, which suggested that they may have been familiar with the programmes of the revolutionary parties:

It is necessary to abolish private property in land and transfer the land to those who will work it with their own family labour.[29]

The land should belong to all and be in egalitarian utilisation.[30]

The land should be taken from private property and assigned to the people.[31]

No specific proposals were made for the disposal of the land once it had become 'the property of the entire people', although one delegate claimed that they wanted nothing to do with doctrines of nationalisation and socialisation, which would scare the mass of the people.[32] The Congress resolved that the issue should be left open for discussion in the localities, at village gatherings.[33]

The most heated discussion concerned the question of compensation for the confiscated lands. It was unanimously agreed that no payment should be made for the takeover of church and state lands.[34] Private lands, however, were a different matter, and a wide range of views was expressed. At the one extreme stood the SR representative and his supporters, who argued that no compensation should be paid for any private land – inherited or purchased, large or small in extent, or owned by gentry or by peasants. Some delegates, indeed, wanted to go even further and have the gentry return to the peasants the redemption dues they had paid since Emancipation.[35] The majority of delegates, however, felt that some compensation should be paid for privately owned lands. For many of the delegates who favoured compensation, the primary concern appears to have been the protection of peasants who had purchased land as their private property. Some drew a distinction between inherited lands, such as those of the

26 *ibid*, p 27.
27 *ibid*, p 28.
28 *ibid*, p 28.
29 *ibid*, p 26.
30 *ibid*, p 36.
31 *ibid*, p 37.
32 *ibid*, p 27.
33 *ibid*, p 38.
34 *ibid*, p 38.
35 *ibid*, pp 26–7, 36.

gentry estates, and land bought by hard and honestly earned money, as in the case of most peasant holdings outside the commune.[36] The opponents of compensation, on the other hand, argued that the very basis of private property in land, whether inherited or purchased, was unjust.[37] The SR representative at the Congress argued that the gentry had appropriated the common land, which was 'as essential for all as light and air', and therefore deserved no compensation, whether their land was inherited or purchased. As for the peasants who had purchased land, there would be no injustice in their treatment. The majority of peasants with private lands held only small areas, and they would receive adequate compensation in their share of the general redistribution of the large estates. Those with larger holdings were kulaks and deserved to be treated in the same way as the *pomeshchiki*.[38] In spite of eloquent arguments by SR sympathisers, the resolution finally adopted by the Congress, with only five dissenting votes, was a compromise: 'Land should be confiscated from private owners partly for recompense, partly without recompense'.[39]

After approving resolutions demanding the introduction of universal, free and secular primary education, and the reform of local government on a more democratic and autonomous basis,[40] the Congress went on to consider the question of tactics. No mention was made of land seizures, but the chairman was warmly applauded for his suggestion that the peasants should seek land and liberty by re-electing their own village and volost′ officials and boycotting the state authorities. Other speakers argued that government force should be met by force, and by organised revolutionary activity. The resolution on tactics, adopted 'after a lively debate', advocated a campaign of political action, in rather ambivalent terms:

> The activity of the Peasant Union, depending on local conditions, may be either open or secret (conspiratorial). All members of the Union should disseminate their views and implement their demands by all possible means, not restricting themselves to opposition to the *zemskie nachal′niki* and other authorities. Among these means, they are strongly advised to make use of their right of drafting communal resolutions at village and volost′ gatherings and at private meetings, concerning the improvement of the state organisation and the amelioration of the condition of the people.[41]

The Congress concluded with a significant exchange which illustrated the self-confidence of the peasant delegates. It was proposed that the Union send a greeting 'to our brothers the factory

[36] *ibid*, pp 27, 29–31, 35–6.
[37] *ibid*, pp 28, 35.
[38] *ibid*, pp 35–6.
[39] *ibid*, p 38.
[40] *ibid*, pp 38–43.
[41] *ibid*, p 47.

workers, who have for so long been spilling their blood in the struggle for the people's freedom'. When the SD delegate intervened to point out that 'without the factory workers the peasants will achieve nothing', he was met with shouts from the floor that 'on the contrary, without the peasants the workers can achieve nothing'.[42]

Revolutionary perspectives

On 6 August 1905 the government issued its long-awaited decree establishing a consultative assembly – the Duma promised in the Tsar's February rescript to Bulygin, the Minister of the Interior. The proposals were totally rejected by the SRs, who planned to turn a boycott of the elections into a general attack on the autocratic government. In the towns, Chernov proposed (in an editorial in *Revolyutsionnaya Rossiya*) an active boycott to be backed up by a general political strike. In the countryside, the electoral gatherings of heads of households should be replaced by protest meetings of the entire village, and the villages should refuse to pay taxes or supply recruits for the army. The peasants should re-elect their own officials, then launch a political strike and boycott of the authorities. Such a movement in the countryside, with the slogan 'land and liberty', supported by a general strike in the towns, would constitute a major assault on the autocracy.[43]

As always, Chernov was reluctant to predict in advance what might be the extent of the achievement of the forthcoming revolution. Before 1905, the party had assumed that the introduction of socialism would be preceded by a transitional period of indeterminate length, in which power would reside in the hands of the bourgeoisie. At the same time, the party hoped that the revolution would go beyond the framework of bourgeois democracy in its achievements in the field of social and, particularly, agrarian reform. The SR minimum programme, which included the demand for the socialisation of the land – an anti-capitalist measure – was designed as a guideline for this transitional period, although the SRs insisted that they could not predict in advance what form of state structure would replace the autocracy.[44]

42 *ibid*, p 48.

43 'Vneshnii mir i vnutrennyaya voyna', *R.R.*, no. 73 (August 1905), pp 3–5.

44 See 'Krest'yanskoe dvizhenie', *R.R.*, no. 8 (June 1902), pp 3–4; 'Sotsializatsiya zemli i kooperatsiya v sel'skom khozyaystve', *R.R.*, no. 14 (December 1902), pp 5–6, no. 15 (January 1903), p 7; 'Proekt programmy PS-Rov', *R.R.*, no. 46 (May 1904), pp 1–3.

In January 1905, immediately after Bloody Sunday, Chernov argued that the party should aim to extend and expand the revolutionary movement as far as possible, with no preconceived ideas concerning its possible limitations. For the true revolutionary, he claimed, there were no limits except the degree of energy, preparedness and consciousness of the masses. It might well be that the revolution would be bourgeois in its outcome, but this did not mean that the party should restrict its programme and tactics in advance to the achievement of a purely bourgeois revolution. The SRs should aim to achieve not only political but also social reforms from the revolution.[45]

The development of the revolutionary movement in the spring and summer of 1905 did nothing to dampen the party's optimism concerning its possible outcome. In May 1905 it was argued in *Revolyutsionnaya Rossiya* that, in view of the weakness of the liberal bourgeoisie, the revolution would have to be made by the workers and peasants under the leadership of the revolutionary intelligentsia. The overthrow of autocracy would therefore also involve the overthrow of the landed gentry and the bourgeoisie who were its main supporters, and this would guarantee the introduction of socio-economic as well as political changes. The extent of the victory – and this was always an important qualification for the SRs – would depend on the strength, energy and organisation of the working masses themselves.[46]

The most radical assessment of the forthcoming revolution came in an article by Mikhail Gots, published in July. Gots attacked both the Bolsheviks and the Mensheviks for their assumption that the revolution would be purely bourgeois-democratic in character, and argued that the working class should be encouraged not only to destroy the autocracy, but also to prevent the entrenchment of the bourgeoisie. He continued, in a passage which foreshadows Trotsky's famous theory of 'permanent revolution':[47]

> The forthcoming revolution will be achieved mainly by the efforts of the workers – the proletarians and peasants. They should take from this revolution all that the social conditions permit them to take – the most important of these conditions being the extent of their own consciousness. They should not

[45] 'Preddverie revolyutsii', *R.R.*, no 58 (January 1905), p 2.

[46] N. Onegin, '"Politika" i sotsializatsiya zemli v nashey programme', *R.R.*, no. 67 (*prilozhenie*) (May 1905), pp 6–8.

[47] See M. Perrie, 'The Socialist-Revolutionaries on "permanent revolution"', *Soviet Studies*, vol 24, no. 3 (1973), pp 411–13.

restrict the scale of this revolution in advance for the benefit of the bourgeoisie, but on the contrary they should turn it into a permanent one, oust the bourgeoisie step by step from the positions it has occupied, give the signal for a European revolution, and then draw new strength from there.[48]

The socialisation of the land through revolutionary expropriation by the peasants would, Gots claimed, be the first blow which the working classes could direct against their exploiters, thus clearing the way for the final overthrow of capital and for the realisation of socialism.[49]

The SRs' plans for a general political strike to coincide with the elections to the Bulygin Duma were forestalled by the spontaneous development of the strike movement in the capitals, which culminated in the nationwide general strike of October. On 17 October, faced with the total paralysis of the country, the Tsar issued a Manifesto conceding full civil liberties, extending the franchise for the Duma, and granting it legislative instead of merely consultative powers. Although the strike was soon called off, the publication of the October Manifesto failed to satisfy even the liberals, let alone the revolutionaries, who openly declared their intention to continue the struggle for a Constituent Assembly elected on the basis of the 'four-tailed' – universal, equal, direct and secret – suffrage.

In spite of their criticisms of its restricted scope, the SRs recognised that the 'liberty' granted by the October Manifesto represented a major achievement for the revolutionary movement, and one which for the first time gave the party a chance to emerge from the underground and operate freely and openly. At the end of October the émigré SR leadership, with the exception of Mikhail Gots, who was too ill to travel, returned to Russia to take over direct control of the party's activities there. *Revolyutsionnaya Rossiya* ceased publication, and Chernov was entrusted with the task of establishing a legal party newspaper in St Petersburg to take its place. On his arrival in the capital, he turned first for advice to the editorial board of *Russkoe Bogatstvo*, Mikhaylovskii's old journal. Here it was suggested that *Syn Otechestva* ('Son of the fatherland'), a Legal Populist newspaper of a similar trend to *Russkoe Bogatstvo*, should be taken over as the official SR newspaper. After negotiations, this was agreed. The new editorial board of *Syn Otechestva* was to consist of Shreyder, its existing editor; Peshekhonov and Myakotin, from the board of

48 'Iz dnevnika chitatelya', *R.R.*, no. 70 (July 1905), p 12.
49 *ibid*, pp 12–13.

Russkoe Bogatstvo; Chernov; and Rusanov, the editor of the SR journal *Vestnik Russkoy Revolyutsii.* From the beginning of November, *Syn Otechestva* was published with the SR slogan, 'In the struggle you will achieve your rights', emblazoned on the front page. A smaller popular edition of the paper, with the slogan 'Land and liberty', was edited by Peshekhonov.[50]

The collaboration between the SRs and the Legal Populists in the publication of *Syn Otechestva* was not unmarked by differences of opinion on policy and tactics. In particular, the Legal Populists hoped that the SRs would take advantage of the new period of constitutional freedom to bring the party out of the underground and turn it into an open and legal organisation. This view was strongly advocated by N. F. Annenskii, a senior member of the board of *Russkoe Bogatstvo*, who at one stage wanted to make the legalisation of the party a precondition for the publication of *Syn Otechestva* as an SR newspaper. Chernov, while agreeing in principle that an open party was desirable, felt that the gains of October were not sufficiently secure for the party to risk taking such a step at that time. His fears were to prove justified, as the newspaper itself survived for only a few weeks, before being suppressed in the wave of government repressions at the end of December.[51] For the time being, the differences between the Legal Populists and the SRs were patched up, but they were to reappear at the party congress in January 1906, and lead to the secession of the 'Popular Socialists' to form a separate party.

The second Peasant Congress

After a partial lull during the harvest months of August and September, the peasant movement broke out with renewed vigour in October, and continued unabated until the end of the year. In some cases, it seems that the revival of the movement was triggered off by news of the October Manifesto, which the peasants interpreted as 'freedom' to take over the land of the gentry estates. In other cases, the movement was more purely political, consisting of meetings and demonstrations designed to put pressure on the government and the Duma for agrarian reform.[52] In the midst of this wave of peasant unrest, the All-Russia Peasant Union held its second (delegate)

[50] Chernov, *Pered burey*, pp 237–55.
[51] *ibid*, pp 247–9.
[52] Maslov, vol 2, p 233 ff; Dubrovskii, pp 51–6. Dubrovskii (p 42) estimates that

congress in Moscow from 6 to 10 November. The increased size of this congress reflected the growth of the local organisations of the Union since August. Of the 187 delegates from 27 provinces, 145 were peasants.

The delegates' reports described the course of the movement in their localities. The disturbances appear to have assumed their greatest dimensions in Saratov, where the movement was largely dominated by the SRs. According to the delegate from Saratov uezd, a state of open defiance of the gentry and the authorities had existed in the province since the time of the October general strike. The SRs had organised combat detachments of peasants, who had seized arms from the guards on the state forests. Officials had been driven out, and new authorities elected; estates had been raided and the *pomeshchiki* forced to leave, the land being declared the property of the entire people. Where money and property were seized from the estates, or from the state liquor shops and post offices, records were made of what was taken and how it was distributed. Although in general the movement had been effectively organised and controlled by the local SR Peasant Union, the delegate admitted that there had been instances when the party had not been able to prevent acts of 'agrarian terror'; there had been cases of arson on several estates, and some of the *pomeshchiki* and their stewards had been beaten up by the peasants.[53] From the reports of other delegates from Saratov, it appeared that arson and bloodshed had in fact been quite widespread in the province.[54]

The picture drawn by the delegate from Sumy uezd, in Khar'kov province, of the movement in his area, was rather different. In Sumy, the publication of the October Manifesto had been greeted by a demonstration of 40,000 peasants, demanding land and liberty. A peasant committee was formed, which organised a strike of agricultural workers on the neighbouring landowner's estate and eventually took over the estate when the steward and other officials fled. Another peasant meeting at the end of October had demanded the convocation of a Constituent Assembly, elected on the basis of universal suffrage, to meet no later than January 1906, and the transfer of the land to communal egalitarian use.[55]

there were 155 incidents of peasant unrest in August 1905; 71 in September; 219 in October; 796 in November; and 575 in December.

[53] *Materialy k krest'yanskomu voprosu; otchet o zasedaniyakh delegatskago s"ezda Vserossiyskago Krest'yanskago Soyuza 6–10 noyabrya 1905 g.* (Rostov, 1905), pp 40–2.

[54] *ibid*, pp 44–7.

[55] *ibid*, pp 42–4.

The delegates from Saratov and Khar'kov, respectively, represented the two major alternatives which were to be advocated in the debate on tactics which began on the third day of the congress: direct revolutionary action involving violence, or peaceful methods of political organisation. In the course of this debate, the SRs were criticised for having encouraged violence and bloodshed in Saratov guberniya. An SR delegate from Saratov defended the party's tactics by pointing out that:

> The SR party would have preferred to keep to peaceful paths and accomplish all its tasks without spilling blood. If the party invites the people to possess the land and to arm, this is only because of the obstacles which the people must and do face in their peaceful seizure of the land, when they plough the gentry's fields and scythe their meadows. Then, comrade peasants, all those who do not wish to give you the land will come out against you. The SR party says to the peasants: we advise you not to attack, but to defend yourselves with weapons in your hands.[56]

In the course of the debate on tactics, it emerged that the SR proposal for confrontation with the authorities, culminating in an armed uprising, was supported by only a minority of the delegates. In a final attempt to sway the congress, the official SR representative drew the delegates' attention to the successes achieved by the workers by direct action:

> The party is in solidarity with you on the question of the transfer of the land to the people on the basis of egalitarian use and on condition that the land is transferred to those who work it, and also on the question of the Constituent Assembly. But we direct your attention to the tactics of the workers: they do not wait for the convening of the Constituent Assembly, but are taking for themselves the eight-hour day, and realizing the freedom of the press, of assembly, and so on – the Constituent Assembly will then only have to confirm all these rights which have been gained. We propose that you include in your resolution that the transfer of the land to the people is the affair of the working people themselves, that this transfer will be accomplished by peaceful means, but, if necessary, violence will be used.[57]

The resolutions on tactics finally adopted by the congress represented a compromise between the views of the liberals and those of the SRs. The Peasant Union resolved to boycott the elections to the Duma and demanded a Constituent Assembly, to be elected on the basis of the fourfold suffrage. The implementation of a just land reform was to be entrusted to the Constituent Assembly. As a provisional measure until the Constituent Assembly met, the Union

[56] *ibid*, pp 61–2. [57] *ibid*, p 81.

resolved that no transactions of rent or purchase should be made between the peasants and the landowners. If their demands were not met, the peasants would call for a general strike, in conjunction with the urban workers. In the case of any persecution of the Union, it would order the peasants to refuse to pay taxes or supply recruits to the army, to withdraw all deposits in savings banks, and close down the liquor shops. However, this catalogue of peaceful means concluded with a barely veiled threat of violence if moderation should fail: 'On the basis of all the information it has received from all parts of Russia, the congress declares that it foresees that the non-satisfaction of the people's demands will lead our country into great disturbances, and will inevitably provoke a general popular uprising, because the cup of the peasants' patience is running over.'[58]

Soon after the end of the November congress, the government began a campaign of arrests of members of the Peasant Union, which virtually destroyed its local and central organisation and forced the postponement of the next congress, planned for the middle of January 1906.[59]

By the end of 1905, the forces of revolution in both town and countryside had been compelled to retreat. The SR Central Committee, after October, had resolved to consolidate the gains of the revolution by organisation and propaganda, rather than seeking to force events further. For this reason, the St Petersburg party committee opposed the decision of the SD majority in the St Petersburg Soviet to call for a second and third general strike in November and December. When the Moscow Soviet decided to stage an armed uprising in December, this decision was supported by the Moscow committee of the SR party, under strong pressure from the youthful 'opposition' faction, but against the advice of the Central Committee.[60] By the end of the year, the return of loyal troops from the Far East after the conclusion of the Japanese war restored the upper hand to the government. December saw the brutal 'pacification' of peasant unrest by military punitive expeditions, as well as the arrest of the leaders of the St Petersburg Soviet, the crushing of the renewed general strike, and the bloody suppression of the armed uprising in Moscow.

[58] N. Karpov, ed., *Krest'yanskoe dvizhenie v revolyutsii 1905 goda v dokumentakh* (Leningrad, 1926), p 78.

[59] E. I. Kiryukhina, 'Vserossiyskii Krest'yanskii Soyuz v 1905 g.', *Istoricheskie Zapiski*, no. 50 (1955), pp 139–40.

[60] Chernov, *Pered burey*, pp 251–9.

11
The nature of the peasant movement[1]

The problem of the 'true' nature of the peasant movement which played such a crucial rôle in the events of 1905 was, as we have seen, the topic of much lively debate within the rival socialist parties, who believed that the socio-political character of the revolution would be determined by the aspirations of the peasantry. In order to assess the extent of SR influence on the peasant movement, and to compare the relative merits of the conflicting SR and SD views of its class character, it may be useful to examine the evidence concerning the social composition of the movement, and the forms which it assumed.

The peasant disturbances which began in the spring of 1905 assumed the same range of forms as the earlier movement of 1902–3, although on a much wider scale, and over a longer period – unrest continued until the summer of 1907, but in terms of the number of incidents, the peak periods were the autumn of 1905 and the early summer of 1906.[2] The Soviet historians Dubrovskii and Shestakov have investigated the forms of the movement and its regional distribution. Their findings are incorporated in Tables 1–3.[3]

Table 1 shows that the great majority of incidents (about 75%) involved conflicts between the peasants and the gentry landowners; the conflicts with state officials, police and troops (about 15%) usually developed as a consequence of their intervention in the move-

[1] This chapter is based on my article 'The Russian peasant movement of 1905–1907; its social composition and revolutionary significance', *Past and Present*, no. 57 (1972), pp 123–55.

[2] Dubrovskii, pp 40–43.

[3] The sources for the tables used slightly different classifications for the forms of the movement, and different criteria for assessing its strength. Shestakov, in common with most pre-revolutionary and Soviet works, refers to the number of uezds affected. Dubrovskii, whose little book provides probably the most systematic account of the movement, uses the more accurate measure of the number of incidents reported; unfortunately, however, he does not provide a breakdown of his data in terms of both form and regional distribution.

TABLE 1 *Forms of the peasant movement in Russia in 1905–7**

Form of movement	No. of instances	Percentage of total	Total no. of instances	Percentage of total
Action against landowners:				
Arson	979	18.1		
Destruction of estates	846	15.7		
Illicit woodcutting	809	15.0		
Strikes by agricultural workers	723	13.4		
Seizure of meadows, pasture, etc.	573	10.6		
Withdrawal of labour from estates	474	8.7		
Seizure of foodstuffs and fodder	316	5.8		
Seizure and tillage of arable land	216	4.0		
Rent conflicts	211	3.9		
Conflict with land-owners and estate officials	205	3.8		
Conflicts over boundaries	52	1.0		
Total	5404	100.0	5,404	75.4
Conflicts with state officials, police and troops			1,041	14.5
Conflicts with kulaks			97	1.4
Conflicts with clergy			33	0.5
Other (attacks on traders, usurers, liquor shops, etc.)			590	8.2
Grand total			7,165	100.0

* The table covers all regions of European Russia except the Baltic and Trans-caucasian provinces. Based on data in S. M. Dubrovskii, *Krest'yanskoe dvizhenie v revolyutsii 1905–1907 gg.* (Moscow, 1956), pp. 65, 67.

ment against the landowners. Attacks on non-gentry 'enemies', such as kulaks, clergy, usurers and shopkeepers were rarer (about 10% of all incidents).

The forms assumed by the movement against the landowners were determined primarily by the system of land-tenure and agrarian relationships in each locality. The movement was strongest in those areas, such as the Central Black Earth, the Volga and the Ukraine (Table 2), where the exploitation of the peasant renters by the gentry

TABLE 2 *Regional distribution of the peasant movement of 1905–7**

Region	No. of instances	Percentage of total
Central Black Earth	2,196	30.6
South-West	985	13.7
Little Russia	850	11.8
Mid-Volga	724	10.3
Belorussia	655	9.1
Central Industrial	482	6.7
Novorossiya	468	6.5
Lower Volga	244	3.4
Lakes	235	3.3
Lithuania	168	2.3
Urals	104	1.5
North	54	0.8
Total	7,165	100.0

* Dubrovskii, p. 60.

landowners was greatest, or where the severest hardships had been caused by the transition from renting to large-scale capitalist farming. Here the predominant form of the movement was the attack on the landowner's estate (Table 3). This often involved the destruction of the manor house and outbuildings to ensure that the 'master' would never return. Sometimes the peasants seized food and fodder from the barns or harvested it from the fields. The frequency of illicit woodcutting and pasturing of animals reflected the shortage of these resources on commune land; peasant appropriation of gentry arable land was less common. Other forms of the peasant movement were wage- and rent-strikes, and boycotts or refusals to work on gentry estates. In some areas, the movement assumed more purely political forms, involving conflict with the state machinery as well as with the gentry landowners. The peasants replaced village and volost′ elders, and other officials whom they considered to be simply the puppets of the state bureaucracy, with their own freely-elected representatives. Refusals to pay taxes were also common. The movement against state intervention in peasant affairs was particularly strong in Georgia, where virtual anarchy reigned in the countryside for much of 1905 and 1906.[4]

On the whole, the forms assumed by the movement corresponded to the measures recommended to the peasants by the SRs, with the

[4] *ibid*, pp 59–83; A. Shestakov, *Krest'yanskaya revolyutsiya 1905–1907 gg. v Rossii* (Moscow, 1926), pp 51–3.

TABLE 3 *Regional distribution of forms of the peasant movement of 1905–7**

Region	Total no. of uezds	No. of uezds affected	% of total	Forms of movement													
				Destruction of estates		Illicit wood-cutting		Strikes		Seizure of pasture and fodder		Illicit tillage		Seizure of grain from fields		Rent conflicts	
				No. of uezds	% of uezds affected	No.	%	No.	%	No.	%	No.	%	No.	%	No.	%
Central Black Earth	75	68	90.7	54	76.5	45	66.2	46	67.6	47	69.1	7	10.3	18	26.5	28	41.2
South-West	36	35	97.2	9	25.7	19	54.3	31	88.6	22	62.9	8	22.9	5	14.3	8	22.9
Little Russia	41	41	100.0	26	63.4	28	68.3	35	85.4	29	70.7	5	12.2	11	26.8	26	63.4
Mid-Volga	51	45	88.2	30	66.7	39	86.7	16	35.6	26	57.2	18	40.0	14	31.1	12	26.7
Belorussia	43	39	90.7	6	15.4	33	84.6	25	64.1	6	15.4	5	12.8	–	–	–	—
Central Industrial	71	45	63.4	4	8.9	38	84.4	8	17.8	19	42.2	7	15.6	–	–	3	6.7
Novorossiya	39	32	82.1	19	59.4	16	50.0	17	53.1	13	40.6	17	53.1	7	21.9	22	68.8
Lower Volga	17	9	52.9	7	77.8	6	66.7	1	11.1	7	77.8	4	44.4	2	22.2	4	44.4
Lakes	34	23	67.6	3	13.0	20	87.0	10	43.5	12	52.2	2	8.7	2	8.7	4	17.4
Lithuania	23	17	73.9	–	–	18	76.5	14	82.4	10	58.8	4	23.5	2	11.8	–	–
Urals	29	11	37.9	1	9.1	10	90.9	–	–	2	18.2	–	–	–	–	–	–
North	19	9	47.4	–	–	9	100.0	1	11.1	2	22.1	1	11.1	–	–	2	22.1
Totals	478	374	78.2	159	42.8	281	75.1	204	54.5	195	52.1	78	20.9	61	16.3	109	29.1

* Based on a table in A. Shestakov, *Krest'yanskaya revolyutsiya 1905–1907 gg. v Rossii* (Moscow, 1926), p. 52.

important exception that the peasants continued to favour 'destructive' tactics, such as arson and raids on estates, as well as the 'constructive' methods advocated by the party, such as strikes and boycotts. Neither was there much evidence of organisation and coordination between districts or even villages, as the SRs had hoped for. The most widespread forms of the movement represented the peasants' traditional 'own means' of local direct action, often involving the methods of 'agrarian terror' which were rejected by the SRs. In most cases in which the peasants seized the land of the gentry estates, they appear to have taken it over as the property of the local commune, rather than as the 'possession of all the people', as the SRs recommended. Only in a few isolated instances does one find reports of the peasants expropriating the land in the manner advocated by the SRs – as for instance in Atkarsk uezd in Saratov guberniya, where the peasants declared that they were taking the land for their provisional utilisation until a Constituent Assembly was convened.[5] Such cases of SR influence on the movement were the exception rather than the rule. Even those forms of the peasant movement which may be classed as 'political' seem to have been essentially anarchic, insofar as they reflected the rejection of the state by the peasants, rather than an aspiration to seize and control it for themselves.

Probably the most valuable source of information concerning the social composition of the peasant movement is the survey conducted by the Imperial Free Economic Society, a learned body with broad liberal and even radical sympathies. About 20,000 copies of a detailed questionnaire on the nature, causes and effects of the movement were sent in 1907 to correspondents and contacts of the Society in 47 out of the 50 provinces of European Russia. Of the 1,400 replies received, 702 contained positive information concerning the existence of peasant unrest in the correspondent's locality. According to the editors of the survey, these correspondents were 'representatives of very heterogeneous strata of the population, various political tendencies and social trends, peasants and landowners, teachers and estate stewards, priests and state officials, extremists of the left and of the right, participants in the movement and police officers, victims of political repressions, and victims of agrarian destruction'.[6]

[5] Dubrovskii, pp 73–4.

[6] *Agrarnoe dvizhenie v Rossii v 1905–1906 gg.* (*Trudy Imperatorskago Vol'nago Ekonomicheskago Obshchestva*, 1908, nos. 3, 4–5) (2 vols, St Petersburg, 1908), vol 1, p vi.

The questions on the survey form included detailed requests for information on the participation of peasant and non-peasant elements in the movement, for example:

Was there any influence from outsiders? How was it expressed?
Which strata of the village took part in the movement: poor peasants, middle peasants, or the prosperous? What was each stratum's attitude towards the movement? What was the attitude of the peasants who had purchased land?
Was any part played by peasants engaged in off-farm wage-work in factories and towns? If so, what?
Was any part played by soldiers and reserves returning from Manchuria? If so, what?
What part was played by the young men? By the old men?
What was the attitude of the women?[7]

The form in which the results of the survey were published makes it difficult to attempt a precise analysis of the informants' answers to these questions. The compilation of a digest of the returns for each region was entrusted to separate editors, who were granted considerable freedom in their approach to the materials. The quality of the editors, like that of the informants, varied considerably: some provided much more detailed and systematic analyses than others.[8] The editors' stated aim was 'not to draw any final conclusions or generalisations, but to set out, systematically and objectively, all the data obtained from the survey, as material which should serve as one of the sources . . . for subsequent scientific study of the agrarian movement'.[9] No attempt was made in the published results to present an overall picture of the movement in any of its aspects; what follows represents this author's personal analysis of the evidence in the regional digests concerning the social composition of the participants in the movement. Table 4 provides a summary of the findings.

Although external influence was frequently cited by correspondents as a factor contributing to the outbreak of peasant unrest, it was by no means a universal factor. Agitation and propaganda in the countryside by non-peasant elements often served as a precipitating factor for the movement, but there were also other precipitants, the most important being the news and rumours of the revolutionary events in the towns, and the occurrence of peasant disturbances in

[7] *ibid*, vol 1, p xv.
[8] The editors included such noted economists as V. G. Groman (Novorossiya), P. P. Maslov (Lower Volga), S. N. Prokopovich (Central Black Earth and Urals) and B. B. Veselovskii (Belorussia).
[9] *Agrarnoe dvizhenie . . .*, vol 1, p ix.

TABLE 4 *Participation in the peasant movement of 1905–6**

Region	No. of guber-niyas	No. of reports	Participants																					
											Village peasantry													
			Outside agitators		Rural intelli-gentsia		Peasant-workers		Peasant-soldiers/sailors		Socio-economic strata								Age groups					
											Poor		Middle		Rich/pros-perous		Women		Young		Middle-aged		Old	
			+	–	+	–	+	–	+	–	+	–	+	–	+	–	+	–	+	–	+	–	+	–
Central Black Earth	6	74	5	2	4	–	6	–	6	–	6	2	5	–	5	6	4	2	5	–	–	–	–	–
South-West	3	54	2	2	3	–	3	3	3	1	3	1	3	–	3	3	3	2	3	–	1	–	1	3
Little Russia	3	183	1	1	–	–	3	–	2	2	3	–	3	–	3	3	3	2	3	–	–	–	1	2
Mid-Volga	5	74	1	–	1	–	3	1	3	1	4	2	3	–	5	4	3	2	3	–	1	–	2	3
Belorussia	7	70	7	2	–	–	6	2	7	3	7	2	7	–	7	6	4	2	5	–	–	–	–	2
Central Industrial	6	70	3	1	1	–	5	–	1	–	1	–	1	–	–	3	2	–	1	–	–	–	–	3
Novorossiya	6	54	4	3	–	–	2	1	1	–	5	2	4	–	4	5	–	–	–	–	–	–	–	–
Lower Volga	3	28	1	–	1	–	–	–	–	–	1	1	–	–	1	3	–	–	1	–	–	–	–	–
Lakes	4	71	3	3	2	–	3	3	2	3	3	–	3	–	3	2	3	3	3	1	1	–	2	2
Urals	3	12	–	–	–	–	2	–	1	–	–	1	1	–	2	–	–	–	1	1	1	–	–	1
North	1	12	–	–	–	–	1	1	1	–	–	–	–	–	–	1	–	–	1	–	–	–	–	–
Totals	47	702	27	14	12	–	34	11	27	10	33	11	30	–	33	36	22	13	26	2	4	–	6	16

* Based on data from *Agrarnoe dvizhenie v Rossii v 1905–1906 gg.* (St. Petersburg, 1908).

Note

1. Figures under the heading 'participants' indicate the number of guberniyas from which the participation (columns headed +) or non-participation (columns headed –) was reported of members of the social group in question
2. Regions are composed of the following guberniyas (See Map, p. xii):

Central Black Earth	Kursk, Orel, Ryazan', Tambov, Tula, Voronezh
South-West	Kiev, Podoliya, Volyn'
Little Russia	Chernigov, Khar'kov, Poltava
Mid-Volga	Kazan', Nizhnii Novgorod, Penza, Saratov, Simbirsk
Belorussia	Grodno, Kovno, Minsk, Mogilev, Smolensk, Vil'no, Vitebsk
Central Industrial	Kaluga, Kostroma, Moscow, Tver', Vladimir, Yaroslavl'
Novorossiya	Bessarabia, Don, Ekaterinoslav, Kherson, Kuban', Tauride
Lower Volga	Astrakhan', Orenburg, Samara
Lakes	Novgorod, Olonets, Pskov, St Petersburg
Urals	Perm', Ufa, Vyatka
North	Vologda

neighbouring localities.[10] Even if the movement was sparked off by external factors, it was usually fuelled by grievances which were peasant, and often purely local, in character. As Groman noted in his introduction to the reports from Novorossiya, the influence of 'outside agitators' was more likely to be claimed by correspondents hostile to the movement than by sympathisers.[11] This phenomenon would appear to be a reflection of the conservative predilection for the 'conspiracy theory' of history, with its corresponding reluctance to admit that social unrest might have its roots in genuine problems and hardships. This is not to say, of course, that 'outside agitation' was simply a figment of the imagination of reactionary Tsarist officials and landowners. Revolutionaries of all parties – or of none – flocked into the countryside from early summer of 1905. Their influence was not always inflammatory; in some cases they tried to divert the violent direct action of the spontaneous movement into more peaceful political channels. The following extract from Groman's introduction to the digest of reports from Novorossiya gives a good survey of the views of various categories of correspondents concerning the nature of the influence of 'outsiders'. It also suggests that that influence often assumed the form advocated by the SRs – attempting to dissuade the peasants from acts of 'agrarian terror', and advocating constructive rather than destructive means of struggle:

> Persons hostile to the movement talk about 'the intoxication of the people by agitators, Jews and students', or talk about 'the leadership of an organisation in Geneva'; those who are neutral divide into two groups: one (the smaller) also says that the disturbances were incited by Jews and vagabonds who threatened with bombs, but the other group (the larger) either simply notes the fact of agitation and the distribution of proclamations, or reports 'public lectures, which attempted to restrain the populace from violence'. The authors of reports sympathetic to the movement define the external influence as follows: 'at the meetings the incomers said that the peasants should organise, but not commit robbery or destruction'; 'the outsiders advised that a strike should be organised if the demands were not met'; 'if the movement owed anything to outsiders, as it undoubtedly did, it was only its organisation and the conscious formulation of its aspirations.'[12]

The outsiders were usually described in the reports only generically, as 'agitators' or 'revolutionaries'. Sometimes the party organisations they represented were specifically mentioned: the

[10] *ibid*, vol 1, pp 48 (Central Black Earth), 173 (Lakes); vol 2, pp 8 (South-West), 289–90 (Little Russia), 418–19 (Novorossiya).

[11] *ibid*, vol 2, pp 417–18.

[12] *ibid*, vol 2, p 418.

Social-Democrats, Socialist-Revolutionaries, the Jewish Bund, or the Peasant Union.[13] The social groups from which the agitators were recruited were rarely mentioned, or mentioned only in terms – such as 'Jews and long-haired students'[14] – which for the Russian conservative were virtually synonymous with 'revolutionary agitators'.[15] The influence of local factory workers was rarely mentioned; nor was it always welcome. Striking railwaymen in Pskov province, who tried to enlist peasant support, suffered severe beatings for their pains.[16]

In addition to this predominantly urban category of complete outsiders, frequent mention was also made of the rôle of the rural intelligentsia as agitators and conductors of revolutionary ideas to the peasantry. The groups most often cited in this connection were village teachers, members of the clergy, medical workers, and employees of the local *zemstvo* organisations. From Voronezh guberniya it was reported that 'agitation was conducted by psalm-readers and seminary students, medical assistants and nurses, doctors and midwives, and railway guards'.[17] The report from Penza noted that priests were very rarely the object of the movement 'because in many cases the priests themselves were "the sources of propaganda", and "in particular their children – seminary students, teachers and schoolmistresses"'.[18] The rôle of the intelligentsia as intermediaries between the town and countryside was also noted – as in a report from Pskov that the local intelligentsia, who distributed pamphlets and leaflets to the peasantry, had been 'infected' from the town.[19] In some cases, a literate stratum of 'peasant intellectuals' (*intelligentnye krest'yane*), especially peasant artisans, performed a similar function to that of the non-peasant intelligentsia.[20] It was reported from Kursk that 'in this locality there were no agitators, but the peasants themselves frankly pointed to their own literate fellows, who had read to them from the "Russian Word", a newspaper widely distributed in our district, the proceedings of the Peasant Congress in Moscow'.[21]

[13] *ibid*, vol 1, p 363 (Belorussia).

[14] *ibid*, vol 2, p 480 (Kherson).

[15] In 1905 the peasants themselves came to use the word 'student' to refer to anyone, including peasants, with radical or oppositional views. 'The term "student" is losing its academic character and is becoming a political category. Of the inhabitants of a whole number of villages it is said that they "have gone and turned into students".' V. G. Tan, *Novoe krest'yanstvo* (Moscow, 1905), p 115.

[16] *Agrarnoe dvizhenie . . .*, vol 1, p 217.

[17] *ibid*, vol 1, p 87.

[18] *ibid*, vol 1, p 121.

[19] *ibid*, vol 1, p 217.

[20] *ibid*, vol 1, p 58 (Kursk).

[21] *ibid*, vol 1, p 56.

An important part in the movement was played by those peasants who had experience of the world outside the village, as seasonal workers in agriculture and industry. In some cases these peasant-workers, returning to their villages in the course of 1905 to help with the harvest, or because of unemployment and the strike movement in the towns, served simply to spread the general revolutionary mood from the factories to the countryside; in other cases, their influence was more consciously political. The editor of the reports from the Central Black Earth region described the nature of their influence as follows:

> The 'ferment' or 'brain' of the movement – as the correspondents phrased it – were the peasants doing seasonal work in the factories, in the mines and in the towns. As more developed persons, they naturally became the leaders of the movement; in some cases they brought into the countryside – along with the newspapers – news about the agrarian and the workers' movement in other places, and unconsciously propagandised the idea of the agrarian movement.[22]

In the Lakes region, peasants working in the towns were said to play an important part as 'conductors of new ideas and trends'.[23] In Pskov guberniya, where many peasants went to work in St Petersburg, correspondents wrote that 'those who had been in the factories in the city urged on the movement, and said that only thus could we achieve equal rights with members of the other legal estates, and obtain the land'; 'those doing seasonal work were insistent that the laws be worked out according to a new system'; and 'an important part was played by the distorted rumours and gossip which were brought by those returning from seasonal work who had been influenced by the propaganda of the various revolutionary parties'.[24]

A similar rôle to that of the peasant-workers was played by the peasant-soldiers and sailors returning to their villages from the Russo-Japanese war. Although in many areas the movement in the countryside had begun before the troops in the Far East were demobilised, 'with their arrival the movement intensified'.[25] In some cases, the troops were active conductors of revolutionary agitation, representing the 'most liberal and aware [*znayushchii*]' element in the countryside,[26] and 'broadening the political consciousness of the peasantry';[27] in other cases, their tales about the military fiasco in the Far East served simply to fuel the existing

[22] *ibid*, vol 1, p 49.
[23] *ibid*, vol 1, p 174.
[24] *ibid*, vol 1, pp 218–19.
[25] *ibid*, vol 1, p 93 (Mid-Volga).
[26] *ibid*, vol 1, p 137 (Saratov).
[27] *ibid*, vol 2, p 336 (Poltava).

flames of discontent in the villages. The soldiers' grievances were often the result of unfavourable comparisons with the Japanese. From Poltava it was reported that 'those who had been prisoners of war in Japan made a strong impression on their audience in general with their tales about the culture [*kulturnost'*] of Japan'.[28] A correspondent from Pskov wrote:

> The reserves returning from the Manchurian campaign had seen better order in the Japanese forces than in ours; they had seen that our commanders were weaker and more cowardly, and were thrashed not by the Japanese enemy, but by their own subordinates; and most likely the campaign was lost through internal enmity.[29]

There was a widespread belief among the soldiers that the Tsar should reward them for the hardships they had suffered by granting them more land. A hostile report from Ryazan' claimed that:

> The soldiers returning from Manchuria – most of whom were liars – exaggerated their hardships, expressed dissatisfaction with their commanders, talked about various abuses of state funds, and extolled their difficulties, for which they said the state was obliged to reward them by giving them the land for nothing.[30]

The troops often returned to find their farms run down, which gave them an additional material incentive for revolt. It was reported from Saratov that:

> In some places the soldiers returned from Manchuria during the movement, and intensified the general excitement. They found their economy devastated: 'There was nothing for them to eat, and no fuel for them to heat their huts.' And then they learned that their wives and families had received no allowances, or had received them only at irregular intervals. The discontented soldiers adhered to the movement and demanded land, saying, 'Why have we spilt our blood, if we do not have the land?'[31]

In other cases, however, the soldiers 'returned from Manchuria with money, feeling fine, and paid no attention to the entire movement'.[32] In one case reported from Novgorod, the soldiers, after an initial expression of support for the movement, thereafter reverted to their traditional repressive rôle, 'turning into watchmen on the invitation of the police; at present they enjoy almost universal hatred from the peasants'.[33]

On the basis of this evidence, therefore, it is clear that the SRs had correctly identified the non-peasant elements who were most likely

[28] *ibid*, vol 2, p 336.
[29] *ibid*, vol 1, p 219.
[30] *ibid*, vol 1, p 66.
[31] *ibid*, vol 1, p 147.
[32] *ibid*, vol 2, p 371 (Chernigov).
[33] *ibid*, vol 1, p 298.

to exert influence on the countryside – the 'intermediary' groups such as the rural intelligentsia and peasant-workers. To these groups the advent of war had brought about the important addition of the peasant-soldiers. Let us now turn to the question of participation in the movement by the village peasantry themselves.

In most cases, the peasants participated in the movement as an entire village or commune,[34] with all socio-economic strata taking part. A typical report is that from the Lakes, where 'The internal stratification of the peasantry in terms of property status did not substantially influence the participation in the movement of the various elements in the village. In the majority of cases, peasants of all strata took part in the movement.'[35] In many individual cases, however, some strata are reported to have been more active than others, and some are more regularly said to have been active rather than passive. Table 4 shows that the most varied evidence concerns participation by the two extreme categories, the rich and the poor. The evidence suggests that participation by these two strata was determined primarily by local conditions, and by the forms assumed by the movement in individual localities.

A considerable proportion of replies depicts the poor and landless peasants as the most active participants in the movement. The reasons for this are usually considered to be self-evident, in that these peasants had 'nothing to lose', and everything to gain, from the movement.[36] There were some forms of the movement, however, from which they were barred by virtue of their poverty: a peasant with no cow could not engage in illicit cattle grazing on the landowner's meadow, and a peasant without a horse was at a disadvantage when it came to carting away timber from the 'master's' forest, or plunder from his manor.[37] Even in wage-strikes, the form of the movement in which the poor were most likely to participate, they sometimes found themselves restrained. A correspondent from Podoliya reported that 'The leaders of the movement were the more prosperous peasants (none are rich); the most timid were the landless, because they cannot exist without their daily earnings, and they were soon compelled to bring the strike to an end, to avoid starvation.'[38] In exceptional cases, the poorer peasants were subsidised

[34] *ibid*, vol 2, pp 21 (South-West), 290 (Little Russia).
[35] *ibid*, vol 1, p 175.
[36] *ibid*, vol 1, p 120 (Penza).
[37] *ibid*, vol 1, pp 77 (Tambov), 109 (Nizhnii Novgorod); vol 2, p 335 (Poltava).
[38] *ibid*, vol 2, p 59.

during a strike by their more prosperous fellows.[39] The poorer peasants, too, were the most dependent for their livelihood on the local landowner, and therefore the most vulnerable to retaliatory measures. Realisation of this would sometimes serve as a deterrent against participation in the movement, as noted by a correspondent from Ufa: 'The meetings are attended mostly by the prosperous and middle peasants. You ask why Savelii (a poor peasant), say, was not there. Well, they say, he rents land from the landowner, and if the latter got to know that he had been at a meeting, then very likely he wouldn't let him have any land, or would only give him some piece of rutted ground.'[40]

In areas of capitalist farming with an extensive landless agricultural proletariat (*batraki*), solidarity with the local communal peasantry was most noticeable when the labourers were recruited from the neighbouring villages; where the work force on the large estates consisted largely of immigrant labour from other areas, as in Novorossiya, conflicts of interest often arose: 'In those cases where the peasants aimed to obtain all the land, they frequently demanded the removal of the immigrant workers, or even made the latter lay off work, so that the landowner could not conduct his enterprise, but sometimes the peasants restricted themselves to demanding that local workers be hired instead of immigrants.'[41]

The rich peasants, especially those who had purchased land as their individual private property and those who employed the labour of others, usually remained aloof from the movement, although it was only in rare cases that individual peasant proprietors were themselves the victims of the movement (see Table 1). Explanations of the passivity of the richer peasants were usually in terms of their general distrust of attacks upon property, which might easily be directed against themselves.[42] More rarely, the non-participation of the richer peasants was attributed to their very affluence. A correspondent from Pskov, describing a local case of illicit woodcutting, wrote: 'Of course, most of the disturbances were by the land-hungry peasants; they are short not only of land, but also of firewood. As for the rich, why should they take part, if they have enough as it is?'[43] In cases where the rich peasants participated in the movement, their avarice, and the fact that they

[39] *ibid*, vol 2, p 23 (South-West).

[40] *ibid*, vol 1, p 164.

[41] *ibid*, vol 2, p 409.

[42] *ibid*, vol 1, pp 58 (Kursk), 398 (Kovno); vol 2, p 306 (Khar'kov).

[43] *ibid*, vol 1, p 220.

possessed the means of gratifying it, were often attributed as an important motive. This was particularly true when the movement assumed the form of pillaging the large estates. A report of an incident of illicit woodcutting in Penza implies that the rich peasants benefited not only from their ownership of horses and carts to bear away the timber, but also from the services of their hired workers: 'They had the most horses and the greatest labour force, and therefore enjoyed the greatest advantage.'[44]

In some cases where the rich participated in the movement alongside the other strata of the village, it appears that although they had purchased land, they still felt themselves to have more in common with their fellow-villagers than with the landlord and shared common grievances against him. A correspondent from Kherson reported that: 'Poor, middle and prosperous peasants took part. Their attitudes were identical because, although the prosperous peasants had bought land through the bank, they had paid dearly for it, and it still did not suffice; therefore they too were obliged to rent land for 15–18 roubles a *desyatina* [2.7 acres] from landowners and the big commercial renters.'[45]

A correspondent from Volyn′ explained that although the local movement had been initiated by the poor and middle peasants, 'the rich took part, as they considered that the landowner had unjustly forbidden cattle grazing in a certain part of the forest'.[46] An interesting distinction between private peasant landownership and the landownership of the gentry, serving to justify the alignment of the peasant proprietors with the communal peasantry rather than with the gentry, was provided in a report from Novgorod: 'All took part in the movement, including the prosperous and those with purchased land. The latter had the same attitude as the poor peasants, saying that they alone had worked for the land they had bought, so that it should not be taken away from them, although it could be taken from others.'[47]

A similar distinction, based on the 'labour principle', was reported from the Central Black Earth region: 'The movement, in the words of a correspondent from Kozlov district, was directed against "those in general who owned or rented land, but did not work it with their own hands, without distinction as to estate [*soslovie*] or rank". Therefore peasant farms worked by family labour were not included among the objects of the movement.'[48]

[44] *ibid*, vol 1, p 129.
[45] *ibid*, vol 2, p 476.
[46] *ibid*, vol 2, p 144.
[47] *ibid*, vol 1, p 300.
[48] *ibid*, vol 1, p 51.

In a few cases, participation in the movement on the part of the richer peasants was the result of pressure exerted by the poorer strata for a demonstration of solidarity. The generally ambivalent position of the prosperous peasantry was exemplified by a report from Saratov that:

The tone of the movement was set by the poor peasants. Sometimes, depending on the circumstances, they would compel the rich to participate in the movement, threatening to deal with them 'as with the gentry landowners'. At other times they would not permit them to take part in the movement, because they took too much of the landowners' property for themselves. 'Sometimes, when the prosperous peasants were away raiding elsewhere, their property would be burned down in their absence.'[49]

Finally, in some individual cases, factors other than socio-economic, such as the influence of ideas, or generational differences, might impel richer peasants to take part in the movement. From Ekaterinoslav it was reported that: 'In those villages which did not act with total solidarity, it was the poor and middle peasants who participated, and, from the prosperous, only individuals for whom the political and social slogans of the epoch served as the impulse.'[50] From Tambov, the interaction of age and economic factors was noted: 'The large landowners among the peasants prepared to defend themselves, but the smaller landowners fell into two categories: the older ones protected their property; the young men joined in with the others.'[51]

The middle peasants, who shared all of the advantages and none of the disadvantages of the poor and the rich strata for participation in the movement, were the group whose active rôle was most consistently stressed. According to one report from Chernigov: 'The poor peasants could not take part in the woodcutting movement, because they had no horses, and the prosperous peasants feared repressions, but the middle peasants said that they would be no worse off in prison, so the wood was chopped by the middle peasants.'[52] A similar report came from Podoliya:

The rich peasants and the poor peasants did not sympathise with the strikes, although they did not display any energetic opposition. The principal strikers were the middle peasants, who had enough work on their own fields, and could therefore hold out for higher wages without suffering particular losses themselves. The poor peasants were especially in need of earnings, and therefore did not sympathise with the strikes.[53]

[49] *ibid*, vol 1, p 146.
[50] *ibid*, vol 2, p 448.
[51] *ibid*, vol 1, p 78.
[52] *ibid*, vol 2, p 371.
[53] *ibid*, vol 2, p 59.

In other cases, however, the middle peasants were less involved in the strike movement, as in this report from Kiev:

> The strike was conducted with solidarity on the basis of class enmity (towards the gentry landowners). But all the same, the active elements were the young and the poor. The middle peasants were not particularly interested in the strike, because they do not go to work on the large estate, neither do they hire workers themselves, but manage their own fields.[54]

It is clear, therefore, that it is very difficult to generalise concerning the differential participation in the movement by the various strata of the peasantry, even if it were possible to establish specific criteria for classifying a peasant as 'poor', 'middle', 'prosperous' or 'rich' – for it seems that no uniform definitions were applied by the correspondents who contributed to the survey materials. The form of the movement, and the extent of social differentiation within the village, appear to have been major factors in determining the nature of the alignments in individual localities. Middle, poor and landless peasants, with the occasional exception of the most destitute, were most likely to take part in wage- or rent-strikes and boycotts, whereas the prosperous and rich, if they took part at all, were more likely to do so in cases of pillage.[55]

Whether the richer peasants, and especially those with purchased land, participated in the movement, stood aloof, or were themselves the victims, appears to have depended on the extent to which the process of social differentiation in the countryside was reflected in the peasants' 'class-consciousness'.[56] Where the prosperous peasants saw themselves, or were seen by their fellow-villagers, as representing simply the most fortunate and successful stratum of the communal peasantry, they would be more likely to participate in the movement and to defend common peasant interests against the gentry landowners and other non-peasant commercial farmers. To the extent that the kulaks saw themselves as a distinct socio-economic group, with similar economic interests to the gentry landowners, from whom they were distinguished only in terms of their ascription to an inferior legal estate, they would be more likely

[54] *ibid*, vol 2, p 106.

[55] These findings correspond in general terms with those of the comparative studies by H. Alavi, 'Peasants and revolution', *Socialist Register* (1965), pp 241–77, and E. R. Wolf, *Peasant wars of the twentieth century* (London, 1971), pp 289–93, both of which stress the revolutionary rôle of the middle peasantry in comparison with the ambivalent position of both the poorer and richer strata.

[56] For a discussion of the manner in which patterns of socio-economic mobility within the Russian peasantry impeded the crystallisation of class-consciousness, see Shanin, *The awkward class*, pp 137–41.

to remain apart from the movement, or to be themselves the object of attack. Factors which might influence the categorisation of the richer peasant in the social consciousness of the village would include: the proportion of his land which was purchased, as opposed to his share in the communal holdings; the degree to which his farm was worked by hired rather than family labour; the extent to which his land was rented to or from others; whether his farmstead was in the village or separate; his commercial interests outside agriculture; and the nature of his life-style.

The ambivalent position of the richer strata of the peasantry constituted a major problem for both revolutionary parties in their attempts to define the class nature of the peasant movement – a problem which neither satisfactorily resolved. Both drew an analytical distinction between the anti-feudal and the anti-capitalist content of the movement, but they differed as to which strata of the peasantry had anti-capitalist as well as anti-feudal interests, and hence disagreed on the overall character of the movement. The SDs saw the alignment of the kulaks with the rest of the peasantry against the gentry as typical of the first, anti-feudal stage of the revolution in the countryside, whereas attacks on the kulaks by their poorer fellows foreshadowed the second, anti-capitalist stage. The SRs, on the other hand, considered the conflict between the kulaks and the gentry to be solely an anti-feudal movement, whereas the movement of the mass of the peasantry against the gentry and the peasant bourgeoisie was both anti-feudal and anti-capitalist. Both parties recognised the revolutionary rôle of the middle peasant, the small independent producer (though the SDs, unlike the SRs, over-estimated the significance of the rural proletariat), but they differed as to whether the aspirations of this stratum – which by virtue of its numerical preponderance determined the socio-political character of the revolution – were capitalist, like those of the kulaks (the SD view), or socialist, like those of the rural proletariat (the SR view). The short answer probably is that they were consciously neither: the negative content of the movement was stronger than the positive. Whether the development of peasant farming in the immediate future was to be along capitalist or socialist lines would be determined by the overall social, economic and political context, and this in turn would be governed by the nature of the leadership and the alliances offered to the peasants.[57]

[57] Witness the diversity of the paths offered to the Russian peasantry within a single generation, the two extremes being represented by Stolypin (1906) and Stalin (1929).

The question of peasant participation in the movement was further complicated by the influence of other factors which modified the impact of purely socio-economic characteristics. Of these, socio-biological criteria, such as age and sex, were probably the most important.

As might have been expected, given the generally subordinate position of women in Russian peasant society, the women as a rule played a more passive part in the movement than the men, although it was only in isolated cases that they actually acted as a restraining influence. Where the women did oppose the movement, it could usually be explained in terms of their lack of awareness. From Ryazan′, a correspondent reported that 'the general mass of women and girls are so undeveloped that they can hardly understand the meaning and significance of the movement'.[58] A similar report came from Tula, where 'the majority of women have difficulty in understanding the movement, and restrain it'.[59] More often, the women shared the attitudes of the men. In the words of a peasant correspondent from Novgorod, 'the women too sympathised with the movement – they live in the same huts as their husbands'.[60] In some cases, the women not only participated along with the men, they were even 'more ardent'.[61] Frequently, although the women did not actually participate themselves, they spurred on their menfolk with taunts and reproaches. A correspondent from Voronezh reported that: 'Anyone who didn't go and pillage was reproved by his mother or his wife, saying that their neighbour was bringing back a lot of goods, whereas he, her husband or son, did not care about his home and family.'[62] In the South, where the women were extensively engaged in agricultural wage-labour, they took an active part in the strike movement, sometimes acting as initiators of a wider movement, as in this report from Kiev: 'At first the participants in the movement were exclusively women and adolescents, but later the whole village joined in. Because the cultivation of sugar-beet employs predominantly female labour, and both the poor and prosperous women do this work, then of course they found support for their demands from all members of their families.'[63]

In other instances where women and children are reported to have been in the van of the movement, it seems that it was not so much a case of the women taking the initiative and setting an example, but

[58] *Agrarnoe dvizhenie . . .*, vol 1, p 66.
[59] *ibid*, vol 1, p 71.
[60] *ibid*, vol 1, p 299.
[61] *ibid*, vol 2, p 61.
[62] *ibid*, vol 1, p 87.
[63] *ibid*, vol 2, p 106.

rather a tactical device adopted by the peasants to explore the ground by sending ahead an advance party composed of the weakest members of the community, against whom the authorities would be more reluctant to initiate punitive action. This would appear to be the most likely explanation for reports such as one from Voronezh that: 'The course of the raids was almost identical throughout the district: first went the young lads and girls, and the women; they rushed into the orchard to pick the fruit, and later they were joined by the adults, and the pillaging began';[64] and a report from Kiev that: 'The movement began with the children going ahead, followed by the young girls and the old women, then by the young lads and the old men.'[65]

The young men of the village usually took a more active rôle in the movement than their elders. Where explanations were considered necessary for the militancy of the young, these were often in terms of the greater literacy and general awareness of the generation which had had the advantage of the expansion of primary education at the end of the nineteenth century. The teenage lads, too, were more likely to engage in seasonal wage-work in the towns, and to be influenced by urban attitudes.[66] Also, a young single man had much less to lose, in case of failure, than men with family responsibilities. According to evidence from Podoliya, the last two factors were more important than the first:

> The most active stratum during the movement, according to the majority of correspondents, were the young. However, the reports connect this not with the greater development and education of the young, but rather with their greater fondness for diversions, or with their position as the group which plays the greatest part in hired labour, or which in general has not yet settled down, in contrast to the proper householders.[67]

Of the two cases in which the young men were said to have played a more passive rôle than their elders, the first apparently referred to the Finnish peasantry in St Petersburg province, where: 'The young men and the old men stood aside, for the local peasants do not permit their youth to do much, and are prompt to subdue them. They do not even give them the right to vote, neither do they

64 *ibid*, vol 1, p 87.

65 *ibid*, vol 2, p 107.

66 *ibid*, vol 1, pp 71 (Tula), 123–4 (Penza), 164 (Ufa). For the hypothesis that peasants affected by 'modernising' factors such as education and the influence of the towns are most likely to participate in peasant movements, see H. A. Landsberger, 'The rôle of peasant movements and revolts in development; an analytical framework', International Institute for Labour Studies, *Bulletin*, no. 4 (1968), pp 55–8.

67 *Agrarnoe dvizhenie* . . . , vol 2, p 61.

give this right to the women.'[68] A report from Perm', however, paradoxically explained the aloofness of the young peasants in terms of their greater political awareness:

According to one correspondent, it was mainly the middle-aged peasants who took part in the movement: 'The young and the old considered such risky action by their middle brothers to be incorrect; the young realised that freedom does not consist in seizing the property of others, while the old men still remembered serfdom, when their burdens were even greater, and they were in bondage to Count Stroganov.'[69]

The old men were usually more passive than the young or middle-aged peasants, but, as with the women, it was only in rare cases that they actively opposed the movement. In Tula province, all the peasants took part in the movement, 'up to and including the old women of seventy-five years';[70] in other cases, the old sympathised, without taking an active part;[71] and in Tver' the old men 'moved significantly leftwards' in the course of the movement.[72] Evidence is contradictory concerning the nature of the influence of serfdom on the older generation. In contrast to the report from Perm' cited above, a correspondent from Tambov noted that support from the movement came from 'the old women in particular, who had experienced the oppression of serfdom'.[73] In other cases, the hostility of the older peasants was explained in terms of the natural conservatism of the aged. It was reported from Pskov that 'the old men are opposed to everything, and say that they lived and were satisfied without all these movements', and that:

Many of the young sincerely believe in the imminence of a new, more perfect and just system of land use, 'but the old men, who are generally sceptical about anything new, did not believe in the possibility of a total transfer of the land into the hands of the peasants, and not only did they not believe in it, but neither did they desire it, feeling that the peasants could not cope with this land'.[74]

The survey materials therefore show that the participation of the peasantry in the movement was determined primarily by the social structure of the countryside and the immediate economic interests of the various strata; other sociological variables, however, such as age and sex, modified the impact of purely socio-economic factors. Access to knowledge about revolutionary unrest elsewhere played

[68] *ibid*, vol 1, p 341.
[69] *ibid*, vol 1, p 165.
[70] *ibid*, vol 1, p 71.
[71] *ibid*, vol 1, p 18 (Vladimir).
[72] *ibid*, vol 1, p 23.
[73] *ibid*, vol 1, p 78.
[74] *ibid*, vol 1, p 219.

an important part – hence the rôle of those groups, such as peasant-workers, peasant-soldiers, and the literate, who served as intermediaries between the village and the world outside, and contributed to the diffusion of the revolution from the towns and armed forces to the countryside, and from one area to another. External influence on the movement was usually confined to the information function of such marginal groups; in some cases, however, where the outsiders belonged to one or other of the revolutionary parties, their rôle was more consciously political. None of the parties – the SRs, the SDs, or the Peasant Union – possessed the resources in 1905 to exert any significant influence on the course of the movement, although the aspirations of the peasantry had to be taken into account both by the government and by the parties in the new political situation which resulted from the publication of the October Manifesto and the establishment of the Duma.

Part IV

THE AFTERMATH OF REVOLUTION
(1906–1908)

12
The party approves its programme

Until the First Party Congress met at the end of 1905, the SRs had lacked an official programme enjoying the general acceptance of the membership as a whole. The main points of the party programme had, however, been developed in a series of theoretical articles in the SR press, and in May 1904 a draft programme, compiled by the editorial board on the basis of an earlier version which had been circulated to local party committees for discussion and comment, was published in No. 46 of *Revolyutsionnaya Rossiya*. The return of the scattered émigrés to Russia in the course of 1905 enabled a party congress to be convened for the first time at the end of that year – not in Russia itself, but just across the border in the comparative safety of Finland. The delegates met in the 'Tourist' hotel in Imatra, which belonged to a member of the Finnish Party of Active Resistance, a body sympathetic to the SRs. The sessions of the congress were held in the dining room of this wooden building, which stood on a snowy slope beside the waterfall which made Imatra famous as a beauty spot.[1] There were 95 delegates, representing 51 party organisations.[2] For many of the delegates, this was their first meeting with the leaders of the party, and with some of the veterans of Populism. According to Zenzinov, the mood was cordial, and even festive. In spite of the recent defeats of the revolution, which were fresh in the minds of all – one of the Moscow delegates, Vadim Rudnev, wore a bandage on his arm, injured in the December uprising – the New Year celebrations took place in an atmosphere of optimism.[3]

The main item on the agenda was the party programme, discussion of which began on 31 December, the third day of the congress. The draft which was presented to the congress by Chernov was based closely on the version published in *Revolyutsionnaya Rossiya*, with

[1] V. Zenzinov, *Perezhitoe* (New York, 1953), pp 265–6.

[2] *Protokoly pervago s"ezda Partii Sotsialistov-Revolyutsionerov* (n.p., 1906), *(prilozhenie)*.

[3] Zenzinov, pp 266–8.

some minor amendments. The programme was introduced by a theoretical section, which outlined the position of Russia, and the SR party, in the international socialist movement. This introduction stressed both the similarities and the differences between the capitalist development of Russia and that of other industrial nations. The programme argued that capitalism, wherever it appeared, had both a positive and a negative aspect. The positive feature of capitalism was that it led to the development of collective forms of labour and production, organised the workers on a large scale, and created the material base for socialism. Its negative characteristics included the anarchy of production, leading to recurrent crises; the exploitation and impoverishment of the workers; and the ruthlessness of the struggle for economic survival. The balance between the positive and negative aspects of capitalism varied in different sectors of the international economy. It was most favourable in the advanced industries and in the countries which had industrialised earliest, and least favourable in extractive industry, especially agriculture, and in the less industrialised nations. In Russia, this balance was especially unfavourable: crises were frequent; the cultural level of the workers was low; and the most primitive forms of exploitation existed in conditions of political oppression by the conservative alliance of industrialists, landowners and kulaks with the Tsarist bureaucracy. Tsarism was a reactionary force not only within Russia, but also in Europe as a whole, and its overthrow would mean a major advance for international socialism. In Russia, the main burden of the task of overthrowing autocracy lay not on the liberal-democratic opposition of educated society, but on the combined forces of the proletariat, the working peasantry, and the revolutionary socialist intelligentsia. It was their duty to ensure that the revolution which unseated the Tsar was accompanied by far-reaching social transformations.

The achievement of socialism – the expropriation of capitalist property and the reorganisation of production and social relations on a socialist basis – represented the party's maximum programme, its ultimate aim, which could be achieved only as a consequence of the complete victory of the working class, organised in a socialist party. Until such time, as long as the organised working class was a revolutionary minority which could exert only a partial influence on social and political developments, the SR party would be guided by its minimum programme, which consisted of demands for reform which would strengthen the solidarity and organisation of the working class in its fight for socialism.[4]

The demands of the minimum programme fell into two main categories: political and legal, and economic. The political section contained the usual democratic demands: full civil liberties; the establishment of a democratic republic, with broad guarantees of autonomy for the regions and localities; a federal structure for the nationalities, with an unconditional right of self-determination; the electivity and accountability of all officials; free legal aid; universal free education; linguistic and religious freedom; and the abolition of a standing army.[5]

In the economic section of the programme, the paragraph which came in for most discussion was that dealing with agrarian policy. In his introduction to the debate, Chernov had drawn the attention of the delegates to the differences between the first draft of the programme published in *Revolyutsionnaya Rossiya* and the version which was now before the congress.[6] The main demand of the agrarian section of the original draft had read as follows:

> In matters of agrarian policy and land relations the SR party sets itself the aim of utilising, in the interests of socialism and the struggle against bourgeois-proprietorial principles, the communal and in general the labour-based [*trudovye*] views, traditions and forms of life of the Russian peasantry, in particular their view of the land as the common property of all who labour. With these in view, the party will stand for the socialisation of all privately owned lands, that is, for their removal from the private property of individuals, their transfer to public possession, and their disposal by democratically organised communes and territorial unions of communes on the basis of egalitarian use.[7]

This demand, however, represented the maximum which could be hoped for within the bourgeois state, and in case the complete socialisation of the land was not achieved at one stroke as a revolutionary measure, the programme also listed a number of transitional measures which the party could advocate as contributing to the realisation of the main demand 'in all its fullness'. Examples of such measures were: the right of communes to confiscate private, state and church lands in order to guarantee their members an adequate

[4] *Protokoly pervago s"ezda . . .*, pp 69–75, 355–61.
[5] *ibid*, pp 75–6, 361–2.
[6] *ibid*, pp 85–6.
[7] 'Proekt programmy PS-Rov', *R.R.*, no. 46 (May 1904), p 3.

allotment; the reduction of rents in relation to the income the land provided; remuneration for improvements made to the land on its transfer from the use of one individual to another; and the introduction of a special land tax to be paid to the communes and local government bodies.[8]

In the revised draft put before the congress, all mention of these possible transitional measures had been omitted – because, according to Chernov, the question of whether the socialisation of the land would be achieved at one stroke, or gradually, was something which depended on external circumstances, and therefore belonged strictly to the realm of tactics, rather than programme. In place of the passage concerning transitional measures, the new version went into much greater detail concerning the actual mechanism by which the socialised land would be controlled. This was necessary, Chernov explained, because the revolutionary events of the past years had brought the party's agrarian programme closer to realisation. Whereas previously the primary need had been to stress the general principle of socialisation, the expropriation of private land was now accepted, at least in part, by both the SDs and the Kadets, the most radical liberal party. It was therefore appropriate for the SRs to explain their positive, constructive proposals for the disposal of the confiscated lands in as great and concrete detail as possible.[9]

In fact, only the first sentence of the original version remained in the new draft, which continued:

> With these in view, the party will stand for the socialisation of the land, that is, for its removal from commodity circulation and its transformation from the private property of individuals or groups to the possession of all the people [*obshchenarodnoe dostoyanie*].
>
> Socialised land will be at the disposal of the central and local organs of popular self-government, ranging from democratically organised non-estate rural communes to the state (for migration and resettlement, control of land reserves, etc.). Utilisation of the socialised land should be egalitarian and labour-based, that is, it should guarantee a consumption norm for the application of one's own labour, individually or in an association, after the payment of rent in the form of a tax for social needs; on the transfer of land from one individual or group to another, remuneration will be arranged for the implementation of improvements in the land. The land will pass into public property without compensation; those who suffer from this revolution in property relations will be granted only the right to public support for the time required to adapt to the new economic conditions.[10]

[8] *ibid*, p 3.
[9] *Protokoly pervago s"ezda . . .*, pp 85–6.
[10] *ibid*, p 77.

In the course of the debate, some of the delegates expressed their dissatisfaction with the new formulation, and especially with its definition of the socialisation of the land. By introducing a reference to the rôle of the state, where the first draft had spoken only of 'democratically organised communes and territorial unions of communes', the revised version, its critics objected, paved the way for nationalisation, rather than socialisation.[11]

SR writings had always stressed the difference between their concept of socialisation and the various proposals for land nationalisation put forward by agrarian reformers in Europe and America, such as Henry George. The value of nationalisation, Chernov argued in *Revolyutsionnaya Rossiya* in 1903, could be assessed only in relation to the class nature of the state which nationalised the land. Thus it was not beyond the realm of possibility that in Russia the land might be nationalised by the existing autocratic state. Such a measure would, of course, be highly undesirable from the point of view of a socialist party, as it would increase bureaucratic interference in the affairs of the peasant commune. Since the party's minimum programme by definition represented those measures which the SRs would find acceptable within the framework of the bourgeois class state – a state which would be essentially only semi-free and semi-democratic – then nationalisation would mean that the ultimate control of the land lay in the hands not of the working peasantry, but of an alien and hostile class. It was for this reason that the SRs demanded the 'socialisation' of the land, not its nationalisation, because the word 'socialisation' did not 'assume the transfer of all proprietorial and disposal rights into the hands of the central power'.[12] For 'It is possible that for a long time to come the central power will be too distant from the people to guarantee the interests of the toiling and struggling peasant masses better than could be done by the lower organs of self-government – the communes and territorial unions of communes, such as the reformed volost′ or *zemstvo*.'[13] Although ideally the higher organs of government should control the lower, in order to erase inequalities, it was difficult for Russian socialists to define their attitude towards the state, since at the present stage in Russia's development they could not predict with any certainty the form of state structure which

[11] *ibid*, pp 181–4, 186–8, 202–5.

[12] 'Sotsializatsiya zemli i kooperatsiya v sel′skom khozyaystve', *R.R.*, no. 15 (January 1903), p 7.

[13] *ibid*, p 7.

would replace autocracy. Therefore, 'we shall adopt a very cautious attitude towards the demand for state control [*ogosudarstvlenie*] of the land'. As long as state power was in the hands of the bourgeois parties, the SRs could demand only the extension of the rights of the organs of local government over the land.[14]

This statement of the issue left open the question of precisely when state power could be considered to be in the hands of the working class rather than the bourgeoisie. Universal suffrage alone was clearly not an adequate criterion, as the experience of contemporary Germany showed.[15] An article in *Revolyutsionnaya Rossiya* in 1905, however, clarified the point somewhat. 'In principle', asserted the author (whom Chernov, albeit with a query, identifies as Zenzinov), 'we have nothing against the nationalisation of the land in conditions where democracy [*narodovlastie*], that is, the exercise of political rights and obligations by all the people, has in fact been realised, and where the people are guaranteed the right to control individual items in the budget, as takes place, for instance, in England.'[16]

In his defence of the agrarian programme at the party congress, Chernov claimed that the question of the possession of the land – whether it should belong to the institutions of central or local government – was in fact not a valid one, and those delegates who had raised it had failed to understand a major principle of SR doctrine. Socialised land did not belong to anyone, and certainly not to the state:

By socialising the land, we place it in a position in which the usual definitions of private rights to its use are no longer applicable. We make the land the property neither of the commune, nor of the region, nor do we simply transfer it to the category of existing 'state property'. We make it *no-one's*. Precisely as *no-one's* does it become *the possession of all the people*.[17]

One delegate had objected that within the framework of the bourgeois state, the only legal concepts of property were those of Roman law; but, Chernov explained, the whole object of the party's minimum agrarian programme was to undermine the bourgeois order from within, by abolishing *de facto* not only private property in land, but also legal rights to such property, and replacing them with new concepts. The drafters of the agrarian programme had taken care

[14] *ibid*, p 8.
[15] *ibid*, p 7.
[16] 'Agrarnaya programma liberalov', *R.R.*, no. 70 (July 1905), p 5.
[17] *Protokoly pervago s"ezda . . .*, pp 219–20. (Emphasis in the original)

not to refer to the 'possession' of the land by the organs of central and local self-government, whose function was simply to regulate the rights of individual members of the working class to use the land.[18]

Some of the delegates who had attacked the new version of the programme, Chernov alleged, had done so from a semi-anarchist position. They had interpreted the party's strictures against the autocratic and bourgeois state as a rejection of the state as such, whereas in fact, Chernov said: 'We are not afraid to work on the basis of the democratic forms of the contemporary state, especially on the basis of its organs of local self-government, in some of which we may have a majority and so hold power considerably earlier than we obtain a majority over the whole country.'[19] In the task of regulating egalitarian use of the socialised land, the institutions of democratic central government would have an important function to perform, as the highest in the hierarchy of collectives. Migration and resettlement, the reserve land fund, and natural resources such as forests, minerals and fisheries, would ultimately have to come under state control. The SR party had no 'superstitious fear' of the state; it simply wanted adequate guarantees of the democratic nature of the state before entrusting it with such regulating functions in the economy. In general, however, the party was in favour of decentralisation, with the minimum of interference by the state in the affairs of local self-government, which had such an important part to play in the political education of the Russian people.[20]

The remainder of the debate on the agrarian programme was concerned with minor details. A proposal by the delegate from Nizhnii Novgorod that the hiring of labour should be explicitly forbidden was rejected. The grounds for rejection were firstly that there were cases where the hiring of labour was essential for the survival of the peasant household – for instance, when the bread-winner was sick or disabled – and secondly that the exploitation of labour would be effectively abolished not by legislation, but by the development of collective and cooperative forms of agriculture.[21] 'Gribovskii', the delegate from Vladimir province, observed that there was little point in granting landless agricultural and industrial workers the right to use the socialised land unless some provision were made for credit facilities to assist them to acquire implements

[18] *ibid*, pp 220–2.
[19] *ibid*, p 234.
[20] *ibid*, p 234–6.
[21] *ibid*, pp 193–4, 237–9, 252.

and animals to work the land.[22] Chernov, in his reply to the debate, pointed out that the organisation of such credit, as well as the development of agricultural advisory services and the development of cooperatives, belonged strictly to the field of local government, which was covered by a separate section of the programme.[23]

A few delegates, doubtless aware of the views on this issue which had been expressed at the Peasant Congress, suggested that some compensation should be paid for the socialisation of lands which the peasants had purchased with earned money. 'Gribovskii' pointed out that the fact that the peasants considered these purchased lands to be their own private property 'might create certain difficulties in the realisation of the reform';[24] and 'Vasil′ev', the representative of the North-West regional committee, claimed that the party's insistence on socialisation without compensation created problems for party propagandists in the countryside, since 'the majority of peasants consider compensation to be just and necessary for lands purchased with earned money'.[25] In reply to this, 'Gur′yanov', for the Central Bureau of the SR Peasant Union, repeated the same argument that the SR representative had produced at the Peasant Congress: that every peasant whose total holding, including purchased land, amounted to less than the labour norm, would receive extra land under socialisation, so that 'purely economic considerations will make the peasant surrender his land as communal property'; purchased lands in a quantity exceeding the labour norm, however, were kulak lands, serving for the exploitation of the labour of others, and should therefore be expropriated on the same basis as *pomeshchik* lands.[26] The advocates of compensation appear

[22] *ibid*, p 192. All of the delegates appeared in the published report of the congress under pseudonyms. On the basis of various sources, however, it is possible to identify many of the major speakers, as in the following list:

'Bazarov'	Rakitnikov	'Rozhdestvenskii'	Myakotin
'Karskii'	Bunakov	'Shevich'	Rubanovich
'Korenev'	Annenskii	'Solomin'	Minor
'Pashin'	Shvetsov	'Tuchkin'	Chernov
'Pomortsev'	Vishnyak	'Turskii'	Peshekhonov
'Roshchin'	Rudnev		

The sources for these identifications are: Zenzinov, pp 263–9; M. Vishnyak, *Dan′ proshlomu* (New York, 1954), pp 121–3; A. V. Peshekhonov, *Pochemu my togda ushli* (Petrograd, 1918), p 4; Spiridovitch, pp 290, 304, 314; O. H. Radkey, *The agrarian foes of Bolshevism* (New York, 1958), pp 24–46. Where speakers can be identified, their real names are given in the text; where they are not identified, the pseudonym is used, in inverted commas.

[23] *Protokoly pervago s″ezda . . .*, pp 239–40.

[24] *ibid*, p 192.

[25] *ibid*, p 197.

[26] *ibid*, pp 197–8.

to have been silenced by this; they did not even force a vote on the issue by proposing an amendment to the draft programme. Indeed, a substantial minority of delegates tended towards the other extreme and were reluctant to have the programme offer even 'public support' to the expropriated landowners.[27] An amendment that the mention of support for the expropriated landowners should be omitted was, however, rejected by 35 votes to 14, with five abstentions.[28]

The only major amendment to be introduced into the agrarian programme as a result of the debate involved a more specific reference to non-arable lands, such as forests, and mineral resources. Several delegates felt that jurisdiction over these should be entrusted not to individual communes, but to the higher organs of government. Chernov gave the proposal his sanction, and the amendment to this effect was approved by 26 votes to 12 with 16 abstentions.[29] Eventually, the following revised version of the agrarian programme was approved by the Congress, with only one opposing vote:

> In matters of the transformation of land relations, the SR party aims to base itself, in the interests of socialism and the struggle against bourgeois-proprietorial principles, on the communal and labour-based views, traditions and forms of life of the Russian peasantry, in particular on the conviction, widespread in their midst, that the land is *no-one's*, and that the right to use it is given only by labour. In accordance with its general views on the tasks of the revolution in the countryside, the party will stand for the socialisation of the land, that is for its removal from commodity circulation, and conversion from the private property of individuals or groups to the possession of all the people on the following basis: all lands will come under the jurisdiction of the central and local organs of popular self-government, ranging from democratically organised non-estate rural and urban communes to regional and central institutions (for migration and resettlement, control of the land fund, etc.); utilisation of the land should be egalitarian and labour-based, that is, it should guarantee a consumption norm on the basis of the application of one's own labour, individually or in association; rent, in the form of a special tax, should be directed towards social needs; the use of lands which do not have a narrowly local significance (extensive forests, fisheries, etc.) will be regulated by the correspondingly broader organs of self-government; mineral resources will remain with the state; the land will be converted into the possession of all the people without compensation; those who suffer from this revolution in property relations will be granted only the right to public support for the time required to adapt to their new conditions.[30]

Having agreed on its agrarian demands, the Congress then went on to consider the remaining sections of the minimum programme. The

[27] *ibid*, pp 201–2.
[28] *ibid*, p 252.
[29] *ibid*, pp 181, 192–3, 235, 249–50, 252–3.
[30] *ibid*, pp 363–4.

industrial section included demands for the eight-hour working day; a minimum wage; a state social insurance scheme; a factory inspectorate to control conditions of work; and the right of workers to form trade unions which would increasingly participate in the organisation of work within the enterprise.[31] Next to be approved was the financial section, which called for the introduction of a progressive tax on income and inherited wealth; the abolition of indirect taxes, with the exception of those on luxury items; and the abolition of protective tariffs and 'all taxes which fall on labour'.[32] The draft version of the section on local government had included demands for the provision of social services; broad rights of taxation and compulsory alienation of property for the local authorities; and the encouragement of democratic cooperative associations at all administrative levels. To this the congress approved an amendment which added provision for 'broad credit for the development of the labour economy, especially on a cooperative basis'.[33] The fifth and final section of the programme consisted of a warning against 'state socialism', which was defined as 'partly a system of half-measures to blunt the awareness of the working class; partly a form of state capitalism, which concentrates various sectors of production and commerce in the hands of the ruling bureaucracy for its own fiscal and political ends'.[34] The SR party would adopt a positive attitude towards such measures of communalisation (*obobshchestvlenie*) only 'insofar as the democratisation of the political structure and the correlation of social forces, together with the character of the corresponding measures themselves, provide adequate guarantees against the increase of the dependence of the working class on the ruling bureaucracy'.[35]

Eventually, on the night of 2 January 1906, the congress approved the programme in its entirety, with only the Maximalist 'Poroshin' abstaining. In the emotional words of Rubanovich, the chairman, the mistress with whom the party had been living for so long was now a lawful wife, and he hoped that the marriage would be a happy one. The programme, he said, was written with the blood of revolutionaries; it was a symbol of party unity. He proposed a vote of thanks to Chernov, as 'the young giant who has for five years carried on his shoulders the entire weight of the theoretical development of our programme'. The congress responded with an ovation for the party leader.[36]

[31] *ibid*, pp 76–7, 362–3.
[32] *ibid*, pp 77–8, 362.
[33] *ibid*, pp 78, 364.
[34] *ibid*, pp 364–5.
[35] *ibid*, p 364.
[36] *ibid*, pp 293–4.

13
Splits in the party

In the course of 1906, the SR party suffered schisms both to the left and to the right, with the formation of the Union of SR Maximalists and the Party of Popular Socialists respectively. Before the First Congress met, both of these groups existed as trends within the party; but with the clarification of the SR programme and tactics at the congress, the gaps between the centre and the extreme wings of the party widened, to the point where organisational separation became inevitable. In the debates between the party centre and the future Maximalists and Popular Socialists, questions of agrarian programme and tactics played a major part.

The Maximalists

Maximalism derived its name from its rejection of the distinction drawn by Chernov between the minimum and maximum programmes of the party: the Maximalists demanded that the socialisation of industry should accompany that of the land. Chernov's distinction between the minimum and maximum programmes implied that the transition to socialism from Tsarist autocracy would be a two-stage process. The maximum programme consisted of socialist measures which the party would implement when it came to power. But a socialist seizure of power 'assumes a persistent struggle, assumes a transitional period – long or short – in the course of which the party will certainly be able to an increasing degree to influence the course of legislation, but must take into account the fact that state power is in the hands of one or other group of the bourgeoisie'. The minimum programme represented the demands which the party would advocate in this period, with the aim of strengthening the position of the working class.[1]

At quite an early stage, criticisms of this distinction appear to

[1] 'Sotsializatsiya zemli i kooperatsiya v sel'skom khozyaystve', *R.R.*, no. 14 (December 1902), p 6.

have been made within the party. In February 1904 – that is, at the time when the first draft of the programme was being circulated to local party committees for comment – Chernov complained in *Revolyutsionnaya Rossiya* that the issue of the maximum and minimum programmes was a controversial question, on which current views were 'insufficiently clear', and even suffered from complete distortion. Some critics were demanding the abolition of the minimum programme, on the grounds that it was not revolutionary, but reformist. This view, Chernov claimed, was mistaken; the demands of the minimum programme might have to be achieved by revolutionary violence; and the transition to socialism might be peaceful – only time would tell. He repeated that the distinction between the two programmes related solely to the two separate periods for which they were designed: the period of socialist victory; and the period of bourgeois rule which would precede it. The minimum programme was intended to serve as a guideline for the party in the pre-socialist epoch – an epoch in which the socialist forces would be organising in the course of a prolonged struggle. Therefore the minimum programme consisted of demands which would help the working class in the period when non-socialist elements still ruled.[2]

A further criticism concerned the inclusion of the socialisation of the land in the minimum programme. Land, in the view of some critics, should not be distinguished from other means of production; the socialisation of industry should take place at the same time as the socialisation of agriculture. The socialisation of industry should therefore be included in the minimum programme. But if the minimum programme included the socialisation of both agriculture and industry, then it would be identical with the maximum programme, and the distinction between the two would become superfluous.[3] This argument, Chernov explained, was based on a misunderstanding of the concept of socialisation and of its relationship to the concept of socialism. Socialisation could be defined as 'the removal of something from the power of private property and its transfer into communal hands'. The character of any measure of socialisation, however, depended on the nature of the 'something' which was socialised. The socialisation of the land was not a socialist measure, because 'socialism is a certain method for the planned

[2] 'Programma-maksimum i programma-minimum', *R.R.*, no. 41 (February 1904), pp 5–6.

[3] 'Sotsializatsiya zemli i programma-minimum', *R.R.*, no. 42 (March 1904), p 3.

organisation of all production by society and for society'. The socialisation of the land would not in itself determine the form of agricultural production; it would determine only the form of property in one kind of natural resource – the surface and depths of the land. Since the socialisation of the land determined simply its ownership, and not the form of its productive utilisation, any analogy between the socialisation of rural land and the socialisation of urban factories was patently absurd:

> The socialisation of factories is the transfer to social control of a whole number of economic enterprises, whole branches of production. This assumes a change in the very basis of the conduct of this production; the replacement in the control of the factory of the personal interest and personal will of the owner by the communal will; the adaption of production to social needs; the planned organisation of production instead of commodity anarchy. The socialisation of the land, however, is only the transfer into communal hands and communal disposal of *one* of the necessary conditions of production, thereby abolishing one of the most harmful and onerous private monopolies.[4]

The socialisation of the factories involved the socialisation of industrial production and was, therefore, a socialist measure; the socialisation of the land did not involve the socialisation of agricultural production and was, therefore, not a socialist measure – for this reason it was included in the minimum programme. The true urban parallel to the socialisation of rural land, Chernov pointed out, was not the socialisation of factories, but the socialisation of *urban* land, that is, its municipalisation or communalisation – since land was a necessary prerequisite of industrial as well as of agricultural production.[5]

In the course of 1904, disputes over programme within the SR party fused with existing conflicts over tactics. Sokolov and Ustinov, the leaders of the 'agrarian terrorists', came to advocate the Maximalist programme of simultaneous socialisation of the land and factories. The tactic of 'agrarian terror' was extended to cover 'economic terror' in general; from the revolutionary expropriation of the land, the future Maximalists moved to the revolutionary expropriation of all private property, including factories. By the application of these means, they hoped that a socialist or semi-socialist revolution could be achieved in the near future.[6]

4 *ibid*, pp 3–4.
5 *ibid*, p 4.
6 Chernov, *Sotsialist-Revolyutsioner*, no. 1 (1910), pp 184–203.

The 'agrarian terrorists' led by Sokolov, who had left Geneva for the North-West region of Russia in the autumn of 1904, soon began to issue proclamations calling for a campaign of expropriations and denying the validity of parliamentary action, in virtually anarchist terminology.[7] In the summer of 1905, Ustinov and other 'agrarian terrorists' remaining in Geneva formed a group of 'Young SRs', who published a journal, *Vol'nyi Diskussionnyi Listok* ('The free discussion sheet'), which advocated the inclusion of the socialisation of industry in the minimum programme.[8] One of the ideas put forward in this journal – which was criticised for anarchist utopianism by *Revolyutsionnaya Rossiya* – was that the forthcoming revolution would be socialist in both the towns and the countryside, with communes (*kommuny*) of peasants and workers socialising both agricultural and industrial production.[9] In December 1905 Ustinov's group seceded altogether from the party and called for the formation of a separate 'Union of Revolutionary Socialists'. The trend had considerable support within Russia, especially in the North-West, where Belostok had become the headquarters of Maximalism. Their forces were increased by the adherence of the Moscow 'opposition', a group which challenged the authority and policies of the official city committee, and which played an important part in the abortive uprising of December 1905. The 'expropriation' by this group, in the spring of 1906, of several hundred thousand roubles from the Moscow Society of Mutual Credit, gave the Maximalists a significant degree of financial independence from the SR party.[10]

At the First Party Congress, only 'Poroshin', the delegate from Vitebsk, represented the 'pure' Maximalist position as adopted by Ustinov and his supporters. 'Poroshin' attacked the existing programme for its 'duality and inconsistency' in basing its agrarian section on the revolutionary principle of the abolition of private property in land, while the industrial section involved simply demands for social reforms such as the introduction of the eight-hour

[7] *ibid*, pp 197–8.

[8] B. I. Gorev, 'Apoliticheskiya i antiparlamentskiya gruppy', in *Obshchestvennoe dvizhenie* . . . , vol 3, p 512; Spiridovitch, pp 394–5.

[9] 'Po povodu "Vol'nago Diskussionnago Listka"', *R.R.*, no. 76 (October 1905), pp 12–14.

[10] Gorev, *Obshchestvennoe dvizhenie* . . . , vol 3, pp 512–13; Spiridovitch, pp 392–6.

day. He advocated the simultaneous socialisation of industry and of land, and the transfer of the land to reformed communes or unions of communes, in the form of 'labour organisations' (*trudovye organizatsii*).[11]

Although 'Poroshin' was the only member of the Congress actually to vote for the inclusion of the socialisation of industry in the minimum programme, he received a certain degree of support in the debates from some other delegates, led by an influential member of the Central Committee, Rakitnikov. Rakitnikov's criticisms of the existing minimum programme derived from rather a different standpoint from 'Poroshin's'. Rakitnikov objected to the definition of the minimum programme as those reforms which the party would try to gain from a bourgeois government. It was understandable, he said, that this should be the criterion for the minimum programme of the SDs, since it was an article of faith for the SDs that the forthcoming revolution would be bourgeois in character. The SRs, however, had always argued that the revolution could and should go beyond the framework of the bourgeois order, and there was therefore no need for their minimum programme to be bound by the assumption of the need for a period of bourgeois rule. The demands of the minimum programme, in Rakitnikov's opinion, ought not to be those reforms which the party should beg from the bourgeoisie, but those which they themselves would implement if the revolution brought them to power. If the minimum programme were so defined, it should include the demand for the socialisation of the factories. In conditions of small peasant farming, however, the socialisation of agricultural production, as opposed to the socialisation of the land, could not take place immediately – on this point, Rakitnikov agreed with Chernov rather than with Ustinov. Industrial production was already collective and could easily be socialised on the morrow of the revolution.[12]

The debates on Maximalism at the congress soon developed into a discussion of its organisational implications. The demand by some delegates from the North-West oblast′ that the Maximalists be expelled from the party, since their refusal to accept discipline made cooperation with them impossible, was rejected by Chernov, and a resolution was passed in favour of the opening of a broad debate on the issue within the party. It was decided to assess the present

[11] *Protokoly pervago s″ezda . . .*, pp 105–7, 181–4.
[12] *ibid*, pp 109–16.

strength of Maximalism by taking a vote on the inclusion of the socialisation of the factories in the minimum programme. From this it emerged that none of the committees represented at the congress possessed a majority of members in favour; that of the committees which were not represented, only Belostok was known to have a Maximalist majority; and that of the individual delegates, only 'Poroshin' advocated the socialisation of industry.[13]

Although the SRs were willing to leave the doors open for further discussions with the Maximalists, the latter were less prepared to continue their association with the party, whose congress had so decisively rejected their policies. Immediately after the congress, in January 1906, Sokolov convened a small conference which decided to leave the SR party and form a separate Maximalist organisation. The 'Union of SR Maximalists' was not officially formed until the autumn of that year, in the wake of two of the most notorious Maximalist exploits: the explosion at Stolypin's villa on Aptekarskii Island in August 1906, and the expropriation on Fonarnyi Pereulok of 600,000 roubles being transported from the St Petersburg Customs Office to the State Bank. The Union proved to be stillborn. Sokolov was arrested on 1 December, and summarily executed the next day. The loss of its leader appears to have demoralised the Union; in addition, many other prominent Maximalists shared Sokolov's fate in the following months. By the middle of 1907, Maximalism as an organised movement had virtually ceased to exist.[14]

The main significance of Maximalism was that it highlighted several apparent inconsistencies which existed in SR theory, in spite of Chernov's ingenious formulations. The Populist writers whose heirs the SRs claimed to be had argued that Russia could avoid a bourgeois stage of development and proceed directly to socialism. To a certain extent, the SRs followed in this tradition, with their assertion that the Russian revolution would be both anti-feudal and anti-capitalist, and that by socialising the land it could go beyond the framework of a bourgeois revolution. The SDs believed that the forthcoming

[13] *ibid*, pp 270–81.

[14] Gorev, *Obshchestvennoe dvizhenie* . . . , vol 3, pp 513–15; Spiridovitch, pp 396–412.

revolution must be a bourgeois one, because the Russian proletariat was still only a small minority of the population. For the SRs, however, no such obstacle existed to the transition to socialism, since according to their definition, the working class – the industrial and agricultural proletariat plus the small producers – already represented the overwhelming majority of the Russian population. Why then did the party not call for an immediate socialist revolution?, the Maximalists reasoned. Chernov's only answer was that the prerequisites for socialism did not yet exist in Russia. In agriculture, the peasant mode of production was individual rather than collective, and it would take a prolonged period of transition before agricultural production could be socialised. The introduction of socialised production in industry also required a high degree of consciousness and organisation on the part of the workers – a degree which, Chernov implied, did not yet exist in Russia, and which could only be created in the course of a long struggle.[15]

Thus although in theory the SRs were prepared to argue that the revolution might go beyond the bourgeois framework, in practice they appear to have believed that the 'backwardness' of the working class would limit its gains in the industrial field to the implementation of progressive labour legislation, and in agriculture to the socialisation of the land. Their slogans were tailored accordingly, and they rejected as demagogic adventurism the Maximalists' agitation for the immediate implementation of socialist measures. Thus there was considerable substance to the Maximalists' claim that the existence of the minimum programme meant that the party, in fact, envisaged that the revolution would be democratic in form, but bourgeois-reformist rather than socialist in content.

Although the Maximalist viewpoint might appear to be more consistently revolutionary, the official party line was certainly more realistic; the reforms which emerged from the revolution of 1905 fell far short even of the SR minimum programme, and the Maximalist perspective of a socialist economy run by free labour communes of agricultural and industrial workers seems totally utopian in the context of 1905–7. Nevertheless, it is not difficult to distinguish, in the debates with the Maximalists at the time of the first revolution, many of the issues which were to split the SR party in 1917.

[15] See the speeches by Chernov and 'Poroshin' on this issue in the debate on Maximalism at the party congress: *Protokoly pervago s"ezda . . .*, pp 253–69, 272–6.

The Popular Socialists

The Party of Popular Socialists derived its origin from the literary group of 'Legal Populists' working on *Russkoe Bogatstvo*, to whom Chernov had turned for assistance in establishing a legal SR newspaper in Russia after the appearance of the October Manifesto. A group of Legal Populists, including Annenskii, Myakotin and Peshekhonov, were invited to attend the First Congress of the SR party, with the right to speak but not to vote. At the congress, they took the opportunity to raise again the question of the formation of an open, legal party, which had been discussed with Chernov in the course of the negotiations over *Syn Otechestva*. The Legal Populists proposed that the conspiratorial organisation of the existing party should be retained for 'destructive work' – by which they presumably meant terrorism – but that a parallel open party, organised on a democratic basis, should be formed to draw the masses into the SR movement. In the discussion which ensued, this suggestion was criticised as impractical, and a resolution proposed by Myakotin that an open political party should be organised was rejected with only one vote in favour, and seven abstentions. A large majority approved a counter-resolution, proposed by Rubanovich and amended by Chernov, that although the party's ultimate aim was the establishment of a régime of political freedom in which it could act as an open organisation, it considered that any transition from the underground to legality was at the present time impossible.[16]

After the rejection of their proposal, the Legal Populists planned to leave the congress. They were persuaded to stay until the following day, when the congress was due to begin its discussion of the party programme.[17] In the course of the next session, various other differences between the Legal Populists and the SRs emerged. Like the Maximalists, the Legal Populists rejected Chernov's distinction between the minimum and maximum programmes, which they criticised as a mere imitation of the SDs' perspective of two distinct stages on the path to socialism. In the tradition of Lavrov and Mikhaylovskii, the Legal Populists envisaged the transition to socialism as a single process, evolutionary or revolutionary; but in contrast to the Maximalists, they believed that the process would be a prolonged one, involving fundamental changes both in the subjective conditions of human consciousness, and in the objective conditions of economic and social existence. They agreed that the

[16] *ibid*, pp 46–66.

[17] Peshekhonov, pp 13–14.

party programme should be divided into two sections, but they disagreed with the definition of the minimum programme as those demands which were realisable within the bourgeois state. Instead, they proposed a more pragmatic distinction between long-term and short-term aims. The party's long-term aim was, of course, socialism, but its short-term aims should be flexibly defined as those which were practicable under existing conditions. For these demands, the Legal Populists preferred the term 'platform', rather than programme.[18]

In addition to these criticisms of the SR programme, the Legal Populists were also in disagreement with aspects of SR tactics. As well as rejecting terrorism and conspiracy, they opposed the party's attitude towards land seizures by the peasants. It will be recalled from the previous chapter that by 1905 the SRs' official position was that they 'welcomed' – rather than 'supported' or 'advocated' – all forms of spontaneous peasant action, including land seizures, but they *advocated* only socialisation, in the form of the declaration of expropriated lands to be in the possession of the people as a whole. The Legal Populists of *Russkoe Bogatstvo*, however, were opposed to the idea that the land could be socialised by any form of direct action 'from below'; they believed that socialisation could be achieved only 'from above', as a result of legislation by a Constituent Assembly. Myakotin raised the issue with Chernov in the course of the negotiations over *Syn Otechestva*,[19] and it was brought to the fore again by the Legal Populists at the First Party Congress. Here Annenskii argued that since socialisation – or nationalisation, as he would prefer to call it – involved the transfer to the people not only of all private lands, but also of the existing lands of the peasant commune, it could not be achieved by direct action, but only by legal means.[20] Myakotin launched an even more scathing attack on the official SR policy of socialisation from below:

> We are told that the socialisation of the land will be achieved by individual local uprisings, and that the Constituent Assembly will sanction it. Individual groups can only take the land as their own property, and it will become the property of these villages, and not of the entire people. We are told that the land will be taken 'for provisional utilisation'. But what if these 100,000 villages

[18] *Protokoly pervago s"ezda* ..., pp 87–96; Peshekhonov, pp 22–3; P. Maslov, 'Narodnicheskiya partii', in *Obshchestvennoe dvizhenie* ..., vol 3, p 153.

[19] Chernov, *Pered burey*, pp 239–41.

[20] *Protokoly pervago s"ezda* ..., pp 89–90.

which have seized the land want to retain perpetual use of it, and come into conflict with the Constituent Assembly? This land certainly cannot then be taken into the possession of the entire people. Consequently, the Assembly can only sanction the *bourgeois* property of individual groups, and in this process not only may the commune vanish without trace, there is also a danger that socialism may be delayed for a hundred years. Thus, only the state can carry out this reform. The seizure and ploughing of land means only that it is being used by the peasants of a certain village, and has nothing in common either with socialisation or with nationalisation.[21]

In reply to Myakotin, 'Starkov', one of the representatives of the SR Peasant Union, reminded the congress that the party advocated not the seizure of land by individual villages, but the organisation of local revolutionary self-government, which would take over the land and implement its egalitarian utilisation.[22] The delegate from Nizhnii Novgorod was actually able to cite an instance of such procedure: a forest had been seized by the peasants, who had placed a guard on it to ensure that it remained intact until the convening of the State Duma, which would decide how to dispose of it.[23] Myakotin was unimpressed; he welcomed such an occurrence, but did not believe that it was typical.[24]

Peshekhonov, in his speech to the congress, stressed that the Legal Populists were opposed not to direct revolutionary action as such, but simply to its advocacy as a means of socialising the land. His own view was that it was the party's task to organise the people, but, having organised sufficient forces, they should call, not for land seizures, but for a seizure of power and the establishment of a Constituent Assembly, which would then decide on the future allocation of the land.[25]

The Legal Populists agreed with the SRs that spontaneous land seizures did have a positive aspect from the point of view of a revolutionary socialist party: by creating a general situation of agrarian crisis they put pressure on the government and on public opinion to implement an agrarian reform in the interests of the peasantry. They believed that the negative aspects – the seizure of land as private property – were more important, and they therefore argued that the party should not advocate any form of direct action by the peasantry with regard to the land.[26]

On this question of land seizures, the party leadership occupied an intermediate position between that of the Legal Populists and that

[21] *ibid*, p 92.
[22] *ibid*, pp 93–4.
[23] *ibid*, p 95.
[24] *ibid*, p 95.
[25] *ibid*, p 94.
[26] *ibid*, pp 89–91.

of the Maximalists, who wanted to encourage all forms of direct action by the peasantry. Later debates at the Party Congress, after the Legal Populists had left, showed that many SRs had come to share their fears about the possible non-socialist or even anti-socialist outcome of spontaneous peasant land seizures. In the course of the debate on the socialisation of the land, the elderly Shvetsov, the delegate from Tomsk – whose speeches on this topic, deriving from many decades' intimate knowledge of the peasantry, were warmly applauded by the congress – raised a point similar to that of Annenskii concerning the socialisation of the peasants' own lands. Neither the communal holdings nor the small plots purchased by the peasants could, he said, be socialised by direct action. Because the peasants had invested both labour and earned money in these lands, they felt that they had property rights in them and would resent any attempt to deprive them of such rights. Similar difficulties, he continued, would be presented by any attempt to socialise private gentry lands which the peasants had seized in the course of the spontaneous agrarian movement, for the peasants felt that they had the same rights to those lands as they had to their own communal holdings:

> The peasants of these communes go and seize the neighbouring privately owned lands, and this is an extension of communal possession of the land, but it does not bring us one step nearer to the introduction of socialisation, because the communes will not be inclined to surrender the land they have seized as the possession of the people [*narodnoe obladanie*]. The peasants of these communes have already developed a sense of property, which was artificially inculcated into them, and they consider the land they have obtained to be their own. The land will have to be expropriated from these peasants, as from other private landowners.[27]

The socialisation of these lands, Shvetsov felt, would have to be a prolonged process, and would constitute a major problem even for a democratically elected Constituent Assembly. Unlike the Legal Populists, he did not reject all forms of direct peasant action; but, because he was aware of the problems which would be created by land seizures, he stressed the importance of the party's tactical directives and insisted on control of the movement:

> This is why the SR party must take on itself the organisation of that spontaneous movement in which the peasantry is now involved, and guide it so that the seizures of the lands of the *pomeshchiki* are not immediately turned to the advantage of the peasant communes, and so that the latter do not use them

[27] *ibid*, p 184.

to extend their own landholding, because this would not be a preliminary to the socialisation of the lands of the *pomeshchiki*, that is, the abolition of landed property, but only an increase in landed property, admittedly that of collective units, the peasant communes.[28]

In the debate on tactics at the Party Congress, there was an open clash between those SRs who, like the Maximalists, believed that the positive aspects of land seizures outweighed the negative, and those who, like the Legal Populists, held the opposite view. The issue was whether or not the party should call for a revolutionary seizure of land by the peasants in the coming spring. On this question, the members of the congress commission on tactics had been irreconcilably divided, in spite of a certain degree of common ground. Both factions agreed that in principle a revolutionary expropriation of the land – in the form of an organised movement for its socialisation from below – was desirable; they agreed too that the spontaneous outbreak of peasant unrest in the spring of 1906 was highly probable, and that the party should do everything it could to control this movement. The difference between them was on the question of whether the party should actually call on the peasants to seize the land.[29]

The Maximalist 'Poroshin', supporting the call for land seizures, argued that the fact that the movement in the spring would be predominantly spontaneous should contain no fears for the party. It was true that some of the forms assumed by the spontaneous movement were undesirable, but the question of desirability was irrelevant, since the spontaneous movement was in any case inevitable. Even a spontaneous movement could play an important part:

> In a revolutionary overturn the rôle of the spontaneous movement can be very great. Before it is possible even to lay the foundations of the reconstructed edifice of the future, it is essential to clear the ground, and this heavy work of the revolution can be achieved by the mass spontaneous movement. In this sense the spontaneous movement plays the rôle of the battering ram which must destroy the wall of capitalist exploitation. On the soil which has been prepared by the spontaneous movement, we, the conscious minority, can begin our further creative work, and in this sense the significance of the spontaneous movement is enormous.[30]

The next speaker in favour of the call for land seizures, 'Glazov', representing the London committee, was apparently hopeful that

[28] *ibid*, pp 208–9.
[29] *ibid*, p 314.
[30] *ibid*, p 321.

the land could be socialised by the spontaneous peasant movement, pointing out that in the SR programme the concept of socialisation was said to be based on the traditional views of the peasants, 'and was therefore *eo ipso* three-quarters spontaneous'.[31] The opposite view was expressed by 'Novgorodtsev', the delegate from Smolensk, for whom 'It is indubitable that the socialisation of the land can be implemented by a conscious, organised movement of the peasantry, and not by spontaneous outbursts. These spontaneous outbursts . . . cannot bring us to the implementation of our agrarian programme'.[32] This view was supported by Osip Minor, from the SR Committee Abroad. The reports from the localities, he said, had shown that SR influence in the countryside was insignificant in comparison with the vast numbers of peasants who had been unaffected by propaganda:

> Our forces are inadequate for the leadership of the movement; it will be spontaneous. And in spontaneity what will guarantee us success? And what sort of success will it be? Will it be a simple seizure of land by the peasants, or will the socialisation of the land be realised in the form and on the scale envisaged by the PSR? Certainly we have no firm grounds for belief that the spontaneous movement will solve the problem in the spirit of the programme of our party. Consciously or unconsciously, we are confusing the impending peasant movement for a crust of bread, for a bag of oats, for a stack of firewood, with a social revolution.[33]

In a vote on the issue, the delegates decided, by a majority of two to one, not to call for land seizures in the spring, and at the next session of the Congress, a compromise resolution, which recommended all party organisations to hold themselves in readiness with a plan of action to be undertaken against the local authorities in the event of the outbreak of peasant unrest in the spring, was unanimously approved.[34]

The general ambivalence of the SRs' attitude towards peasant spontaneity was further illustrated in the debate on 'agrarian terrorism'. Rakitnikov, reporting on behalf of the tactics commission, argued that although the party did not advocate the use of 'agrarian terror', neither did it propose to agitate against it. They realised that there were cases when 'agrarian terror' was an inevitable response to exploitation. Conscious and organised forms of response were preferable, but 'of course "agrarian terror" is better than

[31] *ibid*, p 322.
[32] *ibid*, p 316.
[33] *ibid*, p 323.
[34] *ibid*, p 332.

nothing', and its spontaneous occurrence was therefore in the party's interests.[35]

It is clear, therefore, that many of the attitudes which characterised both Maximalism and Legal Populism – an idealisation of peasant spontaneity, on the one hand, and scepticism towards it, on the other – were shared to a greater or lesser extent by many of those within the main body of the party. The Chernovian position was indeed a compromise between the two extremes. Which group had the most realistic view of the peasantry? Certainly we have no reason to doubt the veracity of the instances cited at the Congress in which the peasants did not appropriate the land they seized, but held it in trust for the Constituent Assembly;[36] on the other hand, the Legal Populists were probably correct to see such cases as the exception rather than the rule. Given conditions of adequate organisation and consciousness, it is not impossible to imagine the socialisation of the large estates being implemented from below, in spite of the enormous problems involved. Such conditions, however, did not exist in Russia in 1905–6, and in their absence the peasant movement could and did degenerate into simple looting, even when, as in Saratov, it was ostensibly under SR control.[37] Writing in 1910, Chernov argued that SR agrarian tactics had, in fact, been proved correct by the experience of the revolution; that in the period of its greatest upsurge, in 1905 and 1906, the peasant movement had followed the course laid down for it in the party's 'plan of campaign'. It was only in the period of the defeat of the revolution, he claimed, that the movement became fragmented into isolated incidents of 'agrarian terrorism' and expropriations.[38] Here, I think one must suspect Chernov of wishful thinking. Many cases of 'agrarian terrorism' occurred in 1905 and 1906, and it was undoubtedly their awareness of this aspect of the agrarian movement that encouraged so many delegates to the Party Congress to share the Legal Populists' suspicion of peasant spontaneity.

In the spring of 1906, the Legal Populists decided to form a separate 'Party of Popular Socialists'. The new party declared itself to be socialist, but its platform of immediate demands was restricted to those reforms which it considered to be feasible and acceptable to

[35] *ibid*, p 336.
[36] *ibid*, pp 95, 195.
[37] This point was made by Peshekhonov at the congress. *ibid*, p 94.
[38] Chernov, *Sotsialist-Revolyutsioner*, no. 1 (1910), pp 192–3.

the masses under existing conditions. Thus, in contrast to the SR minimum programme, the Popular Socialists took into account the monarchist sentiments of the peasantry in asking not for a democratic republic, but for a constitutional monarchy; also their agrarian programme recognised the peasants' proprietorial attitude towards their purchased lands by including provision for compensation to be paid by the state for the socialisation of private lands.[39] The demands of the Popular Socialists were, therefore, closer to those of the peasantry themselves, as expressed through the congresses of the Peasant Union and through the 'Labour group' (*Trudovaya gruppa*) of peasant deputies in the Duma, than were the demands of the SR minimum programme.

Nevertheless, the Popular Socialists were to discover that neither rejection of underground activity nor programmatic pragmatism was sufficient to convert them from a small group of literary intellectuals into a mass party. The party came into existence too late to participate in the First Duma, and the formation of the Labour group as a parliamentary fraction representing the immediate interests of the mass of the peasantry pre-empted the position which the Popular Socialists had hoped to occupy. The similarity between the Popular Socialists and the *Trudoviki* was emphasised when the former drafted the agrarian programme which the latter presented to the Duma. After the dissolution of the First Duma, the Popular Socialists contested the elections to the Second Duma as an independent party, and succeeded in having 14 deputies elected. In the Duma, the small fraction of Popular Socialists occupied a position intermediate between the larger groups of the SRs (34 deputies) and the *Trudoviki* (100 deputies), and lost much of their influence over the *Trudoviki* to the SRs. No Popular Socialists were elected to the Third Duma, and the party as such virtually ceased to exist after 1907, although it was to re-appear on the political scene in 1917.[40]

39 These points of difference had already emerged at the time of the First Party Congress. *Protokoly pervago s"ezda* . . . , pp 87–96.

40 Maslov, *Obshchestvennoe dvizhenie* . . . , vol 3, pp 154–8.

14

The SR agrarian programme in the first two Dumas

One of the first issues tackled by the First SR Congress, in view of its immediate tactical significance, was the party's attitude towards the State Duma, which was to be convened in the spring of 1906. Only one delegate, 'Norring', from Riga, spoke in favour of participation in the Duma, with the aim of using it as a tribunal for revolutionary propaganda.[1] Opinions were divided on whether the party should boycott the elections in their entirety, or participate in the pre-election meetings in order to campaign there against the Duma and in favour of a Constituent Assembly. Although Chernov himself advocated the latter course, his amendment was for once defeated, by 28 votes to 20, and the congress resolved to boycott both the Duma itself and the pre-election meetings.[2]

The results of the elections to the Duma, which were held in March and April 1906, showed how mistaken the boycott policy of the revolutionary parties was. The overwhelming majority of the peasants ignored the boycott appeals and, placing great hopes in the Duma as a means of obtaining land reform, elected their own representatives, mainly non-party men with radical sympathies, to champion their cause.[3] In the Duma, these 'leftist' peasant deputies formed a parliamentary fraction calling itself the 'Labour group' (*Trudovaya gruppa*) or *Trudoviki*. Politically, the *Trudoviki* were to the left of the Kadets. The majority held views similar to those expressed at the congresses of the All-Russia Peasant Union, and some sympathised with or shared the programmes of the SRs and SDs. The fraction, which numbered about a hundred deputies, advocated the transformation of the Duma into a Constituent Assembly, but were willing to work within the Duma framework in

[1] *Protokoly pervago s"ezda . . .*, p 14.

[2] *ibid*, pp 9–23.

[3] On peasant voting in the Duma elections, see Maslov, *Agrarnyi vopros . . .*, vol 2, pp 266–79; B. B. Veselovskii, *Krest'yanskii vopros i krest'yanskoe dvizhenie v Rossii, 1902–1906 gg.* (St Petersburg, 1907), pp 133–9; P. Marev, 'Politicheskaya bor'ba krest'yanstva', in V. Gorn, V. Mech and N. Cherevanin, *Krest'yanstvo i revolyutsiya v Rossii* (Moscow, 1907), pp 99–106.

the hope of achieving necessary reforms, especially in agriculture.[4]

In May 1906, as soon as the radical nature of the Duma became apparent, the SR Party Council – a body which had been established by the Party Congress – met to reconsider the tactics which the party should adopt towards it. Since it was impossible at this stage to reverse the boycott, the compromise decision was that the party should seek to influence the Duma through the 'Labour group'.[5] In this aim, the SRs came into competition with the Popular Socialists. Of the two proposals for agrarian reform which were advocated by the *Trudoviki* in the Duma, one reflected the influence of the Popular Socialists, the other that of the SRs.

On 23 May 1906, the *Trudoviki* presented to the Duma a draft proposal for agrarian reform, with the signatures of 104 deputies. The first paragraph stated the ultimate aim of the group: 'Land legislation should aim to establish a system whereby all the land with its mineral and water resources should belong to the entire people, land needed for agriculture being available for the use only of those who would work it with their own labour. All citizens should have an equal right to such use of the land.'[6] The remaining paragraphs listed the measures which should be taken for the achievement of this goal. It was proposed that all state and church lands should be turned over to a 'people's land fund'; privately owned land in a quantity which exceeded the 'labour norm' for the locality – the amount which could be worked by the family labour of the household – should also be compulsorily confiscated and turned over to the fund. The lands of the peasant communes and land which did not exceed the labour norm were to remain in the possession of their present owners. Compensation for the confiscation of privately owned land was to be paid by the state; the rate and conditions of such payment were to be decided at a later stage. After land 'essential for state and social needs' had been transferred from the land fund to the jurisdiction of the appropriate central institutions, the remainder would be made available to all those who were prepared to work it; local peasants would be given preference over outsiders and non-peasants. Where sufficient land was available, the maximum holding would be governed by the labour norm; if the land was too short in any area to guarantee even the

4 Maslov, *Obshchestvennoe dvizhenie* . . ., vol 3, pp 138–43.

5 *Pamyatnaya knizhka Sotsialista-Revolyutsionera*, vyp 1 (Paris, 1911), pp 56–7.

6 *Gosudarstvennaya Duma, sessiya 1; stenograficheskii otchet* (St Petersburg, 1906), col 560.

'consumption norm' – the amount required to feed the household adequately – the state would undertake resettlement in areas where land was more plentiful. The regulation of landholding would be entrusted to local government institutions elected on the basis of the fourfold suffrage. The draft also suggested the local committees should be democratically elected to prepare for the reform, for instance by assessing the appropriate labour and consumption norms for each locality.[7]

Thus the draft of the 104 clearly illustrated the Popular Socialists' principle of compromise between what was ideologically desirable for the socialist intelligentsia and what was practically acceptable to the mass of the peasantry. The peasants' rights to their communal and purchased lands were guaranteed, and they were also safeguarded against an influx of landless workers from the towns seeking to implement their right to the land. At the same time, recognition was made of the principle of socialisation. The draft of the 104 was passed to the Agrarian Commission of the Duma for consideration.

On 8 June 1906 a group of 33 'Labour group' deputies, representing the minority of SR sympathisers in the fraction, put forward another document for consideration by the Duma. In the 'Declaration' with which they prefixed their proposal, its sponsors declared their support for the draft of the 104. Since only the first paragraph had stated the aim of the desired land law, the rest of the draft being concerned with transitional measures, they 'considered it useful to develop immediately the principles briefly expressed in the first paragraph, in the form of a more detailed and definite "Draft of a basic land law"'. The 'Declaration' also stated that such an agrarian law could be passed only by a 'plenipotentiary Popular Duma', elected on the basis of the fourfold suffrage.[8]

The aim of the draft of the 33, therefore, was to expand on the first paragraph of the draft of the 104, to bring it more closely into line with the concept of socialisation as expressed in the SR programme. The first section declared the 'bases of the land law' to be: the total abolition of private property in land; the declaration of all the land, with its mineral and water resources, to be 'the common property of the entire population'; and equal rights for all citizens to use land for agriculture and building. Detailed legislation governing the use of the land should be passed by an assembly elected on the basis of the fourfold suffrage, and the implementation of the law

[7] *ibid*, cols 560–2.

[8] *ibid*, col 1153.

would be entrusted to democratically elected institutions of local government. The second section defined the rights to land of all citizens. Everyone would be guaranteed the consumption norm as the minimum, and the labour norm as the maximum holding, to be held on a communal or individual basis. Similar rights of access would be granted to building plots, construction materials and fuel, fishing, hunting and gathering, and mineral resources.[9]

Unlike the draft of the 104, the draft of the 33 was not intended as a practical guide to legislation by the Duma; its major function was a propaganda one, as it challenged the constitutional basis of the Duma. It was on these grounds that the Duma, after some debate, decided by a majority of 140 votes to 78 not to pass the draft of the 33 to the Agrarian Commission.[10]

If the SR land programme proved too radical for the Duma, even the more modest proposals for agrarian reform advocated by the Kadet majority in the Duma were too radical for the Tsarist government to stomach. On 9 July, having lasted for only 73 days out of its five-year span, the Duma was dissolved by Imperial decree. The revolutionary parties, and even the liberals, hoped that the dissolution of the Duma would provoke some kind of popular protest. The Kadet and 'Labour group' deputies crossed into Finland and issued the Vyborg appeal asking the people to refuse to pay taxes or supply recruits to the army until the Duma was restored. The Central Committee of the SR party issued an appeal 'To all party organisations', which called for a national armed uprising, with the initiative coming from the countryside. The peasants were to drive out the authorities, seize the land, and then march on the towns, uniting with the troops and the workers in a concerted assault on the government. A few days later, the SRs joined with the SDs, the *Trudoviki*, the Peasant Union and the Railway Union in issuing a 'Manifesto to the entire Russian peasantry', calling on them to rise up for 'land and liberty'.[11] These appeals produced little response either from the urban or from the rural population. The peasant movement, which had continued throughout the spring and early summer of 1906, although on a more muted scale than in 1905, began to fall off in July;[12] the peasants were too busy preparing for the

[9] *ibid*, cols 1153–6. [10] *ibid*, cols 1142–50.

[11] The texts of these appeals, 'K partiynym organizatsiyam' and 'Manifest ko vsemu rossiyskomu krest'yanstvu', are given in an appendix to *Poslednii samoderzhets* (Berlin, 1912), pp 15–19.

[12] Dubrovskii, pp 42, 57–9.

harvest to consider marching on the towns.[13] The main revolutionary events of the summer were the mutinies at the Baltic naval bases of Sveaborg and Kronstadt, which the government succeeded in suppressing without much difficulty.

At the end of October 1906 the SR Party Council met to consider the question of the party's participation in the elections to the Second Duma. After hearing reports from the delegates concerning popular attitudes towards the Duma in the regions, the Council decided to participate in the election campaign. It stressed that this participation did not involve any recognition of the authority of the Duma; the party should simply use the election campaign as a forum for revolutionary agitation for a Constituent Assembly. The Council stressed that participation in the elections and the election of party candidates would not necessarily mean that the party would form its own fraction in the Duma; the question of a boycott of the Duma itself would be decided by the next Party Congress.[14]

The results of the elections showed that the Second Duma would have an even more radical political complexion than the First. The decision of the revolutionary parties to lift their boycott produced about a hundred SR and SD deputies, in addition to another hundred *Trudoviki*; these gains by the left were largely at the expense of the Kadets. On 12 February 1907, about a week before the Duma was due to open, the Second (Extraordinary) Congress of the SR party met at Tammerfors in Finland. In the knowledge that between thirty and forty SRs had been elected, the main task of the congress was to decide on the party's tactics towards the Duma.

The debate on party participation in the Duma showed that there was a small group of delegates still in favour of a boycott. The fate of the First Duma, they argued, had disillusioned the peasants concerning the value of parliamentary activity; the fact that they had taken part in the elections meant only that they wished to demonstrate their defiance of the government by electing deputies even more radical than those in the First Duma.[15] The most emphatic rebuttal of this boycottist argument came in a speech by

[13] This is the explanation given in *Rapport du parti socialiste révolutionnaire de russie au congrès socialiste international de Stuttgart (août 1907)* (Gand, 1907), p 230.

[14] *Pamyatnaya knizhka . . .*, pp 57–9.

[15] *Protokoly vtorogo (ekstrennago) s"ezda Partii Sotsialistov-Revolyutsionerov* (St Petersburg, 1907), pp 14–95.

Gershuni, who, having recently escaped from Siberia, was given a rapturous reception by the Congress. Gershuni warned the party of the dangers of its isolation from the masses:

Here many delegates working among the peasants have conveyed their mood: the peasants expect nothing from the Duma, they believe only in an armed uprising – to say nothing of the workers. But if this is so, one asks, what does it mean? Why is there no uprising, and peasant and worker deputies in the Duma? I do not doubt that the delegates who have spoken here have properly understood and conveyed to us the mood of the peasant and worker masses – but with a slight reservation: the mood of those of the masses whom they, the delegates, have encountered . . . Yes, they have conveyed to you only the opinions of a thousand peasants and workers who are prepared to rise up. But what about the opinions of the tens of millions to whom our delegates *have not talked*, and with whose mood *they are not familiar*? I do not hesitate to state here that the opinions of our delegates may be correct as far as the masses among whom they have worked are concerned; they are totally incorrect in relation to the masses as a whole.[16]

For two years now, Gershuni continued, the party had based its tactics on the assumption that a revolutionary uprising was imminent. This belief had time and again proved to be mistaken; it had derived from an over-optimistic estimate of the mood of the people, based on the psychological 'optical illusion' of local party workers who considered the views of the tiny minority of peasants influenced by SR propaganda to be representative of the mood of the peasantry as a whole. If the party were now to boycott the Duma, the result would be not an armed uprising, but greater apathy than before. The party leadership, Gershuni asserted, must be responsive to the masses:

For what is the SR party? Is it little groups who sit in committees? The party is the organised working class of workers and peasants. *Its will is the will of the party*. And when the party decides whether or not to enter the Duma, this in practice means that the workers and peasants are deciding whether or not to elect. And if the voice of the proletariat and peasantry organised by the party clearly and definitely decides to enter, the committees and central institutions of the party, as executive organs of the working class, should implement its decisions.[17]

In the case of the Second Duma, he said, there was no basic contradiction between the attitude of the party and that of the working masses. The people expected no substantial gains from the Duma,

[16] *ibid*, p 81. (Emphasis in the original.)
[17] *ibid*, pp 83–4. (Emphasis in the original.)

but they saw it as a stage in the revolutionary process and expected their representatives to utilise it as such.[18]

Finally the Congress agreed, with only one dissenting vote, to make use of the Duma for the party's revolutionary ends, by forming a fraction of SR deputies. It was resolved that in its tactics within the Duma, the SR fraction should adopt a middle course between avoiding a dissolution through compromises, on the one hand, and seeking any pretext to provoke a dissolution, on the other. In case of dissolution, the deputies should refuse to disperse and should seek the support of the army and the people.[19]

The main contribution of the SR deputies in the Second Duma came in the debates on the agrarian question. The draft land law which the SR group presented to the Duma had 104 signatures, including those of the majority of the *Trudoviki.* The form of the proposed law represented a combination of the drafts of the 104 and the 33 put forward in the First Duma. The main points of the draft of the 33 were laid out in the first section of the law: the abolition of private property in land, and the guaranteed right of all citizens to the consumption norm as the minimum and the labour norm as the maximum holding. The second section listed transitional measures towards the implementation of the law. These measures were similar to those proposed by the draft of the 104 in the First Duma, the main difference being that no compensation was to be paid for the confiscation of private lands which exceeded the labour norm. The lands of the peasant communes, as well as privately owned and rented land in a quantity not exceeding the labour norm, were to remain in the use of their present owners or users; the remaining lands were to be confiscated and put at the disposal of the state. In the distribution of the confiscated lands, priority would be given to local land-hungry peasants, then to agricultural workers, then to the local non-agricultural population, and lastly, if the supply of land allowed it, to immigrants. In preparation for the introduction of the reform, local land committees were to be democratically elected.[20]

The SR agrarian programme fared rather better in the Second Duma than it had in the First. The SR draft, with its 104 signatures, attracted greater support from the *Trudoviki* than the Popular Socialist project which had been presented to the First Duma, and

[18] *ibid*, p 84.

[19] *ibid*, pp 138–9, 160–62.

[20] For the text of this 'Proekt osnovnykh polozhenii zemel'nago zakona', see *Pamyatnaya knizhka . . .*, pp 71–81.

which, with a few minor modifications, was again presented to the Second Duma by 37 deputies from the 'Labour group' and the Peasant Union.[21] The SRs prided themselves that their draft law presented the socialisation of the land both as an ideal to which the peasants should aspire and as a series of practical measures of reform.[22] In contrast to the draft of the 33 SR supporters in the First Duma, the draft of the 104 in the Second did not insist that socialisation could be accomplished only by a Constituent Assembly elected by the 'four-tailed' suffrage; it referred simply to an 'assembly of popular representatives' as the supreme authority. The SR resolution on land committees, however, criticised the indirect voting system for the Duma and proposed that elections to the land committees be based on universal, direct, equal and secret suffrage, as a safeguard of peasant interests against possible injustices in any land reform approved by an undemocratic Duma.[23]

On 3 May 1907, the draft of the 104 was passed to the Agrarian Commission of the Duma for consideration. A month later, the Duma ceased to exist.[24] From the moment it realised that the Second Duma would be no less intransigent than the First, the government had been seeking a pretext for its dissolution. On 3 June 1907, the Second Duma ended in the same way as its predecessor. The dissolution of the Duma was accompanied by the promulgation of a new electoral law which drastically reduced the representation of the peasants and workers in the elections to the Third Duma. The government took measures to prevent any revolutionary response to the dissolution. On the night of 2 June many SR and SD deputies were arrested. The rump of the SR group issued a manifesto protesting against the dissolution and the new electoral law.[25] The manifesto concluded with a rather lukewarm appeal to the people to organise and defend their rights, but, as with the First Duma, the dissolution of the Second Duma was accepted quietly by the country.

At the beginning of July 1907, the Third SR Council met to decide the party's tactics towards the Third Duma. The Council resolved

[21] *Gosudarstvennaya Duma, sessiya 2; stenograficheskii otchet* (St Petersburg, 1907), vol 1, cols 177–8, 1823–4.
[22] See the speech by Mushenko, *ibid*, vol 2, cols 111–21.
[23] *ibid*, vol 1, col 1100.
[24] *ibid*, vol 2, col 122.
[25] For the text of this manifesto, 'Grazhdane!', see *Znamya Truda*, no. 1 (July 1907), pp 20–1.

to call for a boycott of the Duma, on the grounds that the government's cynical attitude towards popular representation had been clearly demonstrated by the fate of the first two Dumas, that the people were now disillusioned with the quasi-constitutional structure, and that 'the leading strata in the towns and countryside are at present sufficiently prepared to be receptive to the idea of a boycott, and may bring behind them a significant section of the labouring masses'.[26] Again, the SRs' estimate of the mood of the masses proved to be over-optimistic, and the country elected a moderately conservative Duma, which lasted for its full five-year term.

[26] *Pamyatnaya knizhka* . . ., pp 62–4.

15
The commune, socialisation, and the Stolypin reforms

Among the objects of SR attack in the Second Duma were the proposals for agrarian reform introduced by the Prime Minister, Stolypin, in his decree of 9 November 1906. The Stolypin reforms sought to encourage withdrawal from the commune by enabling peasants to claim title to their holdings and consolidate their strips into enclosed individual farms. As an attempt to destroy the communal solidarity of the peasantry, and to foster individualist proprietorial attitudes, these measures ran directly counter to the aims of SR agrarian policy. In order to assess the extent to which the Stolypin reforms threatened SR plans for the socialisation of the land, it is necessary to review the premises on which the party's hopes for socialisation were based, as well as the party's attitude towards the peasant commune.

According to Chernovian theory, SR hopes for the socialisation of the land derived not from the existence of the repartitional commune – this, as we shall see later, simply constituted a bonus – but from their view of the mass of small peasant producers as members not of the petty bourgeoisie but of the working class, and their consequent receptivity to socialist ideas. The peasants' desire for land was a progressive aspiration, with both an anti-feudal and anti-capitalist content, and it was the duty of a socialist party to ensure that any agrarian reform which transferred the land to the peasantry created class solidarity and cohesion and prevented the development of 'property fanaticism'. For this reason, the SR minimum programme advocated the transfer of the land not to individual peasants as private property, but to democratic communal organisations for egalitarian utilisation.[1]

Up to this point, Chernov made it clear that his arguments in favour of the socialisation of the land applied to Europe as a whole, and not specifically to Russia, and he bolstered his articles with references to 'revisionist' European socialists, such as Vandervelde, who

[1] 'Sotsializatsiya zemli i kooperatsiya v sel'skom khozyaystve', *R.R.*, no. 14 (December 1902), pp 6–7.

shared his views about the non-capitalist nature of the economy of the small peasant producers.[2] All European socialists, Chernov argued, should advocate collective rather than individual possession of the land, but the form of collective property in land would depend on individual circumstances in individual countries. Thus the English Social-Democratic Federation was in favour of nationalisation; whereas the Dutch socialists, preferring greater decentralisation, proposed the 'communalisation' of the land, whilst the Belgians envisaged some kind of balance between local and central control.[3] Of these alternatives, the SR concept of socialisation was closest to the Dutch model, which Chernov considered particularly appropriate to Russian conditions for two reasons. In the first place, as we have already seen, the SRs were suspicious of nationalisation until adequate guarantees of democracy – such as those which existed in England – had been introduced into the political system. And in the second place, 'The existence in Russia of communal landownership and the widespread presence of communal traditions and views among the peasantry make this particular type of socialist agrarian policy even more practicable for us.'[4]

Thus it is clear that in SR agrarian theory – in contrast to that of some of the earlier Populists – the existence of the peasant commune played only a secondary rôle to the 'objective' class position of the peasantry as a basis for the socialisation of the land. And insofar as they did take the commune into consideration, the SRs saw its main significance not in the institution itself, but in the complex of attitudes which it engendered. These attitudes represented the 'subjective' basis of SR hopes for land socialisation.

The SRs always insisted that, unlike some of their Populist predecessors, they did not idealise the contemporary commune. They recognised that its operations were as much bureaucratic as democratic, and that repartition had not prevented the growth of individualism and social differentiation in the countryside in the post-Emancipation period. Nevertheless, they believed that the tradition of communal ownership and disposal of the land, and the practice of its egalitarian redistribution, created attitudes in the peasantry which had more in common with socialist than with

[2] *ibid*, pp 7–8. See also 'Klassovaya bor′ba v derevne', *R.R.*, no. 11 (September 1902), pp 8–9.

[3] 'Sotsializatsiya zemli i kooperatsiya v sel′skom khozyaystve', *R.R.*, no. 15 (January 1903), p 7.

[4] *ibid*, p 8.

individualist principles.[5] It was to these attitudes and ideas of social justice, embodied – however imperfectly – in the practice of communal repartition, and also in other aspects of peasant customary law, to which the first sentence of the SR agrarian programme referred:

In matters of agrarian policy and land relations the SR party sets itself the aim of utilising, in the interests of socialism and the struggle against bourgeois-proprietorial principles, the communal and in general the labour-based views, traditions and forms of life of the Russian peasantry, in particular their view of the land as the common property of all who labour.[6]

In the debate on the agrarian programme at the First Party Congress, two delegates criticised this formulation. According to 'Krasova', the representative of the Yaroslavl' committee:

The agrarian section of our draft programme begins with words which indicate that the party derives the socialisation of the land from the subjective psychological views of the peasantry. But the socialisation of the land is derived from purely objective data, and even if there were no commune in Russia, we would still retain the socialisation of the land in our programme. In Europe too, where the commune has long since ceased to exist, we would also advocate measures analogous to those of our agrarian programme.[7]

'Krasova' was supported by 'Tambovtsev', the delegate from Tambov, who argued that all mention of the traditional views of the peasantry should be omitted from the programme, since 'our task with regard to agrarian reform is more profound and more important' than 'simply mounting, if it may be so expressed, and riding these views'.[8] These two humble and solitary voices were ignored by the Congress, and the references to the communal attitudes of the peasantry were retained in the final version of the programme.

The emphasis on communal attitudes in the party programme reflected the reverence which many SRs still retained for the commune as an institution. Although Chernov's theoretical articles in *Revolyutsionnaya Rossiya* gave primacy to the class position of the peasantry as the basis for socialisation, other SRs – particularly the veteran Populists in the party – continued to link their hopes of socialisation to the survival of the repartitional commune. The

[5] 'Krest'yanskoe dvizhenie', *R.R.*, no. 8 (June 1902), p 4; 'Sotsializatsiya zemli i programma-minimum', *R.R.*, no. 42 (March 1904), p 5; 'Russkaya krest'yanskaya obshchina i blizhayshiya zadachi revolyutsii', *R.R.*, no. 53 (September 1904), pp 3–6.

[6] 'Proekt programmy PS-Rov', *R.R.*, no. 46 (May 1904), p 3.

[7] *Protokoly pervago s"ezda . . .*, p 196. [8] *ibid*, p 213.

response of the party to any attack on the commune, real or threatened, was therefore one of dismay, and the fear of individualism in the countryside, whether encouraged by the government or by the SDs, was common to all SRs. Chernov himself shared these apprehensions; he wrote in 1903 that:

For a socialist in the countryside there is nothing more dangerous than the growth of private property and the inculcation into the peasant, who still considers that the land is 'no-one's', 'free' (or 'God's', as the old men express this idea in their archaic formulation), of the idea of a right to trade and speculate in land.[9]

Attacking the SDs, he continued:

Private peasant property is in general an extremely vital force, and by increasing its vitality you of course give it a better chance in the struggle not only against feudalism and capitalism – that is no misfortune – but also against socialism. For by developing private property among the peasantry, in whose psyche there persist communal habits and views, and the concept of the land as the common possession of all, you are making more difficult for yourselves in the future (and even in the present) the propaganda of the communalisation of the land, and also of other means of production.[10]

A threat to the peasant commune from the SDs was, of course, purely theoretical at this time. Much more real was the danger from the government. Even before 1905, the SRs were aware that official opinion was turning against the commune. At the time of Emancipation, the Tsarist bureaucracy had decided to retain the commune and the peasant courts, which relied on customary law; but the reports of local committees established in 1902 to review the needs of agriculture came out generally against the retention of the commune. In 1904 rumours of imminent government attacks on peasant institutions led one contributor to write in *Revolyutsionnaya Rossiya* of the danger to the traditional peasant views on which the party relied, and the need to combat individualism by means of an intensive campaign of socialist propaganda: 'Our task in the present agonising crisis of peasant consciousness of justice [*narodnoe pravosoznanie*] is to support its communal and labour-based principles, which are still preserved in customary law, to preserve it from the infection of individualism, wherever it may come from, and to instil into it new and broader principles of truth and justice.'[11]

[9] 'Sotsializatsiya zemli i kooperatsiya v sel'skom khozyaystve', *R.R.*, no. 15 (January 1903), p 6.

[10] *ibid*, p 7.

[11] 'Iz russkoy zhizni. Krizis narodnago pravosoznaniya i neo-byurokraticheskie eksperimenty', *R.R.*, no. 51 (August 1904), p 7.

The events of 1905 raised the question of the future development of the commune in a particularly acute form. Would there be a revolutionary solution to the agrarian problem, on the pattern of socialisation as envisaged by the SRs; or would the government intervene with reforms to strengthen peasant individualism? Fear of the latter outcome led some delegates to the First Party Congress to adopt a 'now or never' stance on the issue of whether the party should call for a revolutionary expropriation of the lands of the large estates in the spring of 1906. Rakitnikov argued that the revolutionary atmosphere which had been created in 1905 heightened the peasants' desire for radical solutions and presented a unique opportunity for the socialisation of the land, whereas in more peaceful times propaganda proceeded more slowly and gradually and favoured reformist rather than revolutionary solutions. He continued:

> The success of our propaganda among the peasants depends to a considerable degree on the existence within the peasantry of communal and labour-based concepts, and a view of the land as the common possession of all who work. But these communal and labour-based views are involved in a constant and irreconcilable conflict with bourgeois-proprietorial views which are gradually penetrating the more prosperous strata of the peasantry. The development of trade and the consolidation of the position of capital in the countryside (if only in the form of usury) is undermining traditional communal views, and is introducing confusion and disharmony into the labour-based ideology of the peasantry. At a time of revolution such as this the harmful influence of bourgeois principles is erased; seized by a thirst for justice, the revolutionary working peasantry are rising up against bourgeois private property and are trying to uproot the exploitation of man by man. But at another time the corrupting influence of conditions of life appropriate to bourgeois society will make itself felt, the wholeness of the labour-based ideology will be destroyed, and the peasantry will succumb to a system of petty improvements, a system of sops, the main benefits of which will undoubtedly be enjoyed first and foremost by the petty bourgeois strata who do not work, and the more prosperous elements of the working peasantry. The fight for the socialisation of the land, and also the very preaching of socialist ideas, will then encounter obstacles which do not at present exist, and the SR party should not forget this.[12]

Chernov's reply to the supporters of the 'now or never' position referred to both the objective and subjective bases for socialisation. In the first place, he reminded his audience that many Western European Marxists shared the SRs' views on agrarian policy; that even in the West, where there was no commune, agrarian capitalism

[12] *Protokoly pervago s"ezda . . .*, p 330.

was making little headway among the peasantry; and that the French and German peasants were proving more receptive to socialist ideas than the orthodox Marxists had ever imagined possible.[13] And secondly, Chernov had much greater faith than his opponents in the resilience of the commune and the traditional views associated with it; these had, after all, survived the onslaughts of capitalism and bureaucratic interference since Emancipation and even before. 'Why then should I expect their rapid disappearance in an atmosphere of broader and freer communication between the labour-based instincts, traditions and views of the people and the bright thought of scientific socialism?'[14] Chernov contrasted the pre-October 'unfree autocratic plutocratic régime' with the prospective 'free bourgeois régime', and he concluded that from the party's point of view the latter had many advantages, not least the unprecedented opportunity it would provide for the dissemination of SR propaganda in the countryside. He believed that the economic and political crisis would be prolonged, and he argued that no measures of reform introduced by a government which represented the interests of the bourgeoisie and landed gentry would be adequate to satisfy the demands of the peasantry. A temporary victory for the bourgeoisie in the form of a constitutional monarchy would not prevent the solution of the agrarian problem from being ultimately a revolutionary one: 'It does not mark the end of the revolutionary period, but simply heralds a new and more acute stage within it.'[15] Chernov therefore opposed to the slogan 'now or never' his slogan of 'wait and see', which eventually triumphed at the congress.

These views, of course, were expressed before Stolypin's decree of 9 November and before the dissolution of the Second Duma made it clear that the government was not prepared to contemplate any alternative proposals for agrarian reform. By the time the First Party Conference met in August 1908 the Stolypin reforms had been in operation for nearly two years, and the delegates were presented with some rather discouraging evidence that peasant withdrawals from the commune were being forced through by the government, often against the wishes of the mass of the peasantry.[16] Introducing the debate on agrarian policy at the conference, 'Bol'shov', for the

[13] *Dobavlenie k protokolam pervago s"ezda Partii Sotsialistov-Revolyutsionerov* (n.p., 1906), pp 34–5.

[14] *ibid*, p 35.

[15] *ibid*, pp 26–35; *Protokoly pervago s"ezda . . .*, p 313.

[16] *Protokoly pervoy obshchepartiynoy konferentsii Partii Sotsialistov-Revolyutsionerov, avgust 1908* (Paris, 1908), pp 182–9.

Central Committee, admitted that government policy ran directly counter to the SR programme. He remained optimistic, however, concerning the socialisation of the land, even if the government were to succeed in destroying the commune and establishing individual landownership:

> For our hopes and expectations, and our programme, lie not in the fact itself of communal landholding, but in the complex of ideas, emotions and customs, the entire psychology which has been nourished in the peasantry by the whole past history and practice of communal landholding. Even if it were possible to abolish the commune within a short period, this would not in itself erase the complex of ideas and emotions which provide a firm basis for our propaganda among the peasantry.[17]

Even in Western Europe, 'Bol′shov' continued, where private peasant property in land had existed for centuries. 'the ideas of socialism find a fertile soil among the peasantry, as soon as the socialists raise the slogan of the struggle for land'.[18] As examples of this, he cited the recent peasant movements in Hungary and Italy, where gentry land had been seized.

Other delegates were more pessimistic than 'Bol′shov' concerning the chances for socialisation. 'Livin' (a representative of a group of émigrés who in their journal *Revolyutsionnaya Mysl′* ('Revolutionary thought') argued that the party should adapt to the new conditions of reaction by reverting to the *narodovol′cheskii* concept of élite terrorism and regicide) rejected 'Bol′shov's' contention that peasant receptivity to socialist ideas did not depend on the survival of the commune. In the Hungarian disturbances at the end of the 1890s, he alleged, the peasants had demanded the land as private property, which illustrated, in his opinion, 'the negative influence of the absence there of the commune'.[19] The Stolypin reforms, with their encouragement of individualism, represented a real threat to the success of socialist ideas in Russia: 'We stand before a great danger. It will be the greater, the longer Tsarism survives. A favourable resolution of the political issues will therefore influence the solution of the economic problem. The commune can be saved only by the overthrow of the autocracy.'[20]

A more balanced view was put forward by 'Bystrenin' on behalf of the agrarian commission of the conference. The party must bear in mind, he pointed out, that the peasant economy, and peasant psychology, contained both individualist and collectivist features,

[17] *ibid*, p 184.
[18] *ibid*, p 185.
[19] *ibid*, p 189.
[20] *ibid*, p 189.

and that both of these, as Kachorovskii had pointed out in his recent book on customary law, were embodied in the 'labour principle'.[21] The fact that the government was trying to strengthen individualism at the expense of collectivism meant that the SRs must devote themselves with particular vigour to the conduct of a campaign in the countryside to encourage the collectivist aspect of peasant psychology, and to combat the government's efforts to strengthen individualism.[22] A resolution on these lines was approved by the conference. The delegates also resolved to urge the peasants to resist Stolypin's attack on the commune, by refusing to leave it and by boycotting those who established individual farms.[23]

The Stolypin reforms undoubtedly dealt a considerable psychological blow to the SRs. Although in theory the survival of the commune was not essential for the success of the socialisation of the land, we have seen that in practice many SRs associated the two; even those who accepted the primacy of the 'objective basis' for socialisation believed that the existence of the commune made the task of socialist propaganda in the countryside considerably easier, and they were dedicated to its defence against external attack. After 1906, a rather defensive note crept into SR discussion of socialisation, and a series of theoretical articles in a new party journal, *Sotsialist-Revolyutsioner* ('The Socialist-Revolutionary'), tended to place greater emphasis than before on the second plank of the minimum agrarian programme – cooperation.[24]

[21] Kachorovskii argued that the 'labour principle' (*trudovoe nachalo*) in peasant customary law had two components: the 'right to work' (*pravo na trud*) and the 'right of work' (*pravo truda*). The first of these, which meant that all peasants had an equal right to land for subsistence, was a collectivist aspiration, since it implied redistribution of the means of production; the second, however, meant that labour gave rights over the land worked, and was, in conditions of individual or household production, an individualist aspiration. K. R. Kachorovskii, *Narodnoe pravo* (Moscow, 1906), pp 134–203.

[22] *Protokoly pervoy obshchepartiynoy konferentsii* . . . , pp 202–3.

[23] *ibid*, pp 228–9.

[24] See N. Maksimov, 'Razlozhenie obshchiny i nasha programma', *Sotsialist-Revolyutsioner*, no. 1 (1910), pp 131–74; V. Chernov, 'Kooperatsiya i sotsializm', *ibid*, no. 2 (1910), pp 265–314; S. R. Kraynii, 'Sotsializatsiya zemli, kak takticheskaya problema', *ibid*, no. 3 (1911), pp 161–99; N. M., 'Sotsializatsiya zemli i nasha programma-minimum', *ibid*, no. 3, pp 237–300; B. Voronov, 'K teorii kooperativnago dvizheniya', *ibid*, no. 4 (1912), pp 177–255; N. A. A., 'Sotsialisty-Revolyutsionery i kooperatsiya', *ibid*, no. 4, pp 257–92.

16
Party activity in the countryside

The Stolypin coup d'état of 3 June 1907 brought to an end the period of semi-constitutional activity which the SRs had enjoyed during the existence of the First and Second Dumas. In this period the party had been able to agitate widely and openly among the masses, and the relaxation of censorship had enabled them to publish a range of books, journals and newspapers in Russia. In the period of the First Duma, a dozen SR publishing houses were in existence in Russia, issuing over twenty daily and weekly newspapers. In St Petersburg and Moscow, 200 titles of books and pamphlets were published, about 4 million copies in all.[1] Because of police harassment, the main party newspaper had to change its title several times, appearing successively as *Delo Naroda* ('The cause of the people'), *Narodnyi Vestnik* ('Popular herald'), *Golos* ('Voice'), and *Mysl'* ('Thought'); 30 out of the 55 numbers printed were in fact confiscated, but 43,000 copies of the remaining issues were distributed.[2] After the dissolution of the First Duma, the party press went underground again, although a small legal journal continued to survive under the titles *Narodnyi Vestnik*, *Soznatel'naya Rossiya* ('Conscious Russia'), *Novaya Mysl'* ('New thought'), and *Nasha Mysl'* ('Our thought').[3] From October 1906 the central party organ was again published illegally, with the title of *Partiynyya Izvestiya*. Its circulation ranged from 8,000 to 25,000 copies. Three special journals were also published for the peasants and the soldiers, and the St Petersburg party committee published a workers' paper, *Trud* ('Labour'), which had a circulation of 20,000–25,000 copies.[4] Various local party newspapers were also published in the regions, as well as many thousands of proclamations.[5] In 1907 the party publications continued on a predominantly illegal basis. In July 1907 *Partiynyya Izvestiya* was replaced by *Znamya Truda* ('Banner of labour') as the main party organ. In January 1907, a new newspaper

[1] *Rapport . . . 1907*, p 226.
[2] *ibid*, p 228.
[3] Maslov, *Obshchestvennoe dvizhenie . . .*, vol 3, p 118.
[4] *Rapport . . . 1907*, p 234.
[5] Spiridovitch, pp 326–9.

for the peasantry, *Zemlya i Volya* ('Land and liberty'), was launched by the Central Committee. From the beginning of 1908, severe repressions led to the confiscation of most of the party's presses in Russia, and the main focus of the party's publishing activity moved again abroad.[6]

Support for the party increased rapidly in 1906–7, and its policies were widely known and discussed. Membership grew; it was announced at the Second Congress that the Party Council of October 1906 had estimated the size of the party as 50,000 full members, plus 300,000 'persons in the sphere of constant party influence'.[7] By 1906 SR organisations and committees existed in all the major towns and cities of Russia. At the end of 1905 the party had nine regional unions: for the North, Centre, Volga, Urals, North-West, Ukraine, South, Caucasus and Siberia. A tenth union, for the Don oblast', was created at the First Congress; and in the course of 1906 a Turkestan union came into existence. At the Second Party Congress in 1907 twelve unions were represented, the Caucasian union having divided to form separate unions for the North Caucasus and Transcaucasia.[8]

As the party increased in size in 1905–7, its social base broadened to include members of the lower and working classes. Before 1905, the party committees consisted mainly of intellectuals and students, who regarded the 'masses' – the workers and peasants – as the objects of their propaganda and organisational activities. The influx of new membership during the revolution included many representatives of the masses themselves. The reports of the local party organisations in 1907 spoke of hundreds and even thousands of organised workers and peasants.[9] The present writer's analysis of a sample of over a thousand biographies of SRs who were active party members during the revolution of 1905–7 shows that 7.7% were peasants, 45.6% workers and artisans, 12.8% clerical and shop workers, 12.4% members of the minor professions (mainly teachers), 4.1% professional men, and 16.5% students. The workers were engaged not only in their purely class organisations, such as trade unions and the soviets, but also in the party's terrorist organisations and armed militias (*boevye druzhiny*): the SR terrorists were predominantly

[6] *ibid*, pp 498–9, 503.

[7] *Protokoly vtorogo (ekstrennago) s"ezda . . .*, p 120.

[8] *Protokoly pervago s"ezda . . .*, pp 302–7; *Rapport . . . 1907*, p 40; *Protokoly vtorogo (ekstrennago) s"ezda . . .*, pp 178–80.

[9] *Rapport . . . 1907*, pp 53–192, *passim*.

young and working class. The party also recruited extensively among the workers and peasants in uniform – the soldiers and sailors of the Russian armed forces.[10]

The period of liberty was particularly important for opening the lines of SR communication with the peasantry. All the local party committees in 1907 reported some contact with the countryside, the activity being most intensive in traditional SR centres, such as the Ukraine and the Volga. The ideal pattern of rural organisation which had been proposed in 1905 by the congress of the SR Peasant Union was, however, only imperfectly realised in 1906–7. Only the Southern Union reported the existence of a separate regional Peasant Commission. This comprised 10 to 15 peripatetic propagandists and 5 sedentary workers. It had organised 4 peasant conferences, and a regional congress had been held in November 1906.[11] At the guberniya level, several committees had special peasant sections, described variously as Commissions (Moscow, Penza, St Petersburg, Vologda, Khar′kov and Kherson) or Bureaux (Tver′ and Voronezh).[12] The main functions of these sections appear to have been the organisation of peasant conferences and congresses and the distribution of literature. In some other provinces, where no formal peasant organisation existed, the same functions were performed by informal groups. The Nizhnii Novgorod committee had an attached group of twenty militant peasants who made propaganda trips to the villages, and organised a conference.[13] In Samara, in 1906, peasant propaganda was conducted by 'a special organisation of 25 militants'.[14] The Smolensk committee 'had no peasant commission, but three comrades were specially concerned with peasant propaganda, helped by a few peasants and teachers'.[15] In other guberniyas, rural activity was controlled by the local committee itself. The Chernigov committee reported that peasant propaganda was its chief activity, and the upkeep of its militant peasants absorbed 25–30% of its monthly budget, although most militants supported themselves.[16] Peasant conferences at guberniya level were held in Tula, Kazan′, Mogilev, Vyatka, Kursk and Kiev, none of which reported the existence of a separate peasant section.[17] There appears to be little

[10] M. Perrie, 'The social composition and structure of the Socialist-Revolutionary party before 1917', *Soviet Studies*, vol 24, no. 2 (1972), pp 223–50.
[11] *Rapport . . . 1907*, p 161.
[12] *ibid*, pp 63, 74, 94, 105, 110, 150, 155, 163 [13] *ibid*, p 66.
[14] *ibid*, p 95. [15] *ibid*, p 128. [16] *ibid*, p 156.
[17] *ibid*, pp 76, 90, 136, 143, 152, 159.

correlation between the existence, or otherwise, of a formal peasant section of the provincial committee and the vitality of grass-roots activity at the lower levels – uezd, volost′ and village – within the guberniya. This may reflect the fact that some of these commissions were formed 'from above', others 'from below'. Thus the Moscow party committee had a Peasant Commission, although in Moscow guberniya 'propaganda among the peasantry was far from active'.[18] The formation of the Penza commission, on the other hand, appears to have been more spontaneous: 'On 14 July, 30 peasants dedicated themselves to revolutionary activity and formed the provincial peasant commission.'[19]

In many guberniyas, work among the peasantry was organised also at the uezd level, with committees which held regular meetings or conferences of delegates from the village and volost′ Brotherhoods and controlled the distribution of party publications. Party organisations did not, however, exist in every uezd; nor were there contacts with every village or volost′ in uezds with SR committees. The Saratov committee was the exception rather than the rule when it claimed that all villages in the guberniya, except for some in the remote northern uezd of Khvalynsk, had been visited by SR propagandists who had distributed party literature. Even in Saratov, though, peasant Brotherhoods or committees existed in only a minority of villages.[20] The Chernigov committee reported that the eleven uezds in the guberniya could be divided into three categories: four where there were organisations in most villages; four in which about a third of the villages were in process of being organised; and three where there was no organisation, but where party publications were distributed.[21]

Only a minority of the peasants in any village were active members of the SR Brotherhood, although the existence of a party organisation was likely to influence the attitudes of the other villagers. The Samara committee reported that many peasants gravitated around the SR groups without actually belonging to the party, but showing an interest in revolutionary publications and sheltering agitators.[22] In Slobodskoy uezd in Vyatka guberniya, 'the entire population of several villages claimed to be SRs', and 'in some volost′s 50–70% of the population read SR pamphlets and publications and discussed aspects of the SR programme'.[23] From Dmitriev uezd, in Kursk

[18] *ibid*, p 63. [19] *ibid*, p 94.
[20] *ibid*, p 96 and the map facing p 100.
[21] *ibid*, p 156. [22] *ibid*, p 95. [23] *ibid*, p 144.

guberniya, it was reported that the peasants could be divided as follows: politically conscious, 15%; semi-conscious, 60%; and barely conscious, 25%.[24] The Kherson committee reported that in Anan′ev uezd 75% of the peasants were conscious; in Aleksandriya uezd 50% were conscious; in Akkerman uezd 50% of the population was revolutionary; and in Kherson uezd 30% of the peasants claimed to be SRs, and 60% were conscious.[25]

The figures which the 1907 report provides concerning the membership of the party's peasant Brotherhoods – this was estimated in hundreds and even thousands in some guberniyas – must be treated with some caution. It was admitted at the Second Party Congress that the criteria for membership of ancillary party organisations, such as peasant Brotherhoods, were very fluid, and that some Brotherhoods included undesirable elements with little awareness or understanding of the party and its aims. According to one delegate:

> Our party has recently extended its organisation exceptionally far into the masses of the people – and in the countryside in particular. A number of peasant Brotherhoods have been formed, calling themselves party organisations, and receiving the appropriate sanction. But it should be borne in mind that many of these Brotherhoods have been formed, as it were, spontaneously and haphazardly. Their members often not only do not understand the party programme, they even confuse the SR Peasant Union with the All-Russia Peasant Union. Such Brotherhoods can often be counted as party organisations in a barely nominal sense.[26]

Another delegate confirmed that:

> All that is known about some Brotherhoods is that the village was visited by an agitator, that he aroused widespread sympathy, left a copy of the statutes behind him, and that is all.[27]

An even more worrying situation was described by the delegate from Vitebsk. His local committee had decided to demote the 2,300 peasant 'members' of the party in the guberniya to merely 'supporter' (*primykayushchii*) status, after an incident in which members of the Brotherhood elected to the rural electoral college of the Duma had made speeches in the manner of the Black Hundreds (presumably a reference to anti-semitism) at the electoral meetings.[28]

The activity of the peasant Brotherhoods in the villages consisted

[24] *ibid*, p 153.
[25] *ibid*, pp 163–4.
[26] *Protokoly vtorogo (ekstrennago) s″ezda* . . . , p 123.
[27] *ibid*, pp 128–9.
[28] *ibid*, p 116.

mainly in the distribution of propaganda and the organisation of meetings. Many Brotherhoods had small libraries of legal and illegal literature, and some held study circles at which these publications were read and discussed. Funds (*kassy*) were organised to pay for the literature, often on the basis of a monthly subscription of a few kopecks per head.[29] Sometimes the activity of the Brotherhoods was directed towards more specific ends. Attempts were made to put pressure on the Duma. In Nizhnii Novgorod and Pskov, meetings of peasants were held to draft petitions to the deputies.[30] As a protest against the dissolution of the First Duma, the peasants of six villages in Orel guberniya refused to pay taxes or send recruits to the army.[31] In Simbirsk guberniya, peasant insurrectional committees were formed on the dissolution of the Duma, but when a national rising failed to materialise, electoral committees were created for the elections to the Second Duma.[32] In Kiev and Chernigov the peasants collected money to purchase arms. It was reported that in one district of Kiev guberniya 300 roubles had been collected for this purpose, and 50 roubles in another district. A village in Chernigov guberniya claimed to have an armed militia of 80 peasants.[33] Successful agricultural strikes were organised by the SRs in Penza and Kiev.[34] In Penza, 100 peasants under the banners of 11 SR Brotherhoods staged a May Day demonstration in 1906. The Penza committee also reported a degree of self-help among the members of its peasant unions, who cultivated the land of their fellows when they were away on a mission or in prison.[35]

In some areas, the work of the local SR peasant organisations overlapped with that of the equivalent organisations of the All-Russia Peasant Union. According to the party's 1907 report, the two bodies cooperated quite amicably in some provinces – indeed, the Smolensk committee reported that some peasants were unable to distinguish between the party and the Union.[36] At the Second Party Congress, however, it became evident that relationships between the party and the Union had deteriorated, particularly in the southern oblast′, where they had split completely.[37] At the Congress, a representative of the All-Russia Peasant Union accused the SRs of infiltrating the Union and using it as a front organisation for the party, and he demanded an understanding that SRs working under

[29] *Rapport . . . 1907*, pp 67–9, 70, 73–4, 79–80.
[30] *ibid*, pp 68, 109. [31] *ibid*, p 79. [32] *ibid*, p 92.
[33] *ibid*, pp 156, 160. [34] *ibid*, pp 94, 160 [35] *ibid*, p 94.
[36] *ibid*, p 128. [37] *Protokoly vtorogo (ekstrennago) s"ezda . . .*, p 164.

the aegis of the Peasant Union should restrict themselves to advocating the programme and tactics of the Union.[38] In the debate which followed, it emerged that some SRs were in favour of withdrawing altogether from joint activity with the Union.[39] Chernov, however, argued that participation in the Union enabled the party to spread its influence among the 'broad masses' of the peasantry who were not prepared to commit themselves to the narrower party organisation; and SR withdrawal from the Union, he pointed out, would leave the field open for the SDs and Kadets to influence the Peasant Union.[40] After a lengthy and at times bitter discussion, in which allegations and counter-allegations were bandied back and forth between representatives of the party and those of the Union, a compromise resolution was approved which empowered the SR Central Committee to enter into negotiations with the Peasant Union for the regulation of relationships at local and central level.[41]

Although the membership of the village brotherhoods was largely recruited from the peasantry, the 1907 report shows that non-peasants, and members of the rural intelligentsia in particular, continued to play an important rôle as propagandists and agitators in the countryside. A conference of delegates of peasant organisations in Nizhnii Novgorod guberniya consisted of 12 intellectuals, 7 peasants and two workers.[42] The Tula committee reported that peasant propaganda in the province was conducted mainly by 'professional agitators and teachers'.[43] In the Maloarkhangel'sk uezd of Orel guberniya, 'the chief agitators were schoolmasters and enlightened peasants'.[44] The Chuvash organisation in the Volga region reported that propaganda was conducted by Chuvash teachers and students and by a few Russian intellectuals.[45] In Orenburg guberniya, peasant propaganda was mainly conducted by schoolmasters in contact with the local party committee. A similar report came from Olonets.[46] Vyatka reported that in Kotel'nich uezd the propagandists were mainly peasants, but doctors, teachers, medical assistants and church servants also took part; in Yaransk uezd, there were 30 peasant propagandists and 28 intellectual agitators; and in Glazov uezd, 28 militant peasants and 30 intellectuals.[47] In Voronezh, the propagandists were said to be recruited from peasants, schoolmasters,

[38] *ibid*, pp 140–2.
[39] *ibid*, pp 142–4, 164–6.
[40] *ibid*, pp 167–9.
[41] *ibid*, pp 169–70.
[42] *Rapport . . . 1907*, p 66.
[43] *ibid*, p 76.
[44] *ibid*, p 79.
[45] *ibid*, p 88.
[46] *ibid*, pp 102, 111.
[47] *ibid*, pp 144–5.

priests, students and workers.[48] Other committees claimed that all or most of the rural activists were peasants. Pskov reported that over two-thirds of the 480 militants in the guberniya were peasants; in Arkhangel′sk, all militants were said to be peasants; in the North-West region, rural party membership was composed of 'the peasant élite'; and in Kherson, 'the majority of militants were peasants'.[49]

This fragmentary information about the social composition of the party's rural organisation in 1906–7 corresponds in general outline with the picture I obtained on the basis of my analysis of SR biographies. Of 227 SRs who were engaged in propaganda, agitation and organisation in the countryside around the time of the 1905 revolution, 43 were peasants, 57 were workers or artisans, 23 were clerical or shop workers, 64 were professional men, and 40 were students. The 'professional' category was composed mainly of members of the rural intelligentsia: it comprised 50 teachers, 4 medical assistants (*fel′dsher*), 2 midwives, a *zemstvo* statistician, a lawyer, an agricultural expert, a forestry expert, an agricultural technician, a druggist, a pharmacist and a journalist.[50]

The intermediary rôle of the intelligentsia, in fact, proved to be the Achilles' heel of the party's rural organisation after the dissolution of the Second Duma. Arrests and imprisonment removed many SR activists; other fled abroad to escape persecution. The reports of the local organisations to the 1908 party conference showed that in most areas the oblast′ and guberniya committees had ceased to exist, and that survival at the lower levels was very precarious.[51] Chernov summed up the party's organisational crisis as follows: 'The following picture is obtained: the Central Committee is face to face with the organisations in various towns, unconnected one with another, which have irregular relations with the mass organisations proper, and have to a considerable extent lost contact with these organisations.'[52]

Several local committees reported that arrests had destroyed their links with the countryside. Where the party's base in the villages had been slight, the rupture of contacts meant the disappearance of the Brotherhoods. In areas where SR activity was of longer duration and

[48] *ibid* p 151.
[49] *ibid*, pp 109, 112, 122, 164.
[50] Perrie, 'The social composition and structure of the SR party . . .', p 246; 'The Russian peasant movement of 1905–1907 . . .', p 151.
[51] *Protokoly pervoy obshchepartiynoy konferentsii* . . . , pp 23–56, 156–9.
[52] *ibid*, p 57.

where grass-roots support from the peasants was more firmly established, the rural organisations continued to exist in isolation from the urban party structure. The delegate from Saratov reported that although the guberniya and uezd committees had been severely weakened by arrests, party work in the countryside was conducted by the peasants themselves. In some respects, this news was gratifying, but the peasants keenly resented their abandonment by the intelligentsia: 'They complain that they have been deserted, and wonder whether the party itself has collapsed.'[53] The breaking of contacts with the towns deprived the peasants of party literature and of experienced intellectual leadership. In some places, this led to independent local initiatives without party control, some even contrary to party discipline. In Saratov guberniya, 'Well-armed combat groups were formed in Atkarsk uezd. Because of the absence of party leaders, discipline was slack, so that in certain cases they did not refrain from private expropriations. This provoked intensified repression from the police.'[54] The delegate from the Ukraine reported that even the best organised peasants found the party's rejection of 'agrarian terror' difficult to understand, and 'only submit to resolutions against it because of their confidence in the authority of the leaders of the party'. Where the party organisation had been weakened '"agrarian terrorism" breaks out'.[55] In general, he alleged, the mood of the peasantry was more revolutionary than socialist: 'Our party slogan "land and liberty" attracts very heterogeneous revolutionary elements, and the strengthening of the socialist consciousness of the more progressive peasants is the most immediate task facing our party.'[56]

Other delegates disputed this view. If the behaviour of the Ukrainian peasantry had been revolutionary rather than socialist, 'Golubev' alleged, then this reflected the tactical errors of the party leadership in the region, who had insisted on calling for an armed uprising after the dissolution of the Second Duma.[57] The focus of this rising was to have been Voronezh guberniya, where the peasantry was well-organised. In practice, this rising failed to materialise. According to the Ukrainians, the Central Committee failed to support them; according to Chernov, the adventure never had a chance of success, as the Voronezh party committee had over-estimated the strength of its peasant organisations. Whatever the rights and wrongs of the

[53] *ibid*, pp 43–4.
[54] *ibid*, p 45.
[55] *ibid*, p 52.
[56] *ibid*, p 51.
[57] *ibid*, p 127.

episode, the Voronezh countryside had produced only some private expropriations and incidents of 'agrarian terror', before the police struck, arresting over 2,000 peasants and destroying the party's rural organisation.[58]

The real tragedy of the party's situation in 1907–8, in Chernov's view, was that its organisation had become isolated from the masses at the very time when the masses themselves, as a result of their experience of the revolution, were more receptive than ever before to SR ideas.[59] A survey conducted by the Central Committee had shown that the number of conscious, revolutionary peasants was on the increase, and that their influence on their fellow-villagers was also growing.[60] This view was supported by several of the local delegates. 'Nechaich' reported that in Pskov, 'after all they have experienced recently, the self-awareness of the peasants is beginning to become clarified, both socially and politically'.[61] The delegate from Saratov 'noted the interesting fact that among the peasants a break is now occurring with their old way of life. Their attitudes are changing towards women, children, religion, etc.'[62] In areas where the party's rural organisations survived, they showed great vitality (*samodeyatel'nost'*). The delegate from Tambov remarked on the recent change in the character of peasant congresses: 'Previously (before 1906) the peasant delegates for the most part kept silent, and accepted the leaders' proposals without discussion, but now every proposal is heatedly discussed, and the decisions reveal a great maturity of thought and an aspiration to take into account the general mood of the peasant masses.'[63] The delegate from Ryazan' reported that a recent conference organised by the guberniya committee had consisted exclusively of peasants;[64] and in Khar'kov: 'The mood of the peasants is, in general, high. A peasant congress revealed great consciousness and vitality. The small group of *intelligenty* who took part in the congress were completely lost in the strong peasant mass.'[65]

In spite of the brave proposals for restoring the party's organisation and influence which were made at the First Conference, it was not

[58] *ibid*, pp 50–2, 62–3, 103, 106, 127, 130–1, 145–8, 156–7.
[59] *ibid*, pp 56–7.
[60] *ibid*, pp 53–4. A more detailed version of the results of this survey was published later: I. Ritina, 'Iz materialov krest'yanskoy ankety', *Znamya Truda*, no. 26 (February 1910), pp 4–12, no. 27 (April 1910), pp 13–20.
[61] *Protokoly pervoy obshchepartiynoy konferentsii . . .*, p 26.
[62] *ibid*, p 44.
[63] *ibid*, p 44.
[64] *ibid*, p 45.
[65] *ibid*, p 158.

until 1917 that the SRs recovered the popular support they had gained in 1905–7. The revelation of Azef's treachery soon after the conference completed the process of demoralisation which had begun after the Stolypin coup. For the remainder of the pre-war period, the party reverted to its former nature of an underground, conspiratorial organisation, consisting of a squabbling émigré leadership endeavouring to maintain contact with an insecure network of groups and individual sympathisers in Russia.

The party's reports to the Socialist International in 1910 and 1914 were permeated with pessimism about the chances for a revival of the revolutionary movement. In 1910 the SRs claimed to have re-established contacts with the peasantry in the Ukraine, in the guberniyas of Khar'kov, Kiev, Kursk, Voronezh and Poltava; in the south, in Tauride and Kherson; and in the centre and east, in Nizhnii Novgorod, Ryazan' and Vyatka. The former stronghold of the Volga however, was still suffering the repercussion of government repressions, and the party had had little success in restoring its organisation there. The authors of the report expressed the hope that the reactionary policies of the government, and the alienation of the people from the Duma, would eventually provoke a new revolutionary initiative from the masses; but they had to admit that there had, as yet, been few signs of such a resurgence.[66]

By 1914, the situation provided little basis for further optimism. Attempts to organise the peasantry were continuing, apparently over a wider area than four years previously, although the Ukraine remained the most important region in this respect. Among the 'organisations especially dedicated to rural action' the report listed those of Poltava, Kiev, Khar'kov, Chernigov, Voronezh and Kherson, and also the North Caucasus, the Baltic provinces, the north Volga region, Mogilev, Vitebsk, and several towns and villages in Siberia.[67] On the eve of the First World War, the party had to admit that the government's assault on the commune had enjoyed a certain measure of success in destroying the communal solidarity of the peasantry. They could point to only two bright patches amidst the general picture of gloom; the growing militancy of the strike movement in the period 1912–14; and the rapid development of agricultural cooperatives.[68]

[66] *Rapport du parti socialiste révolutionnaire de russie au congrès socialiste international de Copenhague* (Paris, 1910), pp 17–18, 22–4.

[67] *Rapport du parti socialiste révolutionnaire de russie au congrès socialiste international de Vienne* (Paris, 1914), p 12.

[68] *ibid*, pp 3–9.

Conclusion

This study has traced the development of SR agrarian policy from the end of the nineteenth century to the eve of the First World War. In the early stages of the formation of the party, those SRs who retained the Populist faith in peasant revolution had to combat the legacy of disillusionment left by the failure of the 'movement to the people'. It was not until 1902 that the balance between the *narodovol'tsy* and the Agrarian Socialists shifted in favour of the latter. The peasant movement of 1902 conclusively demonstrated the revolutionary potential of the countryside, and the formation of the SR Peasant Union marked the acceptance by the party leadership of the need for an extensive propaganda campaign in the villages. To a considerable extent, the SRs had been taken by surprise by the disturbances in the South, and their policy in the years 1902–4 represented an attempt to harness the spontaneity of the peasantry to the cause of revolutionary socialism. In this, they were hampered by police repressions as well as by shortages of finance and personnel, so that the advent of war in 1904 found the mass of the peasantry still untouched by SR influence. The revolutionary years 1905–7 enabled the party to extend its contacts in the countryside, but only a minority of the peasants elected SR deputies to the Second Duma. 1907 represented the climax of SR development before the war; the Stolypin reaction again forced the party underground, and isolated it from the peasantry.

Most of the problems faced by the SRs in the development of their agrarian policy derived from the complex nature of the party itself. The SRs' programme was socialist, their tactics were revolutionary, and they sought their social base of support in the 'working class' – a concept which included the small peasant producers as well as the industrial, agricultural and intellectual proletariat. The SRs felt capable of attracting the support of the peasantry because they believed that their agrarian programme and tactics corresponded with those of the peasants themselves. Inasmuch as the SRs failed to achieve mass peasant support in 1905–7, the question arises as to how far this was due purely to organisational weaknesses, and how far to an over-estimation by the party of its acceptability to the peasants.

Every party which seeks to make a socialist revolution faces the task of marrying two elements: the party organisation itself, usually comprising, initially at least, a leadership deriving predominantly from the middle class intelligentsia and possessing a theory and strategy of revolution; and the class or classes which, according to the 'scientific' analysis of the party ideologists, are destined to act as the motive force of the revolution. In the nineteenth century, this class was usually identified as the industrial proletariat; the inclusion of the small, peasant producers in the broader category of the working class was a major adaptation by Chernov of orthodox Marxist theory to Russian conditions, and one which earned the SRs the derision of their SD rivals – although the concept was one towards which Lenin had moved significantly by 1917.

The Russian SDs considered the peasantry as a whole to be petty bourgeois; only the agricultural proletariat, in their view, represented a force for socialism in the countryside. The SDs welcomed the peasant movements of 1902 and 1905 as an anti-feudal bourgeois revolution which would clear the way for capitalist agriculture and the development of the class struggle in the countryside. The SRs, on the other hand, saw the movement as both anti-feudal and anti-capitalist; they believed that the peasants desired the abolition of private property in land and a guarantee of equal rights of use for all who wished to work it, and they considered these aspirations to have more in common with the socialist ideal than with capitalism.

In terms of orthodox Marxism, there were two features of the socio-economic position of the peasant which made him a less promising candidate than the proletarian for the socialist society of the future: he owned his means of production, and his mode of production was individual rather than collective. The first of these handicaps Chernov dismissed as irrelevant, since the peasant's means of production, insofar as they were not alienated from the producer and did not serve as a means for the exploitation of the labour of others, did not constitute 'capital'. The second, however, he considered to be more important: it was because of this obstacle that the transition to socialist agriculture would have to be a two-stage process. The first stage was to be the socialisation of the land; the second was to be the socialisation of agricultural production. The merits of the socialisation of the land in Chernov's eyes were twofold. Firstly, such a measure would prevent the development of capitalist relations in agriculture – and indirectly in other sectors of the economy as well – thus undermining the bourgeois order from within. Secondly, the principle of equal access to the land for all who were prepared to work it was considered by the SRs to correspond to the peasants' own ideas of social justice, as embodied in the repartitional commune.

The SRs considered the traditional views of the peasantry to be semi-socialist – they contained both an individualist and a collectivist (egalitarian) component – and it was the party's task to ensure that the latter predominated in any solution of the agrarian problem. The SRs' assessment of the relative weight of these two conflicting elements in the peasants' social psychology ranged from optimism to pessimism in the course of the period under consideration. *Revolyutsionnaya Rossiya* greeted the outbreak of peasant disturbances in Poltava and Khar′kov in 1902 as communal and egalitarian in inspiration, and provided a similarly optimistic estimate of the movement in Kursk in the spring of 1905. By contrast, several delegates to the First Party Congress expressed misgivings about the individualistic avarice which motivated many of the peasants in 1905, and the Stolypin reforms intensified fears that bourgeois-proprietorial aspirations might come to dominate the peasantry. The two attitudes were not logically inconsistent, and indeed the shift from optimism in the period of upsurge of the revolutionary movement to pessimism at the time of its defeat can easily be explained in psychological terms. Nonetheless, a clear divergence may be observed within the party, between those who over-estimated the socialist potential of the peasantry and those who under-estimated it. While Chernov struggled to retain the balanced view of the centre, the two divergent tendencies ultimately found their expression in Maximalism and Popular Socialism, respectively.

A parallel process emerged in the development of SR tactics in the countryside. The SRs identified both a positive and a negative aspect in the peasants' own forms of struggle against the landowners and state officials. They distinguished between constructive and destructive methods and sought to strengthen organised forms of action, such as strikes and boycotts, against 'agrarian terror'. As in the formulation of their programme, so in the determination of their tactics, the SRs sought to base themselves on one element of the peasant tradition – that which they saw as conducive to the socialisation of the land. This resulted in their peculiarly ambivalent policy of 'welcoming' all forms of spontaneous peasant action, 'advocating' revolutionary expropriations of the land and political terror, but 'advising against' acts of 'agrarian terror'.

The party's attitude towards spontaneous land seizures reflects this ambivalence and demonstrates also the transition from optimism to pessimism which has been mentioned above. In the earlier period, land seizures were welcomed as a form of socialisation from below; later, they were seen as a possible obstacle to full socialisation, insofar as the peasants considered the expropriated lands to have become the property of the individual commune, rather than the 'possession of the entire people'. The SRs, therefore, had to tread a slippery path between the idealisation of peasant spontaneity, on the one hand, and scepticism towards it, on the other. Again, Chernov had to defend the centre, with its advocacy of socialisation by means of revolutionary expropriation, while the Maximalists argued that peasant spontaneity could achieve not only the socialisation of the land, but also the socialisation of agricultural production, and the Popular Socialists believed that the land could not be socialised by direct action, but only by legislation.

The successful implementation of socialisation – whether from above, through the Constituent Assembly, or from below, by revolutionary expropriation – depended upon the achievement of socialist consciousness by the mass of the peasantry, through the spread of SR propaganda in the countryside. This did not, in fact, occur; and however utopian they might appear in other respects, the 'agrarian terrorists' were at least more realistic than the SR leadership in their assessment, on the eve of the 1905 revolution, that the party's resources were inadequate for the organisation of a conscious peasant movement. The events of 1905–7 showed clearly that the SRs persistently over-estimated the extent of the political consciousness of the peasantry, and their degree of organisation; this led to the repeated failure of their calls for a general strike and an armed uprising in the countryside. The bulk of the Russian peasantry in 1905–7 appeared still to believe that 'land and liberty' could be obtained within the framework of Tsarism: they ignored the socialist parties' appeals for a boycott of the Duma and staked great hopes on the granting of a radical agrarian reform by the government. The necessity of a political revolution was not obvious to them, and they placed greater reliance on their 'own means' of local 'agrarian terror', as a means of improving their conditions, than on preparations for the elusive national uprising promised by the revolutionaries.

In itself, their failure to mobilise the countryside for revolution in 1905–7 does not prove that the SRs' view of the peasantry was mistaken. Chernov had never claimed that the peasant was an innate socialist; he had simply argued that there were aspects of the peasants' own views – views which were historically and socially determined – which would predispose them favourably towards socialist propaganda. The successes of SR propaganda, admittedly on a limited scale, indicated that sections of the peasantry at least were prepared to accept that the socialisation of the land might, in the long run, constitute a better guarantee of land rights and social welfare than a simple 'black repartition'. The agrarian demands of the All-Russia Peasant Union, and the proposals for agrarian reform presented by the *Trudoviki* in the first two Dumas are further evidence that there was considerable support among the peasantry as a whole for the sort of principles which governed the minimum SR agrarian programme.

Nor was the peasantry entirely apolitical, as its voting pattern in the Duma elections illustrates. The 'modernisation' of Russian society in the post-Emancipation decades – industrialisation, the improvement of communications, and the spread of secular education – was beginning to break down the barriers between town and countryside, between articulate 'society' and the dumb 'people'. Albeit by a process of trial and error, the SRs were able to utilise the new links which had been forged between urban and rural life, particularly through the growth of groups such as the rural intelligentsia and the peasant-workers, in order to spread revolutionary political ideas in the countryside. The task of politicising the peasantry over the vast extent of the Russian countryside was, however, beyond the party's resources in the few short years at its disposal at the beginning of the century. The dissolution of the first two Dumas may have disenchanted the peasants with the Tsar as their benefactor, but by 1907 the government's tactics of a combination of reform and repression had crushed the revolutionary impulse in the countryside. As the events of 1917 were to demonstrate, the Stolypin reforms did not entirely succeed in destroying the revolutionary aspirations of the land-hungry communal peasantry, but they certainly did not make the SRs' task any easier in the intervening years.

The question of whether the SR party was capable of riding to power on the wave of peasant revolution remained an open one after 1907; it would not finally be answered until 1917, in circumstances whose analysis lies beyond the scope of the present work. O. H. Radkey, the author of two invaluable volumes on the SR party in 1917–18,[1] is probably correct in seeing the primary reasons for SR failure in 1917 in the tactical weaknesses and errors of the party leadership, particularly with regard to the issues of coalition with the liberals, and the war. These tactical considerations undoubtedly influenced the peculiarly ambivalent attitude which the SRs adopted towards the agrarian question in 1917; but, as the present study has shown, SR attitudes towards spontaneous peasant land seizures, for example, were highly ambivalent even before the exceptional circumstances of the Great War introduced extraneous influences on SR agrarian policy.

It is always a great temptation for the historian to speculate about the 'might have beens' of history. Radkey, in a couple of articles written over twenty years ago, has raised the question of the probable future development of Russian agriculture if the SRs, rather than the Bolsheviks, had emerged as the victors of the revolution. Would the SRs, he asks, 'have succeeded in placing Russian agriculture on a new and satisfactory basis or would their programme have been exposed as a myth, imposing in its popular appeal but impossible of execution?'[2] Radkey prefers the latter alternative as an answer to his own question. He agrees that the SR agrarian programme held great appeal for the peasants, and he considers that the elections to the Constituent Assembly in 1917 gave the SRs a mandate from the peasantry for the socialisation of the land. However, he believes – and not without some persuasive arguments – that socialisation was a totally utopian and impractical policy. He believes, too, that the SRs idealised the egalitarianism of the peasants, whom he sees as essentially individualist. Radkey argues that had the SRs ever come to power a conflict would have developed between their 'desire to please and lead the peasantry' and their 'fetish of collectivism', between 'devotion to the cause of the peasantry and

[1] O. H. Radkey, *The agrarian foes of Bolshevism; promise and default of the Russian Socialist-Revolutionaries, February–October 1917* (New York, 1958); O. H. Radkey, *The sickle under the hammer; the Russian Socialist-Revolutionaries in the early months of Soviet rule* (New York, 1963).

[2] O. H. Radkey, 'Chernov and agrarian socialism before 1918', in E. J. Simmons, ed., *Continuity and change in Russian and Soviet thought*, (Cambridge, Mass, 1955), p 77.

devotion to socialism'.[3] This conflict, he believes, the SRs would have resolved by abandoning socialism in order to retain peasant support and would have sanctioned a society of small peasant proprietors similar to those of France.[4]

I am unconvinced by this analysis, although I agree with Radkey that the SRs would have regarded a policy of forced collectivisation with 'deepest repugnance'.[5] I cannot accept that the SRs would so easily have abandoned their socialist principles: forced collectivisation was not, after all, the only alternative to individual peasant proprietorship, and many other paths to socialist agriculture were attempted or discussed in Russia in the 1920s. Indeed, it may well be partly because they placed 'devotion to socialism' higher than 'devotion to the cause of the peasantry' that the SRs yielded ultimate victory in 1917 to the Bolsheviks, since, as we have seen, the SR party was concerned as early as 1905 lest short-term support for the immediate aspirations of the peasantry for land might endanger the prospects of achieving their longer-term goal of a socialist transformation of Russian agriculture. Although the Bolshevik 'decree on the land' published on the morrow of the October revolution owed a heavy debt to the SRs' 1917 formulation of their minimum programme for agriculture, the agrarian structure of Russia which emerged from the revolution and civil war bore a stronger resemblance to the peasant ideal of 'black repartition' than to any of the theoretical schemes for nationalisation, municipalisation or socialisation which had so bitterly divided the socialist parties before the revolution; the outcome of the political battles of 1917, however, meant that in the 1920s it was the Bolsheviks, rather than the SRs, who had to face the conflict between peasant individualism and socialist ideology.

In assessing the development of SR agrarian policy in the pre-war period, I have tried not to let my judgments be coloured by hindsight. There were certainly many problems inherent in the party policy; but I do not believe that these were necessarily insuperable. In the event, the SR agrarian programme was never put to the acid test of practical implementation, and one can only speculate about the viability of the socialisation of the land as a transitional step towards collective farming. Insofar as there is an element of

3 *ibid*, pp 79, 80.
4 *ibid*, pp 77–80; O. H. Radkey, 'An alternative to Bolshevism; the programme of Russian Social-Revolutionism', *Journal of Modern History*, vol 25 (1953), pp 37–9.
5 *ibid*, p 38.

utopianism in every revolutionary programme, it is the mixed blessing of unsuccessful revolutionaries that they are spared the disillusionment which derives from the inevitable discrepancy between the socialist ideal and the post-revolutionary reality.

Glossary

The use of Russian terms has been kept to a minimum in the text of this study. English equivalents have been preferred wherever possible, sometimes accompanied, when first used, by the original term in round brackets, to clarify the sense for the reader with a knowledge of Russian. In some cases, short English equivalents may be not only inadequate, but actually misleading, and the following glossary attempts to provide a fuller explanation of certain 'technical terms' for which the Russian words have been retained in the text.

guberniya: province; the main administrative unit in the Russian Empire, comprising several uezds.

intelligent (pl. *intelligenty*): an educated, professional person; a member of the intelligentsia.

kulak: rich peasant. (The problems of defining a kulak more accurately in socio-economic terms are discussed in the text.)

Molokanin (pl. *Molokane*): a member of a sect of 'spiritual Christians', formed in the eighteenth century, which rejected the Orthodox Church, and laid great stress on the authority of the Bible, interpreted in a non-literal sense.

narodovolets (pl. *narodovol'tsy*; adj. *narodovol'cheskii*, pl. *narodovol'cheskie*): a member of or sympathiser with the terrorist Populist group *Narodnaya volya* ('People's will'), formed in 1879

oblast': region; the largest unit in the SR party's organisational structure, comprising several guberniyas.

pomeshchik (pl. *pomeshchiki*): a landowner, a member of the gentry.

raznochinets (pl. *raznochintsy*): an intellectual of non-gentry origins.

uezd: district; administrative subdivision of a guberniya, comprising several volost's.

volost': rural district; administrative subdivision of an uezd, comprising several villages; nominally a unit of local self-government, but subject to bureaucratic interference. Unlike the *zemstvo*, which had a non-estate character, the volost′ was an exclusively peasant institution.

zemskii nachal′nik (pl. *zemskie nachal′niki*): an official, a member of the gentry, with wide supervisory powers over peasant affairs at village and volost′ levels. The institution was introduced in 1889 as part of the counter-reforms of Alexander III.

zemstvo (pl. *zemstva*): elective local government institutions at guberniya and uezd levels, established in 1864 as part of the post-Emancipation reforms of Alexander II. Although members of all estates were enfranchised, the indirect electoral system and property qualifications guaranteed the predominance of the gentry.

Bibliography

The secondary literature on the SR party, especially for the pre-revolutionary period with which this book is concerned, is relatively small, both in Russian and in English. Scholars have not as yet made full use of the existing published sources, and the investigation of archives remains a task for the future researcher. Hence, the major sources for the present work have been the printed primary materials: the SR press, the proceedings of party congresses, the party's reports to the Socialist International, and the memoirs of party leaders.

The bibliography which follows includes only works referred to directly in the footnotes to the text; the secondary literature on pre-revolutionary Russian history, in English alone, is now so vast that it would be futile to attempt, in a work of this kind, a comprehensive survey of all the background material. Articles from the major SR journals, *Revolyutsionnaya Rossiya*, *Vestnik Russkoy Revolyutsii, Znamya Truda* and *Sotsialist-Revolyutsioner*, are not listed individually in the bibliography, although full references are, of course, provided in the footnotes.

Agrarnoe dvizhenie v Rossii v 1905–1906 gg. (*Trudy Imperatorskago Vol'nago Ekonomicheskago Obshchestva*, 1908, nos. 3, 4–5). 2 vols, St Petersburg, 1908.

Alavi, H. 'Peasants and revolution', *Socialist Register*, 1965, pp 241–77.

Argunov, A. A. 'Iz proshlago Partii Sotsialistov-Revolyutsionerov', *Byloe*, no. 10/22 (1907), pp 94–112.

Billington, J. H. *Mikhailovsky and Russian Populism.* Oxford, 1958.

Blackwell, A. S. (ed.), *The little grandmother of the Russian revolution.* London, 1918.

Breshkovskaia, K. *Hidden springs of the Russian revolution.* Stanford, 1931.

Chernov, V. *Pered burey.* New York, 1953.

Chernov, V. *Zapiski Sotsialista-Revolyutsionera.* Berlin, 1922.

Dobavlenie k protokolam pervago s"ezda Partii Sotsialistov-Revolyutsionerov. N.p., 1906.

Dubrovskii, S. M. *Krest'yanskoe dvizhenie v revolyutsii 1905–1907 gg*. Moscow, 1956.

Erman, L. K. *Intelligentsiya v pervoy russkoy revolyutsii*. Moscow, 1966.

Gorn, V., Mech, V. and Cherevanin, N. *Krest'yanstvo i revolyutsiya v Rossii*. Moscow, 1907.

Gosudarstvennaya Duma, sessiya 1; stenograficheskii otchet. St Petersburg, 1906.

Gosudarstvennaya Duma, sessiya 2; stenograficheskii otchet. St. Petersburg, 1907.

Kachorovskii, K. R. *Narodnoe pravo*. Moscow, 1906.

Karpov, N. (ed.), *Krest'yanskoe dvizhenie v revolyutsii 1905 goda v dokumentakh*. Leningrad, 1926.

Kiryukhina, E. I. 'Vserossiyskii Krest'yanskii Soyuz v 1905 g.', *Istoricheskie Zapiski*, no. 50 (1955), pp 95–141.

Ko vsemu russkomu krest'yanstvu ot Krest'yanskago Soyuza Partii Sotsialistov-Revolyutsionerov. N.p., 1902.

Krest'yanskoe Delo. No. 1. Saratov, 1901.

Landsberger, H. A. 'The rôle of peasant movements and revolts in development; an analytical framework', International Institute for Labour Studies, *Bulletin*, no. 4 (1968), pp 8–85.

Lenin, V. I. *Polnoe Sobranie Sochinenii*. 5th edn 55 vols, Moscow, 1958–65.

Lewin, M. *Russian peasants and Soviet power; a study of collectivisation*. London, 1968.

Leykina-Svirskaya, V. R. *Intelligentsiya v Rossii vo vtoroy polovine 19 veka*. Moscow, 1971.

Male, D. J. *Russian peasant organisation before collectivisation; a study of commune and gathering, 1925–1930*. Cambridge, 1971.

Maslov, P. *Agrarnyi vopros v Rossii*. 2 vols, St Petersburg, 1905–8.

Materialy k krest'yanskomu voprosu; otchet o zasedaniyakh delegatskago s"ezda Vserossiyskago Krest'yanskago Soyuza 6–10 noyabrya 1905 g. Rostov, 1905.

Mendel, A. P. *Dilemmas of progress in Tsarist Russia; Legal Marxism and Legal Populism*. Cambridge, Mass., 1961.

Meshcheryakov, V. *Partiya Sotsialistov-Revolyutsionerov*. 2 parts, Moscow, 1922.

Obshchestvennoe dvizhenie v Rossii v nachale 20 veka. (ed. L. Martov, P. Maslov and N. Potresov) 4 vols, St Petersburg, 1909–14.

Ocherednoy vopros revolyutsionnago dela. 1st edn London, 1900; 2nd edn Geneva, 1901.

Pamyati S. N. Sletova. Paris, 1916.

Pamyatnaya knizhka Sotsialista-Revolyutsionera. Vyp 1. Paris, 1911.

Perrie, M. 'The Russian peasant movement of 1905–1907; its social composition and revolutionary significance', *Past and Present*, no. 57 (1972), pp 123–55.

Perrie, M. 'The social composition and structure of the Socialist-Revolutionary party before 1917', *Soviet Studies*, vol 24, no. 2 (1972), pp 223–50.

Perrie, M. 'The Socialist-Revolutionaries on "permanent revolution"', *Soviet Studies*, vol 24, no. 3 (1973), pp 411–13.

Peshekhonov, A. V. *Pochemu my togda ushli.* Petrograd, 1918.

Pipes, R. '*Narodnichestvo*; a semantic inquiry', *American Slavic and East European Review*, vol 23, no. 3 (1964), pp 441–58.

Poslednii samoderzhets. Berlin, 1912.

Protokol uchreditel'nago s"ezda Vserossiyskago Krest'yanskago Soyuza. St Petersburg, 1905.

Protokoly pervago s"ezda Partii Sotsialistov-Revolyutsionerov. N.p., 1906.

Protokoly pervoy obshchepartiynoy konferentsii Partii Sotsialistov-Revolyutsionerov, avgust 1908. Paris, 1908.

Protokoly vtorogo (ekstrennago) s"ezda Partii Sotsialistov-Revolyutsionerov. St Petersburg, 1907.

Radkey, O. H. 'An alternative to Bolshevism; the programme of Russian Social-Revolutionism', *Journal of Modern History*, vol 25 (1953), pp 25–39.

Radkey, O. H. 'Chernov and agrarian socialism before 1918', in E. J. Simmons, ed., *Continuity and change in Russian and Soviet thought* (Cambridge, Mass, 1955), pp 63–80.

Radkey, O. H. *The agrarian foes of Bolshevism; promise and default of the Russian Socialist-Revolutionaries, February–October 1917.* New York, 1958.

Radkey, O. H. *The sickle under the hammer; the Russian Socialist-Revolutionaries in the early months of Soviet rule.* New York, 1963.

Rakitnikova, I. 'Revolyutsionnaya rabota v krest'yanstve v Saratovskoy gubernii v 1900–1902 gg.', *Katorga i Ssylka* kn 47 (1928), pp 7–17.

Rapport du parti socialiste révolutionnaire de russie au congrès socialiste international d'Amsterdam. Paris, 1904.

Rapport du parti socialiste révolutionnaire de russie au congrès socialiste international de Copenhague. Paris, 1910.

Rapport du parti socialiste révolutionnaire de russie au congrès socialiste international de Stuttgart (août 1907). Gand, 1907.

Rapport du parti socialiste révolutionnaire de russie au congrès socialiste international de Vienne. Paris, 1914.

Revolyutsionnaya Rossiya. Nos. 1–77. 1900–5.

Robinson, G. T. *Rural Russia under the old régime*. London, 1932.

Shanin, T. *The awkward class; political sociology of peasantry in a developing society; Russia, 1910–1925*. Oxford, 1972.

Shestakov, A. *Krest'yanskaya revolyutsiya 1905–1907 gg. v Rossii*. Moscow, 1926.

Sletov, S. N. *K istorii vozniknoveniya Partii Sotsialistov-Revolyutsionerov*. Petrograd, 1917.

Sotsialist-Revolyutsioner. Nos. 1–4. 1910–12.

Spiridovich, A. I. *Partiya Sotsialistov-Revolyutsionerov i ee predshestvenniki, 1886–1916*. 1st edn Petrograd, 1916; 2nd edn Petrograd, 1918.

Spiridovitch, A. *Histoire du terrorisme russe, 1886–1917*. Paris, 1930.

Tan, V. G. *Novoe krest'yanstvo*. Moscow, 1905.

Tretii s"ezd RSDRP; protokoly. Moscow, 1959.

Ustav 'bratstva dlya zashchity narodnykh prav'. Geneva, 1899.

Venturi, F. *Roots of revolution*. London, 1960.

Veselovskii, B. B. *Krest'yanskii vopros i krest'yanskoe dvizhenie v Rossii, 1902–1906 gg*. St Petersburg, 1907.

Vestnik Russkoy Revolyutsii. Nos. 1–4. 1901–5.

Vishnyak, M. *Dan' proshlomu*. New York, 1954.

Vtoroy s"ezd RSDRP; protokoly. Moscow, 1959.

Walicki, A. *The controversy over capitalism; studies in the social philosophy of the Russian Populists*. London, 1969.

Wolf, E. R. *Peasant wars of the twentieth century*. London, 1971.

Zenzinov, V. *Perezhitoe*. New York, 1953.

Znamya Trûda. Nos. 1–53. 1907–14.

Index